# No Fighting
# in the War Room

# No Fighting
# in the War Room

## Memoirs of a Spook

Robert J. Woolsey

Writer's Showcase
New York San Jose Lincoln Shanghai

No Fighting in the War Room
Memoirs of a Spook

Writer's Showcase
an imprint of iUniverse.com, Inc.

For information address:
iUniverse.com, Inc.
5220 S 16th, Ste. 200
Lincoln, NE 68512
www.iuniverse.com

ISBN: 0-595-15447-6

Printed in the United States of America

# About the Author

For the past twenty-eight years, Robert Woolsey has been a Trusts and Estates Attorney in New York and New Jersey. For the past two years, he has been an aspiring author. In 1963 he graduated with a BA degree from Saint Peter's College in New Jersey, majoring in German and Classical literature. He was awarded a Fulbright Scholarship to study in Germany after graduation. While abroad, he traveled extensively throughout Europe. He is fluent in Italian and German.

After returning to the US, he studied Law at the University of Virginia Law School, obtaining his LL.B. in 1967. He entered the US Army Intelligence Corps as a First Lieutenant in 1968, and served for two years as a Briefing Officer to the General Staff at the Pentagon , leaving the military with the rank of Captain.

He is a member of the New York and New Jersey Bars, specializing Estate Planning. He is currently practicing law in midtown Manhattan.

In 1996 he returned to his liberal arts background with his first novel, as yet unpublished, a romantic comedy set in Austria entitled *Husband in Waiting*. His latest novel, an autobiographical comedy, is *No Fighting in the War Room*, which describes his life at the Pentagon.

He is unmarried, and lives in Jersey City, New Jersey. His hobbies include foreign languages, cooking, travel, and word games.

# Contents

# CHAPTER ONE

# Hello Columbus

"Y'all goin' to Fort Benning, young man?" the taxi driver asked.

I nodded yes. About five minutes earlier, I'd stepped off Delta Flight 273 from JFK Airport to Columbus, Georgia, courtesy of the US Army. My carefree days as a student were over, and my new life as a soldier was about to begin. The Army, which had been graciously deferring me from military service for almost five years now, had scheduled me for its Basic Infantry Course at Fort Benning, starting tomorrow. Every new officer had to take it. The ROTC commitment that I'd made in the early '60's was only sixteen hours away, at reveille the next morning.

"Look's like this hyeer feller's traveled to some fancy places," the driver said, pointing to my beat up gray suitcase, covered with stickers from different European cities. "Yessir, Paris, Rome, Berlin, Athens, Con-stan-tin-o-*peel*. Well son, welcome to Columbus, Georgia! It ain't no Paris, France, but we're mighty proud of our little town, anyways. Ma name's Bartholomew.

With that, He opened the trunk of his old yellow cab, and unceremoniously flung the gray piece of luggage on top of the spare tire inside. Then he slammed the rear lid shut. I held onto my little brown gym bag, containing a few personal items, as Bartholomew gallantly opened the passenger door and ushered me inside.

1

As I sat in the back seat of the cab, which was carrying me to my doom, I looked out the window and counted the cows on the farms along the countryside. As I did, I ruminated over my life during the past five years, and wondered what the hell had happened. This service in the US Army was supposed to have been a paid two year vacation in Europe. I wasn't any soldier! And now there was a good chance that I'd be shipped out to some combat zone in Vietnam before the Summer. Things were all mixed up. When I graduated from college in 1963, there was no Vietnam mess. My post graduate plan had been so simple. I would spend my first year out of college doing some graduate work at Heidelberg, polishing up my German along the way. For the next three years I would study Law. Finally, before beginning my legal career, I would fulfill my Army commitment with the Intelligence Corps in Germany, at a quiet little desk, at a quiet little base outside Munich, enjoying my weekends and vacation time traveling throughout Bavaria, where I could leisurely guzzle down ice cold liters of Lowenbrau and get fat, while converting my valuable dollars into less valuable German marks. I'd even be able to save some money as a cushion for civilian life when I returned home.

But the "best laid plans" of this particular First Lieutenant had been dashed to pieces. Indeed any young Army officer who harbored any thoughts about relaxing for two years, enjoying Knockwurst and Sauerkraut, would probably have to be satisfied eating C-rations in some sweltering tent outside Saigon.

I hated Law School. I loathed having to learn about compensatory damages recoverable by a plaintiff, when a defendant shipped him a truckload of blue pencils instead of red ones. Could anybody really enjoy studying whether a legal notice had to be sent *via* certified mail? Within ten days or thirteen? But I gutted it out. It wasn't exactly Utopia, but it sure beat the hell out of slogging through some Southeast Asian jungle, swatting away mosquitoes. And so, like any self-respecting coward of the '60's, I stayed in school.

Besides, hadn't the government guaranteed a quick solution to the conflict? Every evening Walter Cronkite would report that General Westmoreland, the George Armstrong Custer of our generation, saw the "light at the end of the tunnel." All that he needed to finish the job were another 100,000 personnel and our boys would be home by the Fourth of July. His assurance of imminent victory became less plausible, when only two months earlier a "totally demoralized and defeated enemy" attacked the city of Saigon, temporarily taking control of the American Embassy there. Time to wire LBJ for 100,000 more troops.

I thought about asking Bartholemew to turn around and go back to the airport. I could catch a flight to New York, and be in Sweden by midnight. Then I could send back a telegram, letting the Army know about my early retirement. I could picture the scene at roll call the next morning at Fort Benning.

*"Lieutenant Woolsey," the Captain would call out." Are you here?Lieutenant Robert Woolsey!"*

*Then some Sergeant would interrupt the roll call.*

*"We've just received a wire from the bastard in Stockholm," he'd say. "Should I read it to you, Sir?" Then the Captain would nod his approval, and the Sergeant would begin.*

*"'Dear Fort Benning Infantry School:*

> *I know that it's very bad manners to tell you this so late, but I've decided to pass on this silly, stupid War. Call me crazy! But I just don't relish the thought of getting a leg blown off, and hobbling around for the next fifty years for some reason that I don't understand. When you guys come up with a logical war, please contact me.*
> *Respectfully,*
> *First Lieutenant Robert J. Woolsey' "*

Of course I didn't have the guts to carry it through. Defecting was tough business. Leaving home for good. Disgracing family and friends. Besides, I loved my country. I just hated the jerks that got us bogged down over in Southeast Asia. No, I'd stay. I had a duty to fulfill, and I was obliged to fulfill it -no matter how unpleasant it might be.

Bartholomew had already driven a couple of miles on the highway to Fort Benning, before I stopped daydreaming. He was rambling on about the points of interest in metropolitan Columbus.

"Ya see that cemetery yonder on the left," he announced. "That there's where ma' late Aunt Gussy and Uncle Wilbur're buried. They was both Methodists, and was laid to rest in th' Methodist Congregational Cemetery. Now, over to the right, if y'all squint yer eyes a mite, ya can see where my Ma and Pa was buried. They was Baptists, jest like me, and are in the First Baptist Pentecostal Cemetery. It's a tad *closer* to town than the Congregational. *That's* where me and the missus'll be laid out."

His voice quivered with pride, as he told me how the dearly departed Baptists of the town were buried closer to the holy shrine of Columbus than their lower caste Methodist brethren. A pride that would no doubt be passed on to Bartholomew's children, and his children's children. It was sort of like Tevye in *Fiddler on the Roof,* praying and hoping that one day he'd be rich enough to buy himself a seat in the synagogue, closer than his less fortunate *landsmen* to the Eastern Wall, facing Jerusalem.

I giggled in the back seat, as I pictured old Bartholomew singing and dancing in the venerable Baptist graveyard, in front of his tombstone, with a long beard, and wearing a yarmulke, and a prayer shawl. "If I were a *dead* man—ya da, biddy, biddy, biddy, biddy, bum…"

The guided tour continued with his pointing out the different iron mills and fertilizer plants scattered along the banks of the Chattahootchee. Those were the days of the environmentally unaware sixties. The pollution and poison relentlessly spewing out from those factories into the poor river, was doing a hundred times more damage to his beloved State of Georgia than General Sherman and all his pillaging Union Army had ever done.

When we finally arrived inside the gates of Fort Benning, Bartholomew stopped the cab so he could have a closer look at my orders, showing exactly where I was to report. Then he drove me to Section C, Building 4. He retrieved my suitcase, and vigorously shook my hand. I paid the fare, and gave him a fifty per cent tip, which I was certain would be added to his funeral fund. I walked to the building entrance that had a directory, assigning the new officers to their quarters.

The place was a motel like set-up with semi-private rooms, decorated in a Ramada Inn decor. Still, it was much more pleasant than the barracks accommodations I had envisioned. Each apartment had wall-to-wall maroon carpeting, twin beds, flanked by a couple of nondescript end tables, a desk with a straightback chair, a small refrigerator, a commode, with a 12" TV on top, and a huge dresser. Adjacent to the room was a private bath. Maybe this wouldn't be the hellhole I'd been dreading these past few months.

There was a knock at the door.

"Can I come in?" asked a deep voice with a distinctly Southern drawl.

"Sure!" I answered back reflexively. I didn't know anybody yet, so I assumed it was Bartholomew. Maybe I hadn't given him the correct fare? Maybe I left my papers in the back seat? Or maybe he just wanted to wish me luck again.

But as the door opened, I saw the imposing frame of a tall blond, crew-cutted cracker, a few years younger than myself. He had watery blue eyes, and still had his high school acne. He was in fairly good physical condition though, except for the tiny paunch that stuck out ever so slightly above his belt. This good ol' boy had obviously imbibed a few six packs in his relatively young life. In twenty years that little paunch was destined to become a full-blown Black Label beer belly. My new comrade-in-arms was named Victor Stimmons, of Raven's Point Alabama. He seemed friendly enough, even after he heard my New York accent and invited me to his room.

Victor had evidently spent a good portion of his pre-induction time getting acquainted with the owner of the town liquor store. His dresser was covered with half- empty bottles of Chivas Regal Scotch, Jim Beam Bourbon, Canadian Club Whiskey, and one bottle of Club Soda. Conspicuously missing were vodka, gin, and rum. Obviously anything without iced tea coloring, that couldn't be mixed with water, was not on Victor's List of Spirits. Next to the booze, there was a bucket of ice, and some plastic cups. I must've been the answer to his prayers for somebody to party with.

"Help yourself!" he said as he poured a stiff, three or four ounces of Jim Beam into his ice filled cup. "Or, if you'd like, there's a whole bunch of malt liquor in the ice box." I guessed that *refrigerators,* that you actually had to plug into an outlet were still a novelty in Raven's Point.

"Do you smoke?" he asked.

I nodded yes.

"Here, take a pack!" he said, opening up a fresh carton of Marlboros. "One great thing about the Army is the price of cigarettes. Only two bucks a carton down at the PX."

I took full advantage of his cigarettes, and his fifth of Chivas Regal as well. I appreciated good Scotch, but I hadn't had any much of an opportunity to enjoy it. In Germany it cost more than liquid caviar. At law school in Charlottesville, it was also beyond my budget. At U. Va. recreational alcohol usually meant a can of Old Milwaukee Beer, or, on special occasions, a shot of Piggledly Wiggledly Bourbon. Maybe once a month my roommate Mike Doyle, would visit his home in Fairfax just outside Washington D.C., with the threefold purpose of seeing his mom; having her do the dirty laundry he'd been piling up for two weeks; and stockpiling some inexpensive D.C. hooch.

Besides liquor and cigarettes, Victor and I had very little in common. He'd never met anyone from New York before—except for Arnold, his cousin Lucy's husband, They'd both attended Vanderbilt University, majoring in Psychology. Arnold wasn't really from New York City, but lived in someplace called Nyack, about an hour or so by car if you took the *New York Turnpike!*

After the obligatory guy talk about football and women, as well as that new TV show *Laugh-In*, the Chivas and the Jim Beam had sufficiently greased the skids for the conversation wheels. We made it through the first two hours, with only a couple of embarrassing pauses, when suddenly Victor blurted out, "So, are you ready to help the good gooks kick the asses of the bad gooks?"

With this short bigoted question, maybe Victor had defined the darker side of why we were in Viet Nam. I had little doubt that in some Pentagon War Room, a group of highly respected Generals, planning our country's strategy were thinking the same thing. Not necessarily thinking of our allies as "gooks" but patronizing them in their heads, as some backward *furriners* that the USA had to rescue.

But I had no desire to discuss the philosophy of the war with Victor. That might lead to some heated debate; and, after all he was my host. He'd already filled me with about half a pint of his best Scotch. So I replied diplomatically, "To tell you the truth, Victor, I think that with my scholastic—that is to say not very practical background—I'd serve my country best by analyzing CIA reports somewhere. When we've reached the point where *my* pitiful carcass has to help the Army to kick *anybody's* ass, we're in deep shit." I stirred the ice cubes in my plastic cup with my finger, and gulped down my last ounce of Scotch. "I'm starved!" I said. "Where's a good place to eat in town?"

Victor was peckish as well. All that Bourbon must've created quite an appetite, and from his capacity to toss down shots, I took an educated guess that he'd probably quaffed three or four before he invited me into his makeshift saloon.

"I know just the place," he said enthusiastically. "It's called the ' *Black Angus Europa*'. You can get a great three inch thick Porterhouse, if you like. Or, for you *Continental* types, they serve frogs' legs and snails. Yucch!"

"The steak part of the menu sounds terrific," I said." Just let me take a quick shower, and put on a shirt and tie. I'll see you back here in fifteen minutes."

The beads of hot water from the showerhead felt incredible as they bounced off my forehead. I'd been feeling icky all afternoon from the plane ride, and I could have easily dawdled in my little shower stall for ten minutes more; but my stomach was already growling over lack of food.

I met Victor back at his room. As we headed downstairs, I assumed we'd be taking a cab to town, but he volunteered to drive us in his huge 1967 Bonneville convertible. Those were the antediluvian days before the designated driver. Vic was pretty shitfaced, but I felt that it would be impolite to turn him down. Besides, I was a lot younger and dumber then—and a bigger daredevil. Anyhow I didn't expect to survive the Viet Nam War. So what the hell! Hey, we might crash, and I might sustain debilitating injuries. Maybe some serious enough to exempt me from military service. We were off on an evening in Columbus.

# Chapter Two

# G.I. Gourmet

We made it into town without mishap. Victor parked the B'ville, and we both stumbled into the restaurant. The sweet aroma of the barbecuing beef was like heaven. The headwaiter motioned to one of his staff to have us seated, and we plopped our famished bodies down at the heavy oak table. A few seconds later, the busboy handed us two Atlas- sized felt menus. Sure enough, the selections were half Texas style—half zee *haute cuisine*. Chili and garlic toast on one side-*Biftek au poivre* on the other. Both sides pretty reasonable.

Vic and I didn't take more than ten seconds to choose the twenty-four ounce Porterhouse- *rare*- but burnt on the outside. A baked potato with sour cream came with the entree. Even before we ordered, we started gobbling down the hot rolls and croissants, heaped in a straw basket at the center of the table.

Just then a *sommelier* made an unexpected appearance, holding out the wine list.

"Do zee Tchentelmen vish to order a bottle uff vine wiss dinner?" he said, attempting to feign a French accent, but sounding very much like a Yugoslavian imitating Pepe Le Pieux. I glanced around the room, to see that ice cold *Mateus* and *Lancer's* were running neck-and-neck as the crowd favorite. I was still polluted enough from the Chivas Regal to make a fool of myself.

"Do you want me to order a bottle of wine, Victor?" I said in a condescending tone of voice, which he fortunately didn't notice.

"Go right ahead!" he replied, trusting my experience, "You probably know a hell of a lot more 'bout wines than I do."

I raised my eyebrows and studied the French Section of Red Wines, and then announced with conviction, "Burgundy, *Chateau Neuf du Pape, 1961,* my good man."

You didn't have to be a gourmet to master the basic roles for selecting a wine. Red wine at room temperature with beef; white wine chilled, with fish or chicken; in foreign wines, the odd numbered years were usually better than the even. When in doubt order the most expensive selection. Never read from the wine list. Make your choice; memorize it; and repeat it to the steward, as though the selection confirms the choice you'd already made.

Anyway, when the *sommelier* returned, I put on a little show for Victor's benefit. The wine steward offered the bottle, label facing up. I pretended to read it through my Scotch-soaked eyes, and then nodded. The waiter removed the cork, which I also inspected, ostensibly to make sure that no little pieces had crumbled into the crimson liquid. Now it was the steward's turn. He poured an ounce of the Burgundy into my glass, which I lifted up, by the stem of course, to the light. I lowered the glass. I inhaled the bouquet like so much cocaine. Then I tilted the glass, which now had served the ceremony well enough to be called a "goblet", ever so slightly to trickle a sip under my tongue. I took a deep breath through my teeth, aerating the wine, and theoretically allowing my palate to savor the body. Unfortunately my tastebuds were so anesthetized by the four or five Scotches from Stimmon's wet bar, that I could have been drinking Listerine and I wouldn't have known the difference. But Victor was impressed as hell by all this bullshit, gaping at me through his bloodshot blue eyes, his mouth wide open. Then to complete my virtuoso performance I smiled and nodded approval to the Yugoslavian *sommelier,* my supporting actor in the scene. He filled my goblet; then the glass of Monsieur Stimmons; covered the bottle with a cloth in the bucket at tableside, and finally backed away, as though departing from royalty. Christ, I almost expected Victor to burst into applause and scream for an encore. He was awestruck. This ceremony would be described by him for years to come to countless audiences over the cracker barrel at the Raven's Point General Store.

# Chapter Three
# Do You Come Here Often?

Victor and I left the restaurant right after dessert, and after splitting the check right down the middle. It was only eight-thirty and he was still in a partying mode. We headed for a local joint called the *Sexy Scabbard*, a neon decorated watering hole for singles in their twenties. Victor couldn't figure why the place had that peculiar name, until I told him that the word for "scabbard" in Latin was "vagina." He roared out loud and slapped me on the back. At last my eight years of Classical Language study had paid off. Cicero and Caesar would have been proud of me. No doubt the owner of the *Scabbard* had been a Classical scholar as well. Probably a defrocked priest, excommunicated for molesting small boys.

We walked up to a no-necked bouncer named Floyd, who checked our ID's, and asked for the five bucks cover charge. When I gave him a ten-dollar bill, I insisted to Victor that it cover the tab for the both of us. After all, he had been my tour guide and chauffeur all evening. And the way that he was continually bragging about his success in the art of getting laid, I was sure that he would try and impress me with his talents by becoming my personal pimp.

Floyd stamped the backs of our hands with ultra-violet sensitive ink, in case we wanted to leave the place and come back. Then he handed each of us a ticket, entitling us to one drink apiece—domestic beer, generic liquor, or non-alcoholic beverage. Additional drinks, hard or soft were $1.50, unless some affluent patron decided to impress a young lady with a Cutty Sark, or a Heineken's, in which case the price was upped to $2.50. Really big spenders, that wanted a Drambuie or Napoleon Brandy, would have to fork over four bucks a pop. I calculated that at those prices in Columbus, Georgia in the year of our Lord 1968, the mark up must have been something like six thousand per cent. After all, a whole bottle of the finest French wine, served by a fancy Yugoslavian waiter at the *Black Angus Europa* was only $10.00.

Some townies and servicemen were already gathered around the three giant horseshoe shaped bars, getting quietly loaded enough to approach the "debutantes" of Columbus. This kind of evening I really didn't need. First of all the deejay was blasting out selections from the Rolling Stones at about eighty decibels; second, I was never any good at picking up women at clubs—even quiet ones; third, I was getting a hangover.

I wasn't in the mood to get drunk anymore. The 24-ounce Porterhouse had absorbed a lot of Victor's fine Scotch, which, by the way would've cost about sixty bucks at the *Scabbard*. So I ordered a Ginger Ale with my free coupon, and was about to take my first sip, when the bartender gave me a nasty smirk, "hinting" that his tip was not included in my coupon. Final reckoning—$10.50 for a six ounce tumbler of Piggledly-Wiggledly Ginger Ale!

I was already depressed, dejected and very horny. The lighting at the club was virtually non-existent, so most of the women seemed reasonably attractive. For that matter so did the men, I suppose. But Stevie Wonder would have been on an equal footing with every guy in the place. Just then Victor came over to me with two of the fairest flowers that Georgia had produced since Scarlett and Melanie—-at least that's how they must have looked to him in his ossified state.

"Bob m'boy, I'd like to introduce yo' Yankee ass to Juanita and Lurleen. Girls, this here's Lieutenant Woolsey. He was a stockbroker in New York City, before comin' down here to serve his country," he said.

Actually they weren't half bad in that dim lighting, except for those damned beehive hairdos saturated with Aqua Net that made the tops of their heads feel like cotton candy.

When Lurleen heard Stimmons' drunken claim elevating me to a stockbroker, she was all over me. Dancing in her head were visions of Wall Street SugarPlums. Who knows? I might become so sexually starved over the next ten weeks to propose marriage to her, and sweep her away from this God-awful town of Columbus. Married to a genuine *financeeer!* Livin' on Park Avenue in a swank five bedroom penthouse apartment, that'd cost at least *eight or nine hundred bucks a month.*

But her dreams of wealth took a downturn, when I ordered her a Seven and Seven, instructing the barkeep to use the house brand of Rye Whiskey. I knew I'd never see her again, but I took down her phone number anyway. I wasn't about to wreck her dream. Tomorrow at work she'd embellish our ten-minute conversation a bit. I would be described to the other girls, as Nelson Rockefeller's grandnephew, who was obviously crazy about her. If she were particularly creative in her little story, she'd go on to portray me as a financial wizard, who'd be running my securities empire by telephone, every minute of my leisure time at Fort Benning. Then she'd brag that I'd take her to dinner at the swankiest restaurant in Atlanta, in my new Mercedes, as soon as training was over.

I was anxious to leave. So I concocted the old, but still reliable excuse that I hadn't slept for the past twenty-four hours, and had to wake up early the next morning. I thanked Victor and told him I'd take a cab back, but he was paying most of his attention to feeling up Juanita. I said I'd see him in formation tomorrow morning.

After I apologized again to Lurleen for leaving so early, I headed for the door, and eventually hailed a taxi that brought me back to Building 4. My new roommate, Wayne Trowbridge, from Sioux Falls South Dakota, was busy unpacking his things, when I walked in the room.

It was about ten-thirty P.M. We talked for about half an hour. Wayne was a newlywed, married to his bride only about two months. She was already pregnant. They both realized the monstrous schedule that he'd have to keep for the first eight weeks, and agreed that she'd join him early in May, after the worst of his ordeal was over. The last week of the course was supposed to be a piece of cake. No more night marches, or obstacle courses to run. It would be mostly administrative crap, as well as platoons playing each other in softball games, and stuff like that.

When I shut off the little lamp on my night table, it took approximately 10 seconds for me to fall asleep.

# CHAPTER FOUR

# First Day of School

At precisely 5:30 A.M., I was awakened by about five hundred loud-speakers blaring away reveille throughout the Camp. This racket lasted almost five minutes. It was more than loud enough to wake up the entire population of Columbus too. Either they all wore earplugs, or all the windows and doors in town were caulked with some kind of miracle soundproof sealant.

Our first day was filled with getting medical exams, taking a battery of tests and receiving at least eight different inoculations, immunizing us against every disease in the world, probably some that hadn't existed since the Middle Ages. We also picked up our uniforms. In one of the long lines, I ran into Vic Stimmons, who told me that he had succeeded getting his sword into Juanita's scabbard last night. But since Victor would have bragged about getting laid from Mother Teresa, if given the chance, I only rated his claim a "5" on the credibility scale. But I had to admit that he was feeling her up pretty good when I left him at the club.

Next day we had our first mail call. Letters were a pretty big deal back then. There were no cellular phones; no phones in our rooms; and most folks couldn't afford extended long distance calls. I got two pieces of mail. One from my mom and dad, wishing me the best and praying for me; and one curious 9"x 11" envelope with no return address.

When I opened it up in the privacy of my room, my eyes bugged out. It was a "pornography package" with a note from my friend Mark, a successful stud on the West Side of Manhattan. He must've gone to the sleaziest section of the sleaziest bookshop on 42nd Street. It contained five perverted photographs, depicting unspeakably raw acts of sex (performed by consenting adults of course). One especially talented young starlet was simultaneously entertaining five gentlemen, all of whom disproved Thomas Jefferson's axiom that all men are created equal. Just *looking* at these things could have meant 3 to 5 at Leavenworth for me. Mark had signed each photo in lipstick, with the words, "Bob, it's not the same without you. Please come back soon. Love. Linda and Debbie. xxxooo"

His little joke gave me a needed laugh. Then I showed the photos to Wayne, who practically came in his pants then and there. Pornography was not the most thriving of businesses in Sioux Falls. Maybe that new poster of Raquel Welch in her cavewoman outfit was as prurient as they got. To be honest that really raunchy stuff didn't appeal to me. I wasn't about to advocate censorship or anything. It just didn't turn me on, that's all.

But old Wayne loved the stuff. He scrutinized every picture from every possible angle, even turning each of them upside down. So I donated them all to him on the spot. He thanked me profusely, and assured me that his wife would get a big kick out of them as well. When they got tired of them eventually, maybe he'd donate them to the local barber shop in Sioux Falls—sort of like gifting over a Picasso to a museum, so that the entire community could enjoy it.

# CHAPTER FIVE

# Sieg Heil

That afternoon we all received an introductory welcome to the Camp by its Colonel commandant, whose name escapes me. He was without question the biggest asshole I ever heard in my life. He'd most likely given that jingoistic, trite, Neanderthal welcome speech to every new group of Lieutenants, since the Viet Nam War began. It was probably based on a World War II version of the same damned thing that he composed twenty-five years ago, when he began his career during the Allied Invasion on D-Day. It was clearly meant to inspire men committed to some divine mission to save the world, like wiping out Nazism. That's probably what the old fart did. Substitute "Ho Chi Minh" for "Adolph Hitler"; "fanatical Viet Cong" for "fanatical Nazis". Our self-delusioned General Patton was living in a fantasy world. Most of the guys in the audience would've chopped off a testicle to get out of going to Viet Nam. Sure some liked military stuff, but not when it meant spending a year overseas, fighting an invisible enemy, that didn't fight like they were supposed to; and doing the fighting for the South Vietnamese Army, that made the Italian Army of World War II look like Caesar's legions in comparison.

This asshole raged on about stopping those Commie bastards before it was too late. If we didn't win this war, he raved, we'd be fighting off hordes of Red Chinese on the streets of San Francisco in five years. Guessing the likely social *mores* of Colonel Attila the Hun, I would've thought that he'd be happy to see San Francisco, with all its *fags and hippies*, burned to the ground.

This would have been the perfect guy to send into battle, but as a Grunt Private, not as a Colonel barking out senseless orders that would just cause more casualties. He was clearly someone born to blindly follow the orders of his superiors. An American *kamikaze*. But our nation had been lucky. As long as this jerk was confined to running this solitary Fort, we were safe. No chance for this moron to press any nuclear buttons. My mind turned off his tirade, and I thought of the movie *Dr. Strangelove* and the character General Jack T. Ripper, who sent out his aircraft loaded with H-bombs to annihilate the Russkis.

In his concluding statements he said something about how, as soldiers, we should all be grateful and proud to serve America in these desperate hours; and how as good Christians, (Jews, I guess were exempt) we should each swear a personal oath to obliterate every man, woman and child Communist from the face of the Earth. But I wasn't too sure how pleased Jesus would have been with such an oath—You know, blessed are the meek and the peacemakers—and all those other gentle types.

At the end of the speech, all the Captains and Low Field Grade Officers, that had to serve under this guy, broke into spontaneous applause. They stood up. Everybody in the Auditorium stood up. *I* stood up; and even joined in the ovation. If there had been torches in the Assembly Hall, it could've passed for one of *der Fuehrer's* speeches at Nuremberg in 1938. Yes, I had joined the mob. I was afraid not to; fearful of being subject to some trumped up Court Martial; the first soldier to be executed since Private Eddie Slovik at the Battle of the Bulge.

But that evening I discovered in a heated bull session that a lot of the guys felt the same way *I* did. They were afraid to make waves too. We all loved our country as much as Colonel Shithead; but we weren't sure fighting a war ten thousand miles away, for some undefined cause was the answer to America's survival. Too bad that the average South Vietnamese had a bunch of crooks as leaders, who'd probably turn tail and head for their Swiss bank accounts at the first sign of an enemy tank.

But I wasn't kidding myself about the enemy either. There weren't any good guys in this war. The VC. and the North Vietnamese were a vicious, and savagely brutal bunch of crazies, who would sacrifice every living thing in their country—or the world for that matter—at the order of Ho Chi Minh. Maybe they didn't have any numbered accounts in Zurich, but they personified a different type of evil, an evil philosophy where human life was expendable; where dissent wasn't tolerated; where questioning one's leaders meant certain death. It was this perverted kind of idealism that would result in the Killing Fields seven years later, leaving two million Cambodians murdered and buried in mass graves.

The lecture was over. We all went back to our rooms. Fortunately, I never saw or heard that crazy commandant again.

# CHAPTER SIX

# Corrupting Wayne

All things considered, Wayne wasn't such a bad guy to live with. He put up with my being a slob, and leaving my socks and underwear on the floor; and my buzz saw snoring didn't seem to bother him.

Out of gratitude I dropped Mark, my friend from Manhattan, a line asking him to send another package of smut for Wayne. A couple of days later I received one more plain brown 9"x 11" envelope containing Wayne's pornographic care package. He was grateful for my belated "wedding presents". But then he figured that he might as well go for the whole nine yards, and ask for something that he knew would *really* turn him and his new bride on. So he made a detailed request. Could I maybe get something showing large breasted black women doing the nasty with oriental men? It seemed that Mr. and Mrs. Trowbridge had a dirty little secret. I told him I'd see what I could do.

So I wrote Mark again, putting in my new requisition. He sent back a postcard that read, "With or without ropes?" What a pal. Wayne said that he'd prefer the ropeless variety. A week later he had the final portion of his collection stashed away in his bottom drawer.

To show his gratitude Trowbridge took me to see *2001: a Space Odyssey.* That was the film that really marked the beginning of special effects. Ten years later George Lucas would make a zillion dollars in *Star Wars* by using all the technology that Stanley Kubrick had started. Ten years before the movie *2001* , that crazy director, Ed Wood had set the standard for incompetence in far out special effects in *Plan Nine from Outer Space.* In that fiasco he got away with showing tin cans dangling from fishing line on the movie screen, and passing them off as flying saucers.

Wayne liked the huge floating spacecraft and the big computers with their lights blinking all over the place, but he had trouble getting Kubrick's message. Wayne was an OK guy, but he wasn't about to be nominated as President of Mensa. For instance, he didn't buy the attempt to portray HAL as a talking super computer. Wayne was convinced that the evil Space Agency in the movie had placed a spy in the spacecraft to manipulate HAL and tell it what to do. After all machines couldn't think, could they? I guess he figured that there was some kind of goofy scientist like the Wizard of Oz running HAL from behind a curtain on the spaceship. Maybe, like Toto, the little dog of one of the astronauts would run out, pull down the curtain with its teeth, and expose the spy. Wayne never could explain how the hero (Keir Dullea) was able to destroy HAL by loosening its nuts and bolts near the end of the movie, if there was some guy manipulating him all the time. But the picture was pretty confusing in other aspects. I'd grant him that.

We got back from the theater in plenty of time to put in the ten minutes of study for the quiz that we'd get tomorrow morning on today's material. The cadre made it a practice to administer a short test every day on yesterday's class. Just to make sure that the guys weren't *totally* asleep. It was pretty basic stuff.

Wayne and I would memorize five or six of the instructors' *key points* that they *always* emphasized by means of a learning device called *mnemonics.* Learn the mnemonic and you passed the test. The Army loved these things. They were a sort of acronym that guaranteed that even the most Forrest Gump-like private could learn. The basis mnemonic, *de riguer* for everybody, was PPPPPP, or "Prior planning prevents piss poor performance. Everybody knows what SNAFU means. Then there was ACSA-Always Carry Sufficient Ammunition. The Army seemed to have a catchword for everything. Somewhere in the bowels of the Pentagon there must've been some sixty-five year old Major hunched over a giant notebook churning them out with a quill pen. This Major from *Sesame Street* probably had daily experiments with words like "BOSYCOITH"—"Beware of shooting your commanding officer in the head"—or "NESDUYA"—"Never ever shove dynamite up your ass!" and catchy things like that. But Wayne and I never failed a test by memorizing this type of crap (for twenty four hours anyway), So it wasn't completely valueless.

On one of those rare occasions during the first few weeks, when Wayne and I weren't totally exhausted to just collapse into bed, we walked over to the PX for a beer. President Johnson just happened to be giving one of his "pep talks" on the war. It sounded like the usual LBJ crap with Johnsonisms like not caving in to the "Nervous Nellies" among us; and how if the brave Republic of South Vietnam fell, than other *dominoes* like Thailand, Burma, and the Philippines would also fall.

As Wayne and I were discussing whether UCLA would *ever* lose a Basketball game, I heard in the corner of my ear, LBJ's voice slowly and deliberately saying "I shall not seek, and I will not accept my Party's nomination for another term as President of the United States." The laughing and drinking crowd came to a hush. Johnson had given up on the war. Wayne and I stayed around for a few minutes to watch the replay and commentary on this unexpected announcement. We left our unfinished beers and went back to our room.

# CHAPTER SEVEN

# Sorry-Members Only

It was Saturday evening of my third week at the Fort, and I hadn't yet begun my habit of going to Atlanta to have fun on my time off. Mike Stern, maybe my best buddy in the platoon, suggested that we go to town, and try out a new place called the *Grateful Grape*. He didn't know much about it, except that it had no admission charge, and it gave fifty per cent off the first drink to servicemen. He had asked a Lieutenant Lucas Perkins, from another platoon, to come along. He was to meet us at the bus stop. Lucas was a little timid at first, but he had a great laugh that was just made for Stern's terrific sense of humor. Luke was from Memphis, Tennessee. Luke was a Negro.

I'd never really thought much about socializing with Negroes (that's what African Americans were called then). I didn't have any black friends. My folks weren't prejudiced, I guess, just a product of a different age. They were born when Teddy Roosevelt was President. They still, out of habit, referred to African-Americans as "colored". But I never heard either one of them use the word "nigger", or any of the other base names that folks in the South *and North* called black people.

I bring this up because the color of Lucas' skin was to have a stunning impact on our evening, but more importantly, it made me take a good, hard look at myself that night—and for years to come.

As we were about to enter the *Grateful Grape*, a Floyd type look alike blocked our way. Maybe there was an admission charge after all. But it wasn't a matter of money that was preventing us from going in. It was race.

"You and the other gentleman can go in," said the gargantuan doorman, addressing me and pointing to Stern. "But he'll have to stay outside", pointing to Perkins.

This was blatant, unadulterated, undisguised bigotry in its cruelest form. Thank God we were just seeing the remnants of it then in the South. Not that it didn't exist in the North too, but there was a difference *below* the Mason-Dixon Line. We Yankees just practiced discrimination in a more refined, genteel way; but practically nobody in up North at that time would have had the gall to say in effect,"Black Man, you can't come into this public establishment." Of course there were some places that black people didn't go. Some places where white people just didn't go to, for that matter. But if somebody black showed up at *Lutece* in New York, no headwaiter would dare bar him or her physically from the door. They'd even call them "Sir", or "Ma'am", and pull out their chair for them, no matter what prejudiced thoughts they might be thinking.

Well, Stern was pissed off as hell. I was too. But Mike became furious. Stuff like this had probably happened to his parents, being Jewish and all, and it *must've* happened to his Grandparents, as they made their way out of the Lower East Side, and into the Great American Dream. I guess that as a WASP I'd had it pretty good most of my life.

"C'mon, let's go someplace else," Lucas said, readily accepting defeat. He'd had that type of shit pulled on him before.

"No,no! This isn't fair!" Stern insisted, thinking perhaps that reasonable adults, talking calmly, presenting arguments *pro* and *con,* could come to some happy conclusion. But Mike wasn't negotiating with some wholesaler in his dad's clothing store. There was no give and take here. He should've known better. It was like Berlin about thirty years before. There were no good, or socially acceptable Jews then; no Jews that maybe didn't have to wear the *Star of David* armbands all the time. Just Jews. At the *Grateful Grape* there were just Negroes.

After a few minutes we all knew that it was futile. Lucas gently nudged Mike; and I tugged on his sleeve.

Then the doorman, performing some warped act of contrition, yelled to us, as we headed away from the entrance, "Hey, why don't you guys try *Gildersleeves*. It's down the street about a hundred yards."

Just then a darker side of my own character revealed itself. For a moment I was annoyed at Lucas. I was actually *blaming* him for ruining my evening. I was pissed off that Mike had invited him along. Maybe I only felt that way for a few moments, but I felt it.

I don't know if there's anything in Psychology like an Apostle Peter complex. But that's what I'd call what I had then. I remembered from Sunday School how Peter got all nervous when they arrested Christ, and pretended not to know him during Pilate's "Ken Starr Investigation". For a few hours anyway, Peter only cared about his owned frightened ass. I felt something like that when I stood up and applauded, after that dumb Colonel Commandant finished his speech. If I'd remained seated, or if I'd stood up and shouted that he'd been spouting a crock of shit, it wouldn't have done me any good. A couple of Army *bouncers* would've grabbed me and marched me to the stockade. My family would've been disgraced, and I would've received a dishonorable discharge. Stigmatized for life.

But the three of us took the doorman's cue, and headed for *Gildersleeves*. It wasn't really such a bad place. It was pretty small though, and was dominated by huge grand piano that *nobody* played all evening. A black bartender, who could read from our faces, what must've happened to us a few minutes before, came over to us from his cash register behind the bar.

"Y'all are welcome here. No sweat. What'll it be? No sweat, "he said putting out our cocktail napkins.

We ordered a Bourbon and Water each. Then another round; and then another after that. After an hour or so we were all laughing and shoving one another. Like little kids at the playground that are bullied away from the swings by the bigger boys, but stop crying eventually, as they discover that good friends can have just as much fun on the see-saws. Heck, if you're with *friends* as a kid, you can have more fun playing with a big cardboard box, than *alone* with some fancy bicycle.

The three of us laughed ourselves silly, as we plotted ways to get even with the *Grateful Grape*. Mike suggested that we rent a white hooker for a half an hour and pay her twenty or thirty bucks. All she'd have to do was make out with Luke about ten feet or so in front of the *Grape's* main entrance. You know give him big French kisses; maybe slide her hand down his crotch. We'd show those bigoted bastards. Or maybe I could find a mouse someplace, go back to the club undercover, and surreptitiously release the little feller as I pretended to tie my shoelace.

But we knew that was just the liquor talking. Hell, if the cops showed up, they'd probably arrest Lucas for consorting with a known prostitute. He'd be thrown in the Columbus cooler. Mike and I would follow him as co- conspirators. In an all *white* cell naturally. Or maybe we'd all be sent to one those renowned Georgia chain gangs. Like Paul Muni in *I am a Fugitive*. Some muscular black fellow prisoner, with arms like Joe Frazier, would have to loosen our leg irons with a big sledgehammer. Then we'd escape with bloodhounds yelping and chasing us through the woods. We'd be caught eventually, after sacrificing our own personal freedoms to save each other. Instead of the electric chair, the judge would sentence us to another ten weeks of Infantry training at Fort Benning.

As for our little caper with that mouse, we'd get life for sure under the pressure of those animal rights activists, for false imprisonment of the defenseless little rodent. Then they'd tack on another ten years for good measure for our crime of releasing a wild beast on private property and threatening the innocent lives of the people of Georgia.

We didn't meet any women that night, but we had fun. I thought again about my mental betrayal of Lucas. In six months the poor guy could be lying dead in some rice paddy halfway around the world, with a bullet in his head. And those bastards at the *Grateful Grape* would still be turning away other Lucases. Those rednecks weren't fit to wipe his boots! And for a moment I'd almost taken their side. I felt like shit. Maybe it was the bourbon. Most likely it was those day old canapés from the snack table at *Gildersleeves'*. I ran to the John and threw up.

# CHAPTER EIGHT

# Going My Way

The next day was Sunday. I knocked at Mike Stern's door about 10:AM. His roommate was out somewhere. I asked him if he wanted to pursue the thing about Luke being ostracized from the lily white club. He thought that it was a great idea, but didn't know who to go to. The Colonel was a loony, but we both doubted that he was prejudiced—unless the Negro was a Communist of course. After a ten second deliberation, we ruled him out. We talked it over a bit more. In the war movies the guys always brought their problems to the chaplain. We both agreed that was a good place to start. Major Dougherty, a Catholic Priest in his civilian days, was probably pretty busy until early afternoon. After all Sunday *was* the only day he really worked.

We went to his office after lunch, about 1:00 P.M. We politely knocked on his door and entered, after he told us to come in. We exchanged salutes , and he asked us to sit down.

"Well lads what is it?" he said like Spencer Tracy in *Boy's Town*. But he had more the manner of the Bing Crosby priest in those late forties flix with Barry Fitzgerald. You know, not as street wise as Father Flanagan.

"We had an unpleasant experience last night, Father—or is it Major - or Father Major?" I said stumbling over my words. Mike and I agreed that I should be spokesman. I wasn't starting off very well.

"A lot of the men, particularly those who watch those World War II movies call me *Padre*," he replied in his thick Boston accent. "You can use that if you like. I'm sure that the Bishop won't mind."

"Well Padre, last night at one of the clubs in town called the *Grateful Grape*," I continued, "Lieutenant Stern, I, and a Negro officer were refused entrance. That's not exactly correct. The other officer, Lieutenant Lucas Perkins was refused. Mike and I were booted out because we insisted that Lucas be allowed to go in with us."

"That kind of outrage is of course reprehensible," he replied. "But what exactly is it that you want the Army, or this humble priest in uniform to do?"

"We both thought that perhaps there could be some kind of boycott against clubs and stores and such that still practice this kind of bigotry," I said. "After all, it is illegal now, and these guys shouldn't be allowed to get away with it. We'd see how long they'd stay in business if all their trade with military personnel were cut off."

"Well Lieutenant," he responded lighting up his pipe, "The word has come down from the Most High that we are all to tread very lightly when it comes to race relations in town. Maybe if it were up to me, I'd take a Company of our Special Forces, and tear down every one of those "white only" clubs stone by stone. But I'm a soldier as well as a priest, and orders are orders. But I *do* pray for racial tolerance, and for the Lord to show us all the way. And I haven't always taken refuge behind this collar you see me wearing. Three years ago I marched with Martin Luther King in Selma, in civilian clothes, holding hands with other ministers and rabbis, against the shouts and curses of the white people, who had been stirred up for days by the Klan.

"But there is change. Negroes are starting to vote here. Four years ago they couldn't set foot in a polling place. That means political power; and huge corporations are letting the word go forth that they'll set up factories and plants down here on an *equal opportunity* basis only. Who knows? In a few years Columbus might have a black sheriff—or even mayor. You young men will be here for a few more weeks. That's a blink of an eye in the history of race down here. You'll be long gone in no time. But I will promise you two things. First, I'll write a letter to a friend of mine in the Justice Department telling him about this "Grape" place; second, I'll continue to pray for an end to the vile things that happened to you last night. Don't laugh! It's what I do best."

Mike and I left the Padre's office barely consoled by his unenthusiastic promise to help. It was very frustrating.

"So, do you think that it might do us any good to go into town and talk to *your rabbi*?" I asked Mike.

"My rabbi's in Long Island," he answered. "Besides, the one in Columbus probably used up every favor that the local town officials might have owed him, getting that new *Bagel Nosh* past the Zoning Board. I guess we'll just have to bite the bullet, as they say."

We started back to our quarters; we both had a lot of stuff to take care of before Monday morning.

"*Shalom,* buddy," I said as we parted company.

"*Pax tecum, mi fili,*" he responded in flawless Latin.

A week later Martin Luther King was shot and killed in Luke Perkins' home town of Memphis.

# CHAPTER NINE

# Beating the System

The first few weeks of training were brutal, at least for me. All my years of smoking, guzzling beer, and avoiding physical activity, had turned my twenty-six year old body into one more akin to that of a puffy, out-of-shape fifty year old man. In fact, there were probably a lot of fifty-year-olds, who'd turn down an exchange. But I noticed a slow, gradual improvement in my physical stamina. By late April I could actually run a mile in under eleven minutes—10:58 to be exact. I even beat out another guy in the platoon. However, my embarrassing last place finish in the obstacle course; and crawling under barbed wire, were enough to earn me the nickname "Ranger"

During week four we all had to pass a map reading exercise. Employing a map, a compass, and a brand new pair of arch supports, I had to locate, in a heavily vegetated area, six "markers". Our supervisor didn't specify what these would be; but we'd recognize them when we saw them. We were all given five hours to "accomplish our mission". The officer in charge gave us a layout of the course. The test area was a little longer than thirteen hundred yards long, and about five hundred yards wide. A straight dirt road divided the course in half. The markers were placed on either side of the road. Upon locating the sought after marker, we'd put it down as an answer on our test sheet. All the tests were different. At the end of the exercise, a siren would sound, and we'd all have to head back to the dirt road, and walk north to the awaiting trucks.

I knew it wouldn't be easy. The whole course was full of chuckholes and brambles; swamp and dense foliage—some created by nature; but *most* of them cruelly devised by some sadistic Infantry landscaper, who was probably cackling to himself right now at the number of sprained ankles, bumped foreheads, and scraped faces and hands, that would result from the exercise. Maybe some poor slob might even suffer a broken pinkie or nose—nothing too serious tho'—the Army didn't really want to maim anybody.

I looked at the set of instructions for Problem #1 "From the starting point, head north-northwest at an angle of 350 degrees for one hundred yards. Stop. Continue at an angle of 200 degrees for 50 yards. Stop. Continue north at an angle of 15 degrees for 180 yards. Stop. West 270 degrees; 120 yards. I was moving in circles. Finally I located the marker "C" on a 3'x5' sign, in black on a yellow background. This little walka-bout had taken me almost an hour. I was tired. I had taken a couple of nasty falls already. At this rate I would fail the course for sure. Damn! I'd have to take it all over again on Saturday afternoon, and ruin my weekend.

I sat down, took a swig of water from my canteen, and tried to think the Army way. Simple; straightforward; no imagination. The captain in charge said that the course was a little more than *thirteen* hundred yards long—markers on each side of the road. Could that mean thirteen markers on each side? Eureka! Twenty-six markers—-twenty-six letters. One placed every hundred yards. I looked down at my map. Marker "C'" under which I was sitting, was three hundred yards north of the starting point. I traced the next set of directions on my map. Two hundred and ten yards; ten degrees north—-blah, blah, blah. Bingo! The next marker/ letter was six hundred yards north of the starting point. About a hundred yards west of the dirt road. It must be the letter

"F". When the geniuses laid out the course, they were more interested in making it physically torturous than conceptually complicated.

Sure as hell, the letters on the other side began with "N" and ended with "Z". Military symmetry; nice and neat. This would be too easy. The angles and distances that I penciled in on my map confirmed my cartographic *coup*. Those guys that deciphered the Japanese code—Bah! Kid stuff! I lit up a cigarette and dawdled in a nearby clearing for fifteen minutes or so; then I moved around a bit and dawdled some more. A couple of my fellow Pathfinders spotted me as they were searching for their own markers. Wayne Trowbridge saw me smelling the wildflowers and shouted out," Hey Bob! You'd better get your ass movin' or you'll be smellin' those same wildflowers on Saturday afternoon!"

"Thanks Wayne! You're probably right, "I answered back, and pretended to continue my Boy Scout routine.

I'd try to make it look a little more difficult. After all, I didn't want to raise any suspicions about my being some Superman Daniel Boone or anything. I went into the brush and completed the test on paper in about twenty minutes. "C", "F", "K", "X", "S", and "P". I had mastered my first lesson in Armythink. What to do to pass the time left in the exercise? I read the only book I had. It was the official US Army map reading manual. The gods *would* have their little joke. A few hours later, the siren sounded, and I walked about a hundred yards to the truck that was waiting for us. Later that day I received word that I'd made a perfect score, tied with two other guys from my platoon. A few of the fellows even stopped calling me "Ranger".

# CHAPTER TEN

# Discovering Atlanta

After about a month as Fort Benning's prisoners of war, a few of us decided to make the two hour trip by car to Atlanta, the Athens of the South. Mike Stern's Mom and Dad were visiting him from Long Island that weekend, so he couldn't make it. But I teamed up with Brian Terhune, Cal Sturgess, and Burt Warren for the ride. Brian picked us all up in the Company Courtyard at noon sharp that Saturday. It was teeming just like it must've been before the Great Flood, and the most logical thing for everybody would have been to cancel the trip, go back to our rooms, get under the covers, and either read or watch the Basketball games on TV.

But we were determined to have a good time in Atlanta, even if we caught pneumonia in the downpour, or were buried alive under a mudslide on the highway. Brian put his headlights on during the ride, but he could barely see the car in front of him. Every half-hour or so, one of us would volunteer to relieve him at the wheel, but he insisted that he was OK. Besides, he wasn't sure if his auto insurance would cover him if the car got involved in an accident, while he was in it but *not* behind the wheel.

It felt *so* good when we drove into downtown Atlanta, and saw real live big city folk without green uniforms. These were the South's most cosmopolitan citizens, who even *invited* the rest of the world to visit their fine city. Of course there were a couple of pockets of metropolitan sophistication back in Columbus- it even had its own symphony orchestra. But it was still a provincial, xenophobic, southern town at heart. Brian headed straight for the brand new *Hyatt Regency* Hotel, with its space age, bubble shaped elevators, where you could view the 360 degree panorama all around you, while the newfangled contraptions zoomed you up to your room at about five or six floors a second.

The four of us were still soaking wet as we registered in the lobby downstairs. Brian and I got a room with two full beds on the 20th floor, overlooking the lobby, the little shops, and the restaurant; while Cal and Burt shared a similar room that overlooked the City, just down the hall.

The bellhop carted our luggage to our room, and placed it just inside the door. My gear was no problem—a small canvas gym bag, containing toiletries, a change of underwear, shoes, and some clean socks; and a garment bag covering a sports jacket, a white shirt, a tie, and a pair of pants. Brian, on the other hand, had brought along his monster, three suit, *American Tourister* world traveler suitcase, that was more appropriate for a two week trans- Panama Canal cruise on the Queen Elizabeth than an overnight stay at the *Hyatt Regency*.

I tipped the bellhop a buck for the both of us; and since Brian had been nice enough to provide the free transportation, the rest of us would see to it that he received a complimentary pass on the first round of drinks that evening.

I couldn't help but chuckle, as I saw Brian unpacking his things.

"Ya' think that you've got enough stuff for the weekend there, Brian?" I asked sarcastically. "It looks like you've got a suit for dinner, a suit to go out nightclubbing in; and you can use that third gray double breasted as a pair of pajamas."

"The suits get all wrinkled unless you stuff the suitcase with three of 'em till it's jam packed, jughead," he replied. "Besides, it's the only piece of luggage I've got. Until now I haven't had a chance to pick up a more compact size. Anyway, you can never pack too much, Bob m'boy. You can't be sure that you won't forget something."

Then I went downstairs *to* the small Odds 'n Ends shop in the lobby. There was an item that I just *had* to buy. After that I took the Star Ship elevator back to our room.

"Ya' mind if I use the bathroom for the next hour?" I asked Brian.

"Course not," he answered. "But do you always take so long to get ready?"

"Not unless I have *this!*" I replied, holding up the package of bubble bath that I bought down in the Odds 'n Ends boutique." I haven't had a good soak in a tub since I left home. And if, when it's your turn to use the head, you find the *Essence of Lavender* too overpowering, I also picked up a can of *Lysol* pine scented air freshener, so you can fumigate the place after I'm through."

Soaking in that big tub, smoking a cigar, and relaxing to the music from my portable radio, was the high point of my military career thus far, but my skin was starting to resemble that of a prune. So I concluded that an hour bubble bath was enough. Besides, I forgot to bring my rubber duck and toy submarines along to play with in the tub.

I got up from the frothy water, showered, went to the sink and brushed my teeth. Then I poked through my toiletry kid for my shaving stuff. I found my razor, but I must've left my shaving cream back at Benning. I would've asked Brian to use the can of *Barbasol* back in his suitcase, but I didn't feel like being lectured on the sins of under-packing, particularly after my smart-alecky remarks; so I lathered my face up real good with the tiny bar of *Ivory* soap, compliments of the hotel, smeared it all over my beard, and shaved the way my dad had when he was a young man. I took my time, was very careful, but nearly bled to death from the four or five nicks that I gouged into my tender skin. As the hot steam in the room hastened the flow of blood, I stuck on the ritual pieces of toilet paper over my face to stem the gushing from the various arteries; and I exited the bathroom.

"It's all yours!" I announced to Brian. He went inside.

About four o'clock there was a knock at the door. Burt and Cal had bought a fifth of *Dewar's*, and were "donating" it as the liquor for a happy hour. They had a large bucket of ice, and four glasses, hygienically sterilized in those little wax paper bags. For a mere five dollars, I could join the party in progress. As our chauffeur, Brian could join in for free. So we sat around for the next hour, and finished about half the bottle among the four of us.

Cal suggested that we get dressed and try this new restaurant that just opened in town, and had been recommended by the *concierge*. A different kind of Chinese place. Not the usual *Egg Foo Yung*, and *Chow Mein* that we were used to; but a restaurant featuring super spicy dishes called Szechwan, heavy on the meat and shrimp, and light on the noodles and rice. If we got there by 6:30, we'd have lots of time afterwards to visit the sin palaces of Atlanta.

Later on we piled into Brian's Pontiac, headed for Peachtree Street, and parked at the corner of Cedar Lane, about a block from the *Szechwan Dynasty*. It had stopped raining, so we didn't need those junky collapsible umbrellas that we all bought for a buck apiece down at the "Odds 'n Ends" shop.

We went in and were seated at a booth for four. The waiter recommended a few dishes, but assured us that *everything* was delicious. The food was glorious. Like nothing else Chinese that I'd ever eaten. Heaping platters of Garlic Shrimp, and General Tso's Chicken, Extra tangy Shredded Pork, and Double Sautéed Beef with Orange Sauce. Every item had been marked as extra spicy with two red stars on the menu. All four of us shared from each other's colossal serving tureens; and our eyes watered as we guzzled glasses and glasses of ice water to neutralize the chili peppers and other Northern Chinese condiments that singed our tongues. But despite our ravenous appetites, we were only able to finish half the portions. Mr. Chang, our waiter, was kind enough to salvage the remaining half in two mammoth doggy bags, and we were on our way.

While standing at the cashier's counter, Cal and I started up a conversation with Beverly and Glenda, a couple of young ladies, who were students at Emory University. Making small talk at a place like the *Dynasty* was easy. The subject was *Food*! We all couldn't help but prattle about the culinary miracles we had just devoured.

Like gluttonous swine we regretted not having been able to sample all of the restaurant's spicy goodies. Glenda regretted not having tasted my Garlic Shrimp, and my palate was jealous of her selection of Scallops with Peanut Sauce.

Our skinhead haircuts, and berry brown tans gave our "occupations" away. We said that we were only in town until tomorrow afternoon, were complete strangers to Atlanta, and were overnighting at the *Hyatt*. This *wasn't* meant as a hint for them to follow us back to the hotel. Really it wasn't. Anyway, *they* suggested that we accompany them back to the visitor's lounge at their dorm. When our appetites got their second wind, we all could sample tidbits from each other's doggy bags, after warming them up on the dormitory kitchen hot plate. As a further inducement coffee and tea were free to all guests. They told us that they had to be back in their rooms by eleven o'clock curfew, to study for their finals, beginning in two weeks.

We told them that *we'd* jump at the offer, but couldn't abandon Brian and Burt, who were just that moment looking very sad and lonely in the other corner of the restaurant. Glenda said that there were lots of available ladies at *Delta Phi Sigma*, who would just *adore* some male company before curfew.

So like Swiss envoys we conveyed their proposals to Brian and Burt, who were, as their body language screamed out, more than a ready to spend a couple of hours at a girls' dormitory. But they hemmed and hawed to save their masculine face, muttering something about coming to Atlanta to get laid, and not to drink tea and nibble *Lorna Doones* at some old college dorm. It didn't take much to convince them otherwise. First of all we explained that their chances of getting sex were practically *nil*, unless they were willing to pay a hundred bucks to a professional, who might very well transmit to them a rash that they hadn't bargained for; second, at the dorm they might actually meet someone nice enough to see again in the next few weeks; finally, if they found the evening of tea and cookies boring, they could take their leave at eleven o'clock, and head for the pick up joint of their choice, where they could spend the next three or four hours practicing their singles' bar dialogue.

So we were all on our way to *Delta Phi Sigma*. When we arrived, I continued having a great time with Beverly. She was a Journalism major, and planned on breaking ground for women on the TV news, as soon as she graduated. She and Glenda had fixed Brian and Burt up with Emily and Mindy on the world's most impromptu blind dates. The girls were good sports about the whole thing, considering that they'd only been given fifteen minutes to look their best for their surprise escorts from Fort Benning.

The eight of us spent the first half-hour or so getting to know one another. Then four of us split off to play a little Bridge. Next to me, Glenda and Cal were the two worst players in the history of the game. Beverly cracked up watching as the three of us competed as to who could make the dumbest bid. Finally we gave up and decided to play "Go Fish". You know the game. "Glenda , do you have any *threes*?No? Then *Go fish!*"

About ten thirty we all noshed a bit from each other's doggy bags. Brian and Burt were trying their best *not* to have a good time, somewhat embarrassed that they had no choice in selecting their *own* female companions. But despite their macho efforts to the contrary, they were enjoying themselves. Brian's ego was at a record high, as Emily doubled over laughing, while he entertained her with stories about his Dublin born parents, and their Irish Catholic outlook on the World. For instance, Mother Terhune would caution Brian's sister, Siobhan, on the evils of wearing patent leather shoes." Sure'an ye moight as well strap mirrors t' yer feeyt," she'd say in her Joyceian brogue." Th' lecherous lads in this parish'll be starin' down at those shoiny thin's all night tryin' to peek up yer legs t'see the treasure of yer womanhood. So at this ev'nin's dance at St Agnes' , ye'll be wearin' those noice brown *felt* pumps that I give ye last Christmas, B'Jeez. "

Brian took down Emily's phone number ( just in case he ever came to Atlanta again); and even gave her a kiss on the cheek, as all of us left the dorm a little before eleven o'clock.

We had all been up for almost eighteen hours now; and had spent the first five of them marching and running, back at Fort Benning. I was ready to call it quits, collapse, and go back to the hotel. Getting Beverly's phone number was enough for me.

I was sure that Brian felt the same way too. But as the driver of our horny detachment, he *had* to take Burt and Cal "on the town". So he dropped me off back at the *Hyatt*, as the remaining musketeers headed off for some carousing at Atlanta's late night pick up spots. I went to bed about 11:30, and was sound asleep, when I heard Brian stumble in three hours later. He didn't want to wake me up completely, so he kept the light off.

"Did you guys score?" I mumbled.

"No!" he answered curtly. "Just a waste of time and money."

I covered my head and went back to sleep.

But that night did change the "Life of Brian". He phoned Emily Sunday evening from Benning. Then he wrote her during the middle of the week. He drove to *Delta Phi Sigma* every weekend after that, for almost two months, to see her; and spent every minute, when he got the chance, talking to her on the telephone. Then in late May he proposed to her over tea and *Lorna Doones* at the dorm. She accepted and they were married a month later, at one of those military weddings, passing under the crossed swords, as they were pelted with rice. She made a beautiful June Bride.

# CHAPTER ELEVEN

# Follow the Yellow Brick Road

A couple of days later, after breakfast, my platoon was instructed to report back to our quarters where a couple of trucks would transport us to our field training exercise—standard gear of helmets, backpacks, and rifles.

We climbed into the metal seated vehicles, which guaranteed us some black and blue marks as well as very sore asses during the bumpy ride. The truck took us to a clearing, where we *devehicled*, and were met by Infantry Sergeant Biffel, who was to be our supervisor that morning.

He led the entire platoon to an area facing three kinds of terrain; a dirt road that was bordered by a few trees—not very many—which curved to the right, and led to the bottom of a moderately steep hill; second, a stretch of thick brush, which we couldn't see through, but which obviously led to the bottom of this same hill; and third, a stinking, fly covered swamp that also seemed to terminate at the bottom of that same hill.

Sergeant Biffel pointed out that the object of this field exercise was to go *via* one of these three routes to the base of the hill; race up same; capture same. He pointed out that the dirt road was the fastest way to the objective, but that it offered practically no cover. The enemy holding the hill, was heavily armed with machine guns, and would have a good view of us along *that* route from the top of the hill. The second and third choices of thick brush and swamp, offered concealment and the element of surprise, even if they might take longer to traverse.

Each squad in the platoon was to commence a staggered advance in about ten minutes. The results of the exercise weren't going on our training scorecards, because only one man from each squad would be making the choice. The choicemaker for my particular squad that morning was me. Sergeant Biffel took each squad leader aside, and asked us the approach we'd take. Bill Safford of the first squad opted for the brush, as did Matt Sherman of squad two; Ollie Taylor of the third decided on that stinking swamp.

I really didn't wish to venture into that suspicious looking thicket. No doubt our hospitable Cadre had planted all sorts of nasty goodies all over the place in there. Barbed wire surprises; clever booby traps; fallen logs to climb over and other stuff which a real squad going into a real skirmish might encounter. On the other hand the swamp was not as much of a hidden adventure, but it must've smelled like hell, and was probably loaded with bugs. I wouldn't have put it past our considerate hosts at Fort Benning to have sprayed the place with Maple Syrup on purpose, to attract just about every fly and mosquito in South Georgia.

The road, as the third alternative, looked pretty safe. Under actual combat conditions, any squad leader would have been out of his mind to take it. Even a blind enemy machine gunner would slaughter your entire outfit in about ten seconds. But this wasn't real war. Those guys on the top of that hill were our own boys. They'd be shooting blanks! Besides, Sergeant Biffel said that this was purely an exercise. The grades wouldn't count.

And so with Robert Frost -like wisdom, I chose "the road."

"Huh?" said the veteran Sergeant, when I told him of my decision. "Ya sure about that, Sir? Ya don't want to change yer mind?"

"No Sergeant. I think I'll take my chances with the first route."

"Very well, Sir. Begin your attack in five minutes at 0820 hours."

I watched with some guilt as the other three squads ventured into their respective predicaments. Then Biffel blew his whistle, signaling my turn to go.

"Follow me men!" I shouted in my best command voice, as I headed for the road and the doom of our entire squad.

"Up the road men!" I continued shouting. "Take whatever cover you can find, but we have to make it to the top of that hill!"

Echoes from *The Charge of the Light Brigade* rang in my ears. *"Cannon to the left of them , cannon to the right of them, cannon in front of them, volley'd and thunder'd"*

Blanks were being fired at us from every angle possible at the top of that hill. We all would have been massacred before we made it fifty yards.

*"Was there a man dismayed? No! tho' the soldiers knew , someone had blunder'd"*

Like sitting ducks we ran and ran, finally making it to the bottom of the damned hill, screaming our lungs out.

*"Ours was not to reason why. Ours was but to do or die"*

"Attach bayonets, men!" I shouted to my suicide patrol, who had all been killed by imaginary bullets a long time ago. Finally, surpassing the bravery of General Pickett and Errol Flynn, we made it to our objective and collapsed.

*"When can their glory fade? Oh, the wild charge they made. All the world wondered."*

Then some other non-com, Sergeant Winslow, told us to sit down, relax, and wait for the others to arrive. It took about another fifteen minutes before the first of the "bush soldiers" made it through *Frontierland*. They fired a few shots in the spirit of the game, but they were almost too pooped to pull the their triggers. Then they joined my squad at the top of the hill. Finally the unit from the Okeefenokee exited from the bog, and began their sloppy ascent up the embankment. They were covered with Georgia's slimiest *dreck* and stunk like the bottom of a septic tank. Every man in the last three squads ripped out his canteen and drained it to the last drop of water; then they collapsed on the hillside trying to catch their breath. The mud on the valiant swamp creatures would start to dry in a few minutes, and by ten o'clock they'd all look like little clay soldiers.

Sergeant Biffel made an announcement over his portable loudspeaker that his critique would start in 10 minutes. I'm sure that he didn't use the word"critique" though.

"Listen up gentlemen! Please listen up!" he said."I thank you all for participating in this morning's exercise. Lieutenants Safford and Sherman, you both got an "A". Twenty per cent casualties. Lieutenant Taylor, you got a "B". thirty per cent casualties. Finally, Lieutenant Woolsey, you got a "D". One hundred per cent casualties. I'd risk a guess that nobody in your squad got through alive. Maybe one could have survived with a shoulder wound. I would've given you an "F", but you *did* complete the maneuver to the top of the hill in pretty fast time——*with all your dead men.*"Then he went on to describe in his homespun way, how the easiest path to achieving one's goal in life is not necessarily the best one. A little non-commissioned philosophy aimed at putting down my foolhardy plan of battle.

I had anticipated all of this crap when I chose the road. It was a decision about playing a game. Nobody got hurt. Nobody got a poor grade. I was the only person that got chewed out. I had decided that I didn't want to suffer any unnecessary pain or discomfort that morning. At the end of it all, I wasn't bumped or scraped or bruised. I wasn't saturated with sweat and foul smelling mud. To achieve this satisfactory result, I had to eschew the *macho* choice of putting my body though an additional thirty minutes of agony for no logical reason whatsoever. Sure, I got an embarrassing evaluation from old Sergeant Biffel, but my IQ could endure the dressing down. The bottom line was that the men under my command made out best of all. They had a pretty easy morning, and received no polite scolding. They had just followed the orders of their mentally unbalanced leader. The lesson learned: Never follow any screwed up Intelligence Officer over any open road, to storm any enemy with a machine gun! And for this we had to waste a whole morning?

That evening after supper, Wayne and I were in our apartment relaxing and taking care of a few personal matters. There was a knock on the door. After we both yelled that it was open, a young Infantry Officer, a First Lieutenant like myself, entered the room.

"Which of you is Lieutenant Woolsey?" he asked.

"That's me, "I answered.

"Oh, they didn't tell me that you were a *First* Lieutenant." He replied.

This piece of information was obviously a very important one in this guy's Bible of military protocol. He had some kind of bone to pick with me, but now he'd have to do it as my equal, not as my superior.

"Why the hell did you have to act like some wiseass, and spoil the field exercise that I planned this morning by using the road?" he barked out.

He was upset as hell. He could see from my Intelligence Emblem, that I wasn't ever going to lead anybody up any hill during my tour of duty in *that* branch of the service. Not unless ninety five per cent of all the combat officers in the whole army were suddenly stricken simultaneously with bubonic plague, and I was one of the few lieutenants left to command the charge, would his precious exercise have the slightest relevance to me.

"I might have been stupid in my judgment," I said quietly, "But you did offer the road as a viable alternative to getting up that hill."

I couldn't believe that I was actually defending my position to some goon whose nametag read Lieutenant Vukov. How low had my suasory powers sunk from arguing in Moot Court the legal correctness of the *Miranda* decision, before a panel of federal judges—to matching wits with Beetle Bailey. I was willing to drop the whole thing, but he forged on.

"You Ivy League smart guys think that you own this Army, don't you? Are you trying to fool with a couple of hundred years of Infantry tradition?" he asked, the veins popping out all over his forehead.

I didn't want to aggravate this guy too much though. He was built like a Pittsburgh Steeler under his GI Joe fatigues that were perfectly creased, like they'd been soaked in starch for a couple of days. And his boots were unbelievable. They must've had a hundred coats of shoe polish. Maybe that's what saved me. If this cretin had decided to mop the floor with me, I might have scuffed the *Kiwi* dazzle of his shoeshine; or maybe have bled all over his nice stiff uniform.

"I'm sorry that you feel that way Lieutenant Vukov," I said trying to apologize. "I guess we Intelligence types have no concept of Infantry tactics. Sorry! But you *did* offer the squad leaders the option of choosing route number 1. I foolishly chose it, and was roundly criticized in front of my entire platoon for my mistake. *Mea culpa, mea maxima culpa.*"

"Don't think that I'm takin' any of your horseshit in *French* either, Mr. Wiseguy," he shot back.

We were getting nowhere. He wouldn't accept my apology. He did not want to know from logic. I'd have to try another strategy. The old sympathy ploy. Maybe out of pity he'd leave me alone.

"I'd like to continue this with you, "I said, "but you've caught me at a very bad moment. I was in the middle of writing a letter to my younger sister. The poor kid has terminal hematoma of the gastrocnemius. We don't expect her to survive the summer." I bit my lip to suppress the smile, wondering if he'd fall for somebody dying from a bruised calf muscle. "My letters mean so much to her. Now that mom and dad are both gone, I'm the only one she has. Before I came down here, I promised her a letter a day. I've kept my pledge so far. I really can't disappoint her."

Vukov must've flunked freshman Biology. He bought it. He was an incredible jerk, but I noticed that he was wearing a wedding ring.

*Somebody* loved him. Besides, my phony tearjerker was loaded with all sorts of good things for him to appreciate. Family values. Sibling love. Duty. Loyalty. I was tempted to throw in some crap about John Wayne being my sister's favorite movie star and my taking her to see the *Green Berets* when I got back, but I didn't want too push the envelope too far.

He muttered something about not forgetting my name, and how a smartass like myself wouldn't last in this man's army, but he made an informal about face, grabbed the doorknob, and left the room.

As he was leaving, every fiber of my pun loving body was holding back the urge to yell out, "Have a good evening –Lieutenant *Fuck-off!*", but reason prevailed, I kept my mouth shut, and he was gone, never to be seen by me again.

I've often wondered what happened to him after the war. I had a gut feeling that he somehow survived. I picture him retired and living in Florida, driving his wife crazy. Maybe he was selling life insurance over the phone to keep himself busy.

My imagination created two sons for him. One was busted selling coke about fifteen years ago. Then he got some girl pregnant, and they both moved out to Colorado somewhere. He drives a pickup for a living. Every year Vukov makes his Christmas phone call, and begs to see his grandchildren, offering to pay everybody's round trip fare to St. Petersburg, if only they'll come to visit.

The other son was probably kicked out of the house ten years ago, when he was caught being sodomized in the living room by his gay lover. Vukov set up a wall of complete denial. Doesn't even acknowledge his son's existence anymore. And then he pretends not to hear, when a new acquaintance, hearing his last name, asks whether he's related to that successful designer in Los Angeles who owns Vukov's Fashionwear.

# CHAPTER TWELVE

# Phone Sex

"Hi, Beverly, this is Bob!" I announced over the telephone later that evening. "Last Saturday? Szechwan food? World's worst Bridge player?"

"Oh sure! Hi! I thought that you'd be out digging foxholes or shooting things someplace. Is training over?"

"No," I answered, "but I've got a few minutes before I hit the sack, and I felt like talking to somebody worth talking to. I just finished a discussion with a real jerk—Infantry type. I wanted to speak with a pleasant, intelligent, warm, funny person—woman type. Ya busy?"

The only phone around was in the lounge downstairs. A pay phone with absolutely no privacy. Fortunately the place was practically empty, except for Don Santini and Jack Tillitson playing cards in the other corner of the room.

"I should be studying for next week's final on *Modern American Playwrights*," she answered. "What do you know about *Death of a Salesman?*"

"Arthur Miller wrote a drama about a salesman named Willi Loman. In the end the guy died!" I said.

"I don't think that information is gonna get me past a "C" on the exam," she laughed. "But, I mean, don't you think that maybe Arthur Miller is America's greatest living playwright?"

"I don't know," I said. "It's sort of hard to take some writer seriously who used to screw Marilyn Monroe. Not just that he was screwing her, but that he actually *married* her to do it.

"For instance, I can just picture him typing away in his den, working on some scene in the second act of his latest play, getting disgusted, ripping the sheet of paper out of the roller, crumbling it up, and tossing it into the trash basket. Then he gets up from his desk, and tiptoes upstairs into Marilyn's bedroom. While she's fast asleep in some flimsy negligee, he wakes her up and whispers something in her ear. He needs inspiration. She knows exactly why he married her. So she goes to her clothes closet for a few minutes, comes out, and puts a record on the stereo. Next thing you know, she's performing a striptease to "Diamonds are a Girl's Best Friend" sashaying around the room, and dropping bracelets and jewelry all over the place, before she peels off her silk evening gown. Then *he* makes love with her, rushes back to the typewriter, and completes the second act.

"Whenever I try reading his stuff, or even *talking* about it, I just picture him with Marilyn, and his credibility goes down the drain."

"Well, you're no help!" she said. "Professor Guaneri practically worships Arthur Miller. And I've got to get at least a "B" in his course, if I stand any chance of winning that grant for Journalism at Yale Graduate School. Even though I'm acing all my other classes I don't see Professor G giving me anything higher than a "C". I think that the *real* reason is that he doesn't approve of independent women.

"But I do need that grade! Do you think that I should have sex with him?" she said, trying to shock me.

"Maybe you should talk it over with your career counselor?" I replied, playing along. "Are you a virgin?"

"*Weelll*—almost!" she said. "The very first time shouldn't count. It happened during my high school prom. Charles McElroy was my date. He was the big shot quarterback at Stonewall Jackson Memorial then.

We'd had a couple of beers in the front seat of his dad's *Chevy Impala* and were necking like crazy.

"Then he takes out this prophylactic from his wallet that he'd probably been carrying around since freshman year, tears the foil open, and puts the thing on. I put up the minimal struggle expected from a "respectable, young, Southern lady", but I was curious to see what it would be like. Most of my friends had done it by their junior year. He *did* have protection; I was going away-almost three hundred miles—to Emory in September, and I could always rationalize to myself that my downfall was the result of two cans of beer. So I did it. Five minutes later-if that long—it was over, and Charles lay passed out on the seat.

"I think that you men would call it something like an "exhibition game" in pro football. It really didn't count in the standings. Anyway, I've had only two lovers since then; so by today's standards I'm still qualified to wear a white wedding gown.

"So what's up, General?" she asked.

"Well," I said, still a little dazed from her capsule sexography, "Maybe you'd like to talk in person with me this Saturday night. You pick the topic—*Death of a Salesman;* legroom in Chevrolet Sedans; pro football—whatever you prefer.

"Brian's going up to visit Emily this weekend, so I think that I can bum a ride with him. But I'm pretty sure he'd rather be alone with her, and not chauffeuring the two of us around Atlanta. So maybe we could just talk, or find a pizza place within walking distance of your dorm. I'd like to see you again."

"Pizza and cokes are my *favorite* date. What time?"

"I'll get Brian to drop me of at seven thirty. OK?"

She agreed and we both hung up the phone. I looked around the room. Santini and Tillotson had finished playing cards.

# CHAPTER THIRTEEN

# Buck's Finest Hour

The end of our training was approaching. The whole company would be sent out on night maneuvers culminating in a make believe assault on an enemy stronghold the next day. Twenty-four hours of war games. I dreaded it. We were given the entire afternoon to try and squeeze in whatever sleep we could before *Operation Overnight* took place.

The cadre chose as our Company Commander for this awesome task, a guy with the mouthful name—First Lieutenant Buckminster Worthington III. For once the Army had made the perfect choice.

Buck was a member of my squad. He was an attorney from Boca Raton Florida, and had just the right mixture of command presence, intelligence, understanding, tact, and physical endurance to have made it to the top of any army. He called me "Counselor".

A couple of weeks earlier we'd spent the morning on one of those goddam obstacle courses that were *sooo* exhausting. And they were always *uphill*. Didn't the enemy ever make camp *downhill*? I was dragging ass but good after about fifteen minutes of climbing and crawling and swearing.

Then I stumbled and hit the ground hard. My lungs were screaming for more air, but I was already gasping at full throttle. Sorry guys, but that's all the oxygen I can give you. The Cadre were shouting at everybody to keep moving. Only a hundred yards more to go. In a few moments I would hear the merciless shouts of Major Randolph, our instructor that morning, to *get our asses in gear.* Sweet man.

Just then Buck came running over.

"What's the matter, Counselor? You'd rather be taking the bar exam?" he asked.

"I can't make it Buck. Just let me lie here and die," I said.

With that he lifted me up to my feet, unstrapped my pack, improvised a big loop, and attached the twenty-five pounds of my gear to his own pack.

"C'mon Counselor. It's less than a hundred yards to the Court House."

Without having that excess baggage to weigh me down, I could make it. No ponderous chains on the ghost of Jacob Marley.

Buck and I finished the course. I restrapped the backbreaking load to my shoulders. Good as new. Major Randolph didn't say anything about Buck's largesse. He was probably pleased at what had happened. Guys fighting in the field are supposed to help each other out. It fosters *Esprit de Corps.* Troop morale. Placing the unit above the individual. Maybe it was that little episode that won him the company command for *Operation Overnight.*

As the big *enchilada,* Buck could choose his own assistants for the exercise. These assistants would have the best jobs in the whole *Operation.* No responsibility, and you got to ride around in the *jeep!*

"Lieutenants Woolsey and Santini!" Buck announced in front of the whole company," You guys will help me carry off the operation. Meet me at Point Alpha at 2130 hours."

Ah! Podiatric music to my ears. My toes thank you; my metatarsals thank you; my ankles thank you and *I* thank you.

A lot of Army crap was bearable if you could do it sitting down. Planning an Operation, reading the maps, establishing co-ordinates, and stuff like that were a mental challenge. And that was really where the battle was won. In the commander's brain. After all, Hannibal got to be a big shot General in History by *riding* on an elephant, not trying to *lift* one. Buck ran the whole show, but asked us for any advice we might give him, and whether he'd made any big screw-ups in his plan.

We were off on our campaign. Santini and I would have to leave the comfort of the jeep at times to co-ordinate with the platoon leaders, but mostly we just sat in the back seat and drank coffee.

At 0400 hours we'd reached Stage One. Make camp for four hours and be ready to go at 8:00 A.M. Buck spent that time with the Cadre supervisors. Don and I returned to platoon headquarters.

Each day the company changed its platoon leaders. The leader of our fourth platoon that day was Second Lieutenant Henri Talley, from New Orleans. Henri liked to boast about how his great-great-great-grandparents were French aristocrats who left their snuff and powdered wigs behind at the Court of King Louis XVI, and snuck away in a ferry to Dover, England, barely escaping the guillotine. Within two months they were roughing it in the Mississippi Bayous.

I took all of Henri's blue blood with a grain of salt. I suspected that Henri's ancestors were most likely *given* their release from *Devil's Island*, in exchange for their helping to build the New World colonies of France in Louisiana.

Don and I entered Henri's large tent, which he was sharing with Ollie Taylor. We were all hungry as hell. I got out my drab green cans of cold C-rations, which all tasted like pork and beans to me. But Henri's gourmet palate, inherited from his French ancestors wouldn't permit him to eat such pedestrian chow. First, he unfolded from his back pocket, a 2' x 2' white cloth, and lay it on the grass inside the tent; Then he took out several tins of smoked salmon, *escargots*, and strawberries that he had bought from the delicacy shop in town. Next, he opened the cans and began to feast. Unfortunately there wasn't room in his pack for an *espresso* machine (war is hell), but he did have a couple of packets of the instant stuff that he dissolved in boiling water. *Maxim's* in the boondocks. For a minute I thought that he'd order Ollie Taylor to start playing violin music to go with the candlelight that illuminated the tent.

Santini suggested that we might play a few hands of Poker, like he always did, but everybody else was exhausted. So we all sacked out, and awakened to Henri's wrist alarm buzzing at precisely 0745 hours. Don and I buried our empty tin cans and headed back to Buck's jeep. Stage Two was about to begin.

Buck was busy calling imaginary artillery support and air strikes on the doomed enemy position. By 11:00A.M. the assault had begun. Buck, Don, and I were driving all over among the platoons, which each had its own particular assignment. A lot of blanks were fired. Cherry bombs were detonated to simulate artillery fire and bombs dropping. The enemy under siege soon realized that the situation was hopeless and surrendered. Would that the *real* Viet Cong had been so co-operative.

To make the whole thing look believable, the Cadre had rounded up some enlisted men from the base, and dressed them in black pajamas, and coolie hats. As the barefoot prisoners paraded past our jeep they shouted out their rehearsed lines from a prepared script. "Go to hell, Imperialist Yankee dogs," or "Mickey Mantle eats shit!" I think one talented young hopeful felt the *motivation* of the scene, and created an *ad lib.* "Stupid GI ! While *yoo* chasing People's Army through jungle, some draft dodger fucking *yoo* wife back home."

The director of the play even got some oriental grunts from Benning to add yellow skinned realism to the cast of P.O.W's.

But the spectacular was over. So was our pleasant jeep ride. The instructors informed Buck that an enemy shell had blown the vehicle sky high. We'd all have to return to base as plain old infantrymen again. Henri remained the platoon leader and led us back through the woods for a few hours. At 9:00 P.M. we reached our final checkpoint on the map. Trucks were waiting for us to take us all back to the post. They drove us to Section C. I headed for that nice, soft, beautiful bed; undressed and was sound asleep before my head touched the pillow.

# Chapter Fourteen

# ...the Envelope Please

Two months had already gone by. I was feeling pretty good about myself, a far different creature from the chubby, dejected nebbish that landed at Columbus Airport in early March. I was part of a clique of friends. Vic Stimmons wasn't among them. I had lost twenty pounds. My waist had trimmed down from 36" to 32". I slept great. But I still was scared shit about being shipped out c/o PO Box xxxx ,Saigon. Particularly now that LBJ had announced that he wouldn't run again. There'd be a new administration. Maybe even a quick end to the war. Something like Eisenhower stopping the Korean "Police Action" back in 1953.

Then came the fatal day when our assignments were handed out. I picked up my sealed envelope. My hand shook as I tore it open. I took a deep breath. "AND THE WINNER IS—-BOB WOOLSEY!" The small 3"x 5" card read simply—"You are report to the office of ISB, Room B245, Pentagon, Washington D.C. on July 1, 1968, after your six week period of training in Army Intelligence at Fort Holabird, Maryland. An officer will contact you within the next thirty days regarding your assignment."

It was Saturday—about 1:00 P.M. A few of my friends—Don Santini, Dick Wampler, Mike Stern, and a couple of other grateful troops chipped in and bought a virtual distillery of the best liquor in town. Wayne Trowbridge was living with his wife now at the Holiday Inn on the Interstate, so my room became the logical choice for our mini banquet hall. We laughed and drank and hugged each other. We spilled liquor all over the place. We'd clean it up later, when we were sober.

Somebody suggested that we make a list of everybody that we knew from the entire Company that would be playing soldier stateside. After a few names, it became clear to everybody in the room that we had been the beneficiaries of the Army's weird process of selection, so simplistically bizarre in the way that it determined everybody's fate.

All personnel assigned stateside had a last name beginning with the letters "S" through "W" (There were no "Y's" or "Z's" in the Company). We talked it over among us, but nobody could come up with a name from the letter "R" on down. I guess the Army needed a hundred and twenty Lieutenants to fill slots in Viet Nam. An efficient solution was to start at the beginning of the Alphabet and stop when you reached 120. The remaining personnel would be scattered to different posts throughout the U. S. About half of us were headed for Washington D.C., the rest to random bases from New York to California. *Kismet.*

# Chapter Fifteen

# No Swimsuit Competition?

The next to last day at Fort Benning, the platoon threw itself a sort of picnic/ beer bash. We had the corny tugs-of -war between squads, and even a sack race. The highlight of the afternoon was when Barney Watson, the self styled Don Rickles of the unit, presented the "Distinguished Achievement Awards". He set up a little stage, that was nothing more than a 5' x 5' plywood target laid on top of some empty paint cans. The podium was a couple of old footlockers tipped on their sides and stacked on top of one another. On the back of the" stage" was an easel holding up a thin cardboard sign that Mike Venturi had painted in honor of the occasion. It was the Infantry Logo with some modifications. The *genuine* article was an unsheathed sword, blade up, on a shield background. The words "Follow Me" were emblazoned on the shield. Venturi had replaced the sword with an erect penis in front of a tasteless scrotum, that bore the words "Up Yours".

The audience was pretty sloshed by Award Time, but the raucous crowd came to a hush when Barney rapped his beer can on the podium a couple of times and asked the guys sprawled out on the grass for their kind attention. A few hecklers shouted for the red eyed Master of Ceremonies to commit some unnatural sex acts on himself, but they quieted down after a few seconds.

A cardboard box next to the podium contained the prizes. Since Barney knew the recipients in advance, he didn't need the suspense-filled moment when he opened the sealed envelope or anything. He just began with a couple of old jokes, before announcing the first winner.

Henri Talley received the Master Chef Award, a can of dog food, with a piece of adhesive tape slapped over the label that read "Beluga Caviar". Polite Applause. The Sportsman's Trophy went to Don Santini. It was a deck of marked playing cards, which he graciously acknowledged by holding it up in plain view of the crowd. Mr. Congeniality was Vic Stimmons, who got a pack of condoms, and a small vial of water marked "Penicillin". Wayne Trowbridge received a lifetime membership in the Legion of Decency for his efforts to stamp out the depiction of lewdness in the arts.

Sharpshooter of the Year Award , a loaded water pistol, went to Ed Walzak, who couldn't hit a barnside at three feet with a telescopic site. Rumor was that he finally passed the marksman test, after the enlisted man administering Ed's "make up exam" bent the rules a bit. You were supposed to shoot within 18 inches of dead center with five out of ten bullets. The exasperated Corporal in charge gave him a few extra rounds of ammo. When that didn't work, he moved the target to within spitting range. At last. Sergeant York reincarnated.

The Pathfinder Award for map reading, a five and dime compass that read "North" in every direction went to Cliff Tubman, who would *still* be out wandering over that damned course today, if I hadn't told him of my little "short cut". Buck Worthington was given the General Custer Award for Leadership, a *Superman* comic book. The cardboard box was empty, and the audience gave out with a big cheer.

"Hold on Gentlemen, Hold on. We have yet one more Distinguished Award to present," Barney shouted." Last and certainly *least*, I have the distinct honor and privilege to present the coveted plaque behind me, painted by none other than our very own Michelangelo Da Venturi, and glorifying the Fort Benning Infantry School, to the Soldier of the Year. Congratulations, BOB WOOLSEY!"

The crowd went wild. I stood up and took the prize that Barney had just rolled up like some oversize diploma, secured by a rubber band. I thanked the now *standing* ovation with an embarrassed wave of my hand.

As I looked around at all the guys giving me a mock salute and smiling at me, I realized that it was indeed quite an honor.

# CHAPTER SIXTEEN

# Next Stop Baltimore

Some guys from our Company taking the course at Fort Holabird got together and rented a large three bedroom Townhouse in Towson Maryland, just outside of Baltimore. How we managed to finagle a large, modern six-room apartment, with two and a half baths for only six weeks, was beyond me. Maybe the owner of the place took pity on us boys in uniform, and was satisfied just breaking even with these short-term leases.

During the week vacation between Fort Benning and Fort Holabird , I bought myself a used 1967 Bonneville, something like the one I fell in love with while being chauffeured around by Vic Stimmons, my first night in Columbus. The damned thing only got about nine miles to the gallon , but since it only cost me four bucks to fill my gas tank at the Army base, economical mileage was never really a consideration when I purchased it. Besides, I had saved about two months pay at Benning, and my share of the rent was only $40 a month.

The Intelligence Course at Holabird was a joke. Six weeks of rest and relaxation. We did have to attend classes in uniform every morning at 9:00 A.M. , but in the entire history of the U.S. Army, probably going all the way back to George Washington, nobody'd ever flunked the Intelligence Course at Fort Holabird. I bet that a lot of the guys going to 'Nam would have gladly failed it over and over, if it would have postponed their trip.

Since I had the big convertible, I drove everybody to class each morning. Classes ended at 4:30 P.M., so we were all back at the townhouse by 5:00P.M., opening our cans of Budweiser by 5:01 P.M.

With New York City only three hours away by car, and now that I enjoyed the luxury of having both *Saturday* and *Sunday* off, I spent most weekends with my friends and family back home. But a couple of times I experienced the temptations of the flesh that existed on Baltimore's "Block"—a two hundred yard gauntlet of whorehouses and Strip Clubs, one of which, the *Two O'clock Club*, featured the busty Blaze Starr. She was the *femme fatale*, who almost converted Earl Long, the infamous Governor of Louisiana, from alcohol to sex. She was sort of immortalized a few years back , in that motion picture *Blaze* starring Paul Newman. Anyway, when Ms. Starr selected me from all my buddies in the audience, to pluck a long stemmed rose from between her boobies with my teeth, I immediately lost the nickname "Ranger" and was dubbed "Blaze" by my cronies, the rest of my time in Baltimore.

# CHAPTER SEVENTEEN

# Lightning Strikes Twice

Very early in the morning, on June 6, 1968, as I ambled down the stairs for a glass of nice cold Tropicana in the 'fridge, I was surprised to find Andy Wertheimer, one of our resident alcoholics, staring at the TV.

"Anything special on the tube?" I asked.

"Some guy called Sirhan something or other shot Bobby Kennedy in the head. He's not expected to live," he answered.

A lead sinker dropped to the pit of my stomach. I was hoping for a quick end to the war, now that LBJ was out of the picture. His Vice President, Hubert Humphrey, a shadow of the once courageous politician, who bravely shouted down Strom Thurmond and his racist Dixiecrats at the Democrat Convention in 1948, couldn't win the upcoming election. I just knew it. And Dick Nixon, whom I trusted just about as much as that shithead Commandant at Fort Benning, would easily outfox any of the other "ivory tower" candidates. Bobby Kennedy was ruthless too. But he could bring the Democratic Party together. Blacks loved him, ever since his vigil that horrible night, when Martin Luther King was shot, only three months ago. Hard-hats and traditional Democrats trusted him too. They knew deep down that he wasn't any pinko comsimp like these smartass college kids , burning flags and occupying buildings on campus. No sir! Bobby was one of them.

I had it already figured out, until that chilling moment , when Andy told me the news. Wallace and Nixon would battle over the Southern

states. Let 'em. First , Kennedy would win the primaries. He had all the
money in the world to spend on winning most of the delegates outside
the South. California and New York were already in his pocket. LBJ
would spend the primary and election campaigns in seclusion at his
ranch. Bobby'd win the Nomination. Then he'd make his acceptance
speech at the giant podium in Chicago, in front of a huge backdrop
showing his dead brother. The band would play the theme from
Camelot. The crowd wouldn't be able to hold back the tears. Humphrey,
who still had a modicum of decency left, would raise Bobby's right
hand ; Gene McCarthy would raise his left. A picture impossible even
for Tricky Dick to overcome. Kennedy would have won the election ,
and stopped the war.

    But that was all over now. As I sat in front of the TV, listening to
Walter Cronkite, weeping as he told of Kennedy's death, and as I
watched over and over the footage of him lying there on that kitchen
floor of that Los Angeles hotel, blood gushing from his skull, I knew it
was over. I'd survive my two years at the Pentagon, lost among all the
Generals, but Viet Nam wouldn't go away. Dick Nixon would be
President next year. Christ, we'd still be fighting in Korea , if he'd had his
way. Viet Nam would be with us for a long time. All because some
stupid assassin with an imaginary grievance shot Bobby Kennedy. I
sipped my orange juice and cried. Then my body shook, and I sobbed.
So did Andy.

# CHAPTER EIGHTEEN

# First Encounter with Spooks

While I was dozing off during a boring lecture on interrogating a prisoner, there was a slight rap on the classroom door.

"Excuse me, "the instructor said as he walked over to the door and opened it.

Two young officers handed him some kind of ID or other; then they whispered in his ear for a few seconds.

"Lieutenant Woolsey!" said the instructor.

"Yes sir!" I said as I stood up to attention.

"These two gentlemen would like to speak to you for a few moments. You're excused from the rest of the class. You also have permission to be absent from any other classes, while they might have need of you. Carry on!"

The two First Lieutenants seemed to have a great deal of influence over the captain that was teaching the class. Neither of them looked like your standard officer types either. You know, hair a little bit too long; uniform a bit crumpled. 180 degrees opposite Lieutenant Vukov.

They both escorted me upstairs to the main conference room, which they had reserved that morning. We went in and sat down.

"Bob, I'm Jeff Pritchard," said the slightly older one," and this spook here is Gary Maggio."

"What's a spook?" I asked.

"It's a person in the Intelligence business," he answered. "From CIA on down. As Army Intelligence spooks we're only small fry. And we're pretty low key. No glamorous sports cars with ejector seats or briefcases that explode. Gary and I don't have sex every night with Ursula Andress or Pussy Galore either. But we *do* read the enemy's mail, and have bugged an embassy or two, so we are spies. In a couple of weeks you will be too. We're here to tell you a little bit about your new job starting July 2. It's at the Intelligence Support Branch-ISB for short. Colonel Black, the head of the outfit hasn't decided where to put you exactly, but it will be either as an Oral Briefer, or as the new head of our Western Europe desk."

"But I haven't had any experience analyzing Intelligence anyplace. I doubt whether I'm ready to take on everything west of the Iron Curtain," I said.

"Relax," Jeff said. "The West Europe slot is most likely the easiest one we've got. Diplomatic Reports about who's sleeping with whom. Piddling shit. No war's about to break out in Italy or France. All the important stuff's going on in Southeast Asia. Maybe a little interest in China and the Soviet Bloc. The remaining ten per cent is scattered through Africa, Latin America and the Middle East. Besides, I said that there's a good chance you'll be assigned to just broadcasting your own reports every morning to the General staff. Look, you're not due to report for another couple of weeks. Your last day here is June 24th, Stop up for a visit. You've already received top clearance, so we can give you a little tour of the place. Ask the Sergeant at the door for me or Gary."

"Thanks for the briefing," I said. "By the way, you guys didn't seem to have any trouble getting past my class instructor. Just what did you show him at the door?"

He produced a fancy laminated card with his photo next to the Great Seal of the United States. The ID read:

"*This will serve to identify Jeffrey R. Pritchard, a special officer, author-ized to collect highly sensitive Intelligence data on behalf of the military forces of the United States of America. He is permitted to carry a firearm at all times. He is further authorized to use any and all means to protect and defend the Security and National Interest of the United States. You are to extend to him your unqualified co-operation*

*Clark C. Clifford*

*Secretary of Defense"*

"Wow!" I said, just like a little kid meeting a genuine G-man. "Will I get to carry one of those?"

"Sorry, Bob," he said," but that's one of the perks that they stopped issuing at the beginning of the year. It seems that some of the boys were abusing the card. After a couple of jerks used theirs to get into the Redskins' games for free, the Defense Department put a halt to issuing any more. See ya after June 24th."

# Chapter Nineteen
# A Slight Change in Orders

The day arrived for my mini-graduation from the University of Fort Holabird. It was to take place at 12 noon, so we had the entire morning to ourselves. We had to wear the dress blue uniforms, that they forced us to buy at Fort Benning. I had to admit that even I looked pretty good wearing mine. Deep blue; white trim; a couple of gold braids here and there; black silk stripes running down the outside of the pants legs; and fancy white gloves. Just what we needed on a hot sizzling summer afternoon in Baltimore.

I even thought that I looked military enough to give my shoes a quick shine. Just a dab of Kiwi polish on the shoe tips; and a fast buff with the soles of the socks I was wearing, was enough I thought. No need to get carried away.

About eight or ten of us gathered in the officers' snack bar. Just a Coke machine, a coffee machine, and a couple of snack dispensers. It was Sunday, and the main lounge was closed. Because this was a *special* day, we were permitted to shed our heat absorbing jackets, and loll around in shirtsleeves. Some of us were so bold as to loosen our neckties. Both of these liberties would have merited us a quick death before a firing squad at Fort Benning, where even regarding one's wardrobe, Military Discipline was King. I hung my jacket on the coat rack.

Two of the guys had made a special effort to invite Lieutenant Tom Stebbitz to the pre- graduation get together. Tom was a thoroughly

68

loathsome character, who'd been with us through basic training at Benning. What made him particularly detestable was his accosting the men in the other platoons, whom he *knew* had orders for Viet Nam, and flaunting the fact that he'd been assigned as a General's aide in Washington D.C.. Jim Turner and Paul Strauss had schmoozed themselves the use of a printing machine at the *Holabird Newsletter* a couple of days earlier. They cut Stebbitz a brand new set of orders that looked as official as hell, which read more or less:

*To Second Lieutenant Thomas B. Stebbitz:*         *25 June 1968*

*Due to an administrative error, your orders to report for duty on 2 July 1968 at the Office of Major General Lewis Percival, Room C314, Pentagon, Washington D.C. have been canceled. Instead you are to report for duty at Army Headquarters, Post 37, Company A, Tring Nam Sanh, Republic of South Viet Nam. Details regarding transportation to said assignment will be transmitted to you with in 48 hours of this notice*

        *Lt. Colonel Homer Babbitt*

        *Army Department of Personnel*

"Some guy from Personnel was looking for you, Tom," Turner said. "I had to sign for this. Here!" Then he handed Stebbitz the envelope. He opened it and stared down at the news.

Tom turned white. Then he opened his mouth wide, and let out a silent scream. Tears started to pour from his eyes, as he looked helplessly around the room, crumbling his phony orders in his left hand.

Turner and Strauss panicked. In Stebbitz' condition he was liable to run down to the pistol range and blow his brains out. Turner grabbed the official looking papers and began tearing them into little pieces.

Then he said shamefully, "These orders are phony bullshit, Tom. I'm sorry."

Luckily for Turner, he was about 6'4" and weighed around 220 lbs. Stebbitz was 5'8" and weighed around 140 lbs., with his shoes and clothes on, after coming in from a heavy rain. But he was so relieved, that he might just have kissed Jim on the lips for confessing the plot that meant he wouldn't have to go to Viet Nam after all.

I was the butt of a much more good natured prank that morning. While my jacket hung on the coat rack, Don Santini replaced the "Woolsey" nametag with one that read "Blaze", commemorating my evening of glory on the "Block". Strictly out of the Third Grade. If I didn't notice it , I'd receive my little diploma, wearing my new ID. I did notice it, but didn't let on. At least two of these clowns *would* be going to Viet Nam on *real* orders in a few days. Maybe this tiny laugh at my expense would be the last one they'd have for a long, long time.

# CHAPTER TWENTY

# Playing the Angles at the Pentagon

When I reported for duty at the Pentagon in late June, I told the Sergeant manning the door that I was supposed to see either Lieutenant Pritchard or Lieutenant Maggio. He buzzed the intercom, and within two minutes Jeff and Gary met me in tandem. They both gave me a friendly slap on the back, and we were off to see Colonel Roger Black, the head of our merry band. He was a tall white haired gentleman who was just then engaging in some mild sexual harassment with his cute secretary. Jeff and Gary politely interrupted him in mid flirt. He gave me a friendly smile, offered me coffee, and gave me a brief tour of the place, after letting Pritchard and Maggio get back to their work.

Afterwards he took me back to his office that he shared with Mr. Johnson, a civilian Intelligence expert that had been with the team that cracked the Japanese code during World War II. They seemed like a couple of nice guys. Black handed me a stack of papers to fill out so that I could get paid, and get my ID badge allowing me entrance into even the most arcane recesses of the Pentagon. It just wasn't quite impressive enough to get me into RFK Stadium for free, like Jeff's and Gary's.

When I returned all the red tape, Colonel Black told me about my new assignment. He and Johnson had given it a lot of thought. I was to join the Oral Briefing team instead of taking over the Western Europe desk. The most important changes in the office of Army Intelligence would be taking place within the next couple of weeks. General

Westmoreland had done such a remarkably unsatisfactory job in Vietnam, that he'd been" kicked upstairs" to become Chief of Staff of the whole Army. And he brought his entire crew along with him. Among his Generals was the new Intelligence Chief, Major General Joseph McChristian, whose name alone struck terror in the hearts of every spook that had ever served under him. He didn't tolerate mistakes. And a *dumb* mistake by a subordinate could mean an assignment gathering data at Thule Air Force Base in Greenland. It could also mean that an Army *Major* with ten years in service would retire as an Army *Major* with *twenty* years of service, saying "Yes sir" and "No sir" to guys in their early thirties.

But it seemed that McChristian pictured himself as a soldier/ scholar. Maybe a re-incarnation of Julius Caesar or Frederick the Great. *And* the good General liked to be surrounded by young officers who had impressive academic credentials. The old guy couldn't give a damn whether I could run an obstacle course or find a tree stump in the dark. Finally a place where I could actually put my talents to use!

I could see Colonel Black now making with the brownie points. "This is your new Oral Briefer General. Lieutenant Woolsey. First rate officer. *Magna cum laude.* Fulbright Scholar. Virginia Law School. I hope the General approves of my choice." And then the hoped for response. "Fine choice, Black , fine choice." Whew! No midnight plane to Greenland.

Anyway Colonel Black explained what our *official* mission was( in addition to brownnosing the General).We amassed information from the CIA, DIA,NSA, and other Intelligence sources to produce a "Black Book" every morning. A lot of the information was obtained from state of the art radio intercepts as well as from satellites that could spot a football from about twenty miles up in space. The most hush-hush top secret codeword stuff we had. Of course if I let any of all this slip out, my remains would be found splattered at the bottom of the Washington Monument.

Before I left the place, the Colonel introduced me to Major Donald Cachuk, my new boss at the briefing team. Cachuk was a career Army bureaucrat, an Artillery Officer who was shuffled into this particularly sensitive position by another Army bureaucrat that must've been dozing off at the computer when he pressed the button selecting him. The Major wasn't a complete jerk of the Vukov variety, but he was in the lowest of the bush leagues compared to the other sterling officers that I'd met briefly during my first couple of hours at ISB. But the Army *had* saved Donald Cachuk from a career for which he was more well suited—sitting at a Post Office desk, canceling stamps and sorting envelopes.

Cachuk clued me in as to what I'd be doing until General McChristian lay down the law. I'd come in every morning at 0400 hours. We'd review the raw Intelligence data that was laid out on our desks by Sergeant Haskell. Then we'd cut and paste what we considered to be the important stuff, to make a twelve minute oral briefing. Whoever wasn't actually *giving* the briefing would put together some 8"x 11" transparencies on a rear projection screen showing suspected enemy positions in Vietnam and stuff. Then after we'd spent seven or eight minutes announcing the important Southeast Asia poop, we'd report on some new Soviet tank being developed.(show generic picture of Russian tank). Or their might be a possibility of Golda Meir being Israel's next Prime Minister.(Show outdated slide of Mrs. Meir; probably her graduation photo at Milwaukee High School); and so forth. Often *our* briefing covered a lot of that in the black book, but it differed at Cachuk's whim. So we had twenty experienced desk officers working on a different product than ours. You didn't need a degree in business management to see that this was stupid. Particularly since Cachuk's knowledge of critical nuances in world affairs ended with his knowing that the Americans were the "good guys" and the Russians were the "bad guys".

This 4:00 A.M. business didn't sound too pleasant either. *Two whole years* of the graveyard shift. Good-bye social life!

Cachuk wished me a good time on my week furlough. Then he said to be back at 4:00 A.M. sharp on July 2nd. He also told me that I'd have to pick up late intelligence reports from the classified terminal at Room B 425 D, so I'd have to be in the building by 0330 hours. He scribbled down the directions for me. If there was anything important in the reports, then I'd have to take the *appropriate action*. I went home for a few pleasant days, before attending Emily and Brian's wedding in Boston that Saturday.

# CHAPTER TWENTY-ONE

# "Banned" in Boston

The banns joining Brian Terhune and Emily Walker had been published, and the wedding formally set for Saturday, June 30th, at two P.M. at the Church of St. Agnes in South Boston. A buffet dinner was scheduled at *The Sons of Erin Hall* at five o'clock. A huge crowd was expected. Emily's family consisted only of her folks, two sisters, a widowed Aunt and one cousin. On the other hand, in good Irish Catholic tradition, Brian's clan (Terhunes and O'Malleys) was an enormous assortment of ten brothers and sisters, almost two dozen Aunts and Uncles, and hordes of cousins of varying degrees. And these comprised *only* the relatives on *this* side of the Atlantic. Had the gala affair included those folks still living on the *auld sod* in County Kildare, Brian and Emily would have had to rent Fenway Park for the afternoon.

Among the invitees in attendance were Cal Sturgess, Mike Stern, and myself. Mike was taking his car, and would see me in Boston. He was staying with his Uncle Jeffrey and Aunt Rose. Cal would fly in to Logan Airport. By sheer coincidence it all worked out perfectly for me. You see, Beverly(the sweetheart of Delta Phi Sigma ) had received that "B" from Professor Guaneri that she wanted so badly. So she'd been awarded that fellowship to the Yale School of Journalism. I don't know if she had to sleep with the Professor to get the grade. But if she did, the fact that she didn't get an "A" in the course, could have meant that she wasn't the most co-operative bed partner, and had some points deducted in the sexual favors portion of the "exam."

Anyway, Beverly was now taking summer classes in New Haven, the very heart of Connecticut Yankeedom. When I learned, in early June, that she'd been invited to the wedding by Emily, I telephoned to ask if she'd be my date.

"That'd be simply lov-er-ly, General," she said. "When should I be ready?"

"Eleven o'clock Saturday morning should give us plenty of time to get to Boston," I said. "By the way, are you staying overnight?"

"Yes I am," she said. "Mindy Rutledge and I've booked a room for the night at the Marriott off Route 93."

"Now ain't that a stroke of good luck," I said. "Cal Sturgess and I are staying at the same place. Are you in the wedding party?"

"I just missed out," she said. "I guess you might call me 'first alternate'. Emily's sister Rachel is Maid of Honor. Her other sister Leah is first bridesmaid, and Mindy filled the final bridesmaid slot. It doesn't look like I'll be seeing much of Ms. Rutledge. Not unless Rachel or Leah breaks an ankle and I have to pinch hit as designated bridesmaid. Oh well, one can only hope.

"But it'll be just so precious hearin' those sweet voices from Dixie again. Up here at Yale everybody sounds like William F. Buckley Jr.

"And I just can't wait to see y'all too, *Honey Chil'*," she cooed in her best southern drawl. "Y'all have a safe trip! You *heearh!*"

"You betcha, Bev!" I said. "I can't wait."

Beverly really sounded homesick. The poor kid was probably phoning home every night. And summer school was a pretty lonely place anyhow. I called her a couple more times before the wedding, to try and lift her spirits a bit.

The afternoon when I concluded my little tour of ISB, I took a little ride into Fairfax County. All my luggage from the Townhouse in Towson, Maryland was packed in the trunk of my Bonneville. I decided to do a little shopping in Northern Virginia before heading home to New Jersey.

The Saturday of the wedding I left Jersey City for Boston *via* New Haven, Connecticut. At about a quarter to eleven I rang the doorbell to Beverly's apartment.

"It's open *dahrlin',*"she yelled from the bathroom. "Y'all come right in, and make y'self to home."

I twisted the knob and pushed the door open, over the worn carpeting, and went inside. Except for a few personal items, like family photos and an embroidered map of Alabama hanging on the walls, the place was furnished courtesy of her Yankee landlady. There were paintings of clipper ships hanging all over, and one portrait of a particularly dour looking sea captain above the mantelpiece. I sat down on the beat up, flowered Victorian sofa to the right of the door. Three ladderback walnut armchairs were placed about the room. Near the far corner, between the window and the mantelpiece, there was a dilapidated tea table flanked by two equally dilapidated cane back side chairs. In the other corner stood the room's showpiece—a grandfather clock whose monotonous tick-tock defined the very essence of the place.

"I'll be right out, Bob," Beverly said. Then she made her entrance, looking more gorgeous than ever.

"Well, wadya'll think, General?" she asked. "Is Emily gonna be absolutely green with envy of me in this dress?"

"They just might have to keep you outside the church," I said. "That strapless creation could cause unbridled chaos among the bachelors inside; and the priest saying Mass, might very well renounce his vow of celibacy right then and there."

"You're so sweet," she said.

Then I walked over to the big brown shopping bag that I'd set next to the front door. Beverly looked at me with a puzzled stare.

"These are just a few trinkets that I picked up for you from Northern Virginia," I said. "A coupla trifles from probably the last *Stuckey's* in Dixie. To sort of remind you of the *ol' homestead* in Alabama."

I opened the bag and began to remove the various items. First, there was a package of *Colonel Culpepper's Grits*; then I produced a genuine *Stuckey's* Pecan Pie; a box of Goo-Goo clusters; a paperback of *Absalom, Absalom* by William Faulkner; two sweet potatoes; a moon pie; a pint of *Southern Comfort*; a box of cotton balls; and a package of *Dixie Cups*.

She laughed as each memento from the south was presented, interrupting her laughter with an occasional "Why you sweet thing", or "You darlin' man you!" Then she gave me a big hug and kiss after I announced that the presentation was over.

"We have to hustle, honey," I said. "Boston is an easy town to get lost in- even though Brian gave me a whole page of directions to the church, including Revolutionary War landmarks, gas stations, and Irish pubs that we have to pass along the way."

She draped a silk shawl over her bare shoulders; I took her hand and led her down to my car.

Brian had requested that I wear my dress blue uniform for the ceremony, *not* because he was supermilitary or anything, but because he wanted me to be part of the troop holding up the "canopy" of crossed swords, that he requisitioned at the Fort Devens Arsenal. Actually it was Emily's idea. She wanted to always remember this unique form of departure that the newly married couple would make from the church.

Brian said that everybody at the Fort wanted to help out with this sentimental custom. They searched the Base from top to bottom and located about a dozen World War I sabers stashed in the back of the supply room. Brian just had to dust them off, shine them up with a little *Brasso*, sign a receipt, and bring them back within a week after the wedding.

The Army baffles me sometimes. One minute the seem to be run by unfeeling, stoic *apparachiks* like Vukov or Cachuk; and the next they're a bunch of softies turning an Army installation upside down to cater to the sentimental whim of a new bride. Go figure.

Beverly and I arrived at St. Agnes in plenty of time. We entered the church, and were confronted with the burning question of the afternoon by Brian's younger brother Patrick, one of the ushers, who asked, "Bride's side or groom's?"

Beverly had known Emily a lot longer than I'd known Brian, *and* she was willing to go *escortless* at the tail end of the wedding just so I could hold up that sword for five minutes-so we sat on the *Bride's* side of the aisle. We waited and looked around the modest sized cathedral, while I eavesdropped on a couple of folks on Brian's side whispering about how it seemed like only yesterday that he played one of the three kings at the second grade Christmas pageant; and how the audience all laughed when he forgot his lines and presented the little baby Jesus with the gift of "Frankenstein."

Emily's family had made the bulk of the concessions, during the hasty wedding plans. True, Brian and his family were paying for the affair, but the small Walker contingent had to trek all the way up North from Tuscaloosa, to a strange city, new relatives, and some unfamiliar Yankee Roman Catholic Church, smelling of incense. Mother Terhune had tried to calm their misgivings by assuring them that if they followed her lead, stood up when *she* did, knelt when *she* did, didn't become flustered when the little bells rang, and remembered to say "Forgive us our trespasses, as we forgive those who trespass against us" and not "Forgive us our *debts,* as we forgive our *debtors,*" during the Lord's Prayer, they'd be OK. Oh! They also had to Amen the Prayer after "and deliver us from evil" and make sure not to drag it out with "for Thine is the Kingdom etc. etc." as in the Protestant version.

The newlywed Terhunes would start wedded life as a mixed marriage couple in a remote Fort near Lubbock Texas, more than a thousand miles from Boston and Tuscaloosa; in a place where neither of them had any desire to be—for two whole years. But despite their living in the middle of nowhere, going to different churches every Sunday, and learning each other's cultures from scratch, I knew that they'd make it. Brian adored her; and she worshipped him. After the wedding vows, their love just seemed to fill every corner of St. Agnes'. And when we all smiled our congratulations at the receiving line, he caressed her dainty hand in that big Celtic paw of his, like he was holding a butterfly. And she'd blush and peek up at him with a shy, innocent glance. But not wanting to stare too long, and ignore the folks on the receiving line.

After the ceremony, and the reception line, I excused myself from Beverly, and headed for my post at the stainless steel canopy formation (left hand side; third sword from the end; next to Mike Stern). It took all of five seconds for the Bride and Groom to pass under the arch. But during that time the photographer must've taken a dozen shots, as they crouched and hurried down the church stairs. I sheathed my blade, talked to Stern for a few seconds, and returned to Beverly.

"Well, we've got a couple of hours to kill before we pig out on Corned Beef and Guinness' Stout at the *Sons of Erin Hall,*" Beverly said. "Let's head back to the *Marriott.* Mindy's already committed to attending a little tea reception the rest of the afternoon at Mama Terhune's. She told me not to wait for her."

"Cal won't be back until dinner either," I said. "*American Airlines* misplaced his luggage, and he's off to Logan Airport to find it." We headed back to the Marriott.

I escorted Beverly to her room, and she invited me in. She wanted to freshen up a bit.

"Help yourself to a glass of the *Southern Comfort* you bought for me, General!" she said." There's a glass and some ice in the Styrofoam bucket. I'll be out in five minutes. Pour one for me too." She entered the bathroom.

When she came out, I had her glass of liquor ready for her. As she took it from my outstretched hand she stroked my fingers. Her eyes were a little misty-probably from her thinking nostalgically about

Emily, the good times that they had at Emory, and the college girl life that would never be again.

I looked down into those moist hazel eyes and cupped her cheek in my hand. I bent over and kissed her on the forehead; then on her lips. She kissed me back.. I grasped her hand, as I led her over to the bed. The Venetian blinds were open. I shut them and went back to her. Then I embraced her bare shoulders and we kissed for several minutes. We sat down on the edge of the bed and I began to unzip her strapless dress. I was nervous. So was she. We hadn't made love with each other before. After we eased ourselves across the mattress, I kissed her now uncovered breasts. I fumbled to remove my own clothes, and was as clumsy as *all* men are, taking them off, in their haste to make love to a beautiful woman.

"Take it easy darling," she said. "I'm not going anywhere. This is a voluntary seduction. I knew that it was going to happen, the minute that you gave me those grits and all that other thoughtful stuff this morning. Thank you dear, I really needed that. I was one step from deserting Yale and heading back to Alabama and home."

We were both naked as I kissed her again. "I can promise you that I'll try to make this more pleasant than that 'exhibition game' in Charles McElroy's *Impala*, Bev," I said. "I want it to be the ' Super Bowl' for the both of us."

"I have no doubts, darlin'," she said. "Anyhow, you *were* just wearing your country's uniform. I know that you'll do America proud."

We made passionate love for the next hour and more, but it was getting close to *Sons of Erin* time. And she had to make some patchwork repairs to her now disheveled hairdo.

"That was so wonderful, Bev," I said as I redressed.

"For me too, Bob," she replied. "But I do feel a little guilty at having had sex, before Emily and Brian did. After all, it is *their* wedding day."

Then I took off my wristwatch.

"Look," I said, "I'm setting my trusty five dollar *Timex* to three A.M , 'Woolsey Standard Time'. So now we can pretend that we didn't make love until tomorrow. OK?"

"You'll make a good lawyer," she answered, and kissed me again.

We were off to see the sons of Erin.

# CHAPTER TWENTY-TWO

# An Affair to Remember

We arrived at the hall about twenty minutes past five. I parked the car and we went inside. Most of the guests had already arrived, and were busy taking full advantage of the "happy hour." Since about four-thirty the three bartenders had been busy at their fast drink assembly line with man#1 taking the order and plunking in the ice; man#2 pouring the liquor; and man # 3 adding water or mixer. Occasionally man #2 had a breather when somebody requested a simple Coke or Seven-Up.

The cocktail list was short and inexpensive. Old Mr. Boston's Scotch, Gin, Vodka, Rye Whiskey and Rum. With a crowd of over three hundred people, the barkeeps didn't have enough time for Singapore Slings, Old Fashioneds, or any other fancy pink concoctions with little umbrellas in them. And the Terhunes certainly didn't have the wherewithal to provide unlimited shots of Bushmill's or Canadian Club to the unending line of thirsty guests. At five thirty or so- when the pay as you go signal sounded- the patrons could order all the overpriced brand names of first rate liquor they wanted-provided they were willing to shell out the going price that the Sons of Erin had fixed.

Before heading to the bar I took Beverly to our table at the other end of the room. The banquet hall was enormous. In addition to filling the St. Patrick's Ballroom with about twenty round tables, the management removed the portable partition abutting the Blarney Salon to accommodate ten more tables; and the other partition separating the Leprechaun Lounge from the main room, to squeeze in eight more.

The Bride and Groom hadn't arrived as yet. Bev and I took the roundabout, less congested route over the parquet dance floor, past the unoccupied dais and the band, that was a curious quintet of accordion, saxophone, drums, flute and piano. They called themselves the Bostones. The piano player, Malcolm, was to double as master of ceremonies for the evening. For an extra fifty bucks it was his unenviable job to oversee the party and keep it moving. He had to introduce the individual members of the bridal party, as they paraded up to the dais; supervise the pre-meal wedding customs; and coax as many of the men as he could to dance with their wives, instead of getting drunk at their tables. Then he had to feed the wedding cake to Emily and Brian; get the single guys out on the floor to catch the garter; organize the stampede of single woman as they trampled over each other to catch the Bride's bouquet; and take requests from the crowd. The group was playing Penny Lane by the Beatles,

Finally we reached our table. Already seated were Mike Stern, Cal Sturgess, and Jim Turner, the brains behind the forged documents caper with Tom Stebbitz. The women at the table were Brian's cousins, Kathleen and Carrie as well as Glenda Whittaker. Kathleen was to be Mike's "partner" for the evening, and Carrie had been purposely chosen for Jim Turner. She was about six feet two in high heels, and would be just perfect −sizewise- for the 6'4" Turner. She might even have to tilt her head up ever so slightly to look into his eyes. Glenda was Bev's friend whom I'd met that first evening at Delta Phi Sigma.

"Well, Glenda, have you been brushing up on your Bridge game?" I asked her.

"Not really," she replied. "But I am becoming an absolute whiz at Go Fish. Maybe you, Bev, Cal and I could arrange a little tournament together."

"It'll have to take place in New Haven, Glen, " Bev said. "With my workload I doubt if I'll be able to even make it home for Christmas."

"Excuse me for few minutes," I said to the group at the table. "I've got to go fetch Bev and me a couple of gin and tonics before the 'free booze' sign is turned off."

I went to the bar by myself. I figured that Bev needed a break from my company for a while. After all, she'd been with me for over six straight hours now. And I was sure that she had a whole bunch of post graduation gossip to discuss with Glenda.

When I returned, after about ten minutes, Malcolm was standing at the bandstand microphone ready to introduce the wedding party. He tapped it a couple of times. "Is this thing on? Can everybody hear me?" he asked. Then the mike squealed out that horrible whistle that mikes always do, before the guy on drums adjusted the sound. The band started playing The Look Of Love, and the ushers made their entrance as Malcolm announced each of them one by one. Then the bridesmaids were introduced as they took their places next to their respective ushers.

Next came Brian in his dark blue uniform, and he stood at the front of the dais. Finally Emily entered to the increasing applause of the crowd, and joined Brian.

"I would now request that the new Bride and Groom, Mr. and Mrs. Brian Terhune dance to the wedding song that they've chosen," Malcolm announced.

Emily and Brian walked to the dance floor as the Bos-tones began to play What the World Needs Now Is Love Sweet Love, by Burt Bacharach. This had been the campaign theme of Bobby Kennedy, whose quest for the Presidency had been so brutally terminated only three weeks ago. The male guests wiped tears from their eyes, and the women cried and hugged each other. Maybe Bobby had been a Senator from ' New York ', but he would always be an Irish boy from Boston to just about everybody in the hall.

After Brian and Emily had danced to a few bars, Malcolm interrupted. "Now would the Groom's mother, Maureen O'Malley Terhune, dance with the Groom." The band switched to playing When Irish Eyes Are Smiling, while Brian and his mother fox-trotted around the floor.

"Now would the Bride please dance with her father, Mr. Jefferson Walker," Malcolm said.

Emily and her dad danced as the band played Stars Fell On Alabama for the next two minutes. Then the quintet resumed playing What the World Needs Now…, as the whole wedding party, and Mama and Papa Terhune, and Mr. and Mrs. Walker all waltzed around until the music stopped.

"Would everyone please be seated?" Malcolm asked. "At this time I call on Father Donovan to bless the festivities. Father, if you please."

The priest who married the new couple rose at his place on the dais and began his speech.

"On this glorious occasion when these two wonderful young people have been joined by the holy sacrament of matrimony…blah, blah… confident that their devotion to each other and in the years to come will enable … blah blah…through the trials, tribulations, joy and mutual love, sharing each moment…blah blah… constantly renewing their vows in their life together forever. And now if you all will rise, let us pray."

Then Father Donovan crossed himself. So did Kathleen and Carrie at our table, and most of the other people in the hall.

"Hail Mary, full of grace, the Lord is with Thee. Blessed art Thou among women and blessed is the fruit of thy womb, Jesus," he began.

Kathleen and Carrie responded with the others. "Holy Mary, Mother of God, pray for us sinners, now and at the hour of our death, Amen. They crossed themselves again.

"Thank you Father," Malcolm said. "And now if you all will remain standing, I call upon Brian's brother Sean, the Best Man, to toast the newly wedded couple."

Brian's oldest brother stood up and lifted his glass. You could see how uncomfortable he was in his tuxedo. He was a building contractor in Chelsea, and probably hadn't worn a suit-much less a tuxedo- for a couple of years. We all raised our glasses, half filled with domestic champagne as he spoke.

"Here's to my dear brother and wonderful new sister-in-law," he said. "May they have a long life together, and many healthy and happy children!"

We all drank.

"And now, everybody have a good time," Malcolm said, and resumed his place at the piano.

During the invocation and the toast the caterers had served the soup. True, it was to be a buffet style meal, but the management had thought it more prudent, if the staff served the first course. Many of the guests had spent well over an hour at the open bar, and could hardly be trusted to accurately ladle the New England Clam Chowder into their shaky soup bowls. The Sons of Erin could just picture gallons of the hot, sticky stuff spilling onto their carpeting and shiny hardwood floors, and then being stepped on by shoes that would track it all over the hall.

Before we began the first course at our table, Kathleen said out of the blue, "Let's choose to see who gets the centerpiece."

"The charming Miss O'Malley has a splendid idea," Mike Stern said. "Let's get the business of the wedding trophies taken care of. And I volunteer my services and my hat for the drawing."

Cal, Jim, and I booed, and the girls laughed.

"There, there, ladies and gentlemen," Mike continued. "Last summer at my Temple's renovation drive I was in charge of the raffle of a brand new RCA color TV. The whole drawing went off without a snag, up to and including the magic moment when I picked the ticket of my favorite cousin Ruth from the silver bowl containing the stubs. The entire congregation commended me for running an honest, impartial drawing. Except for a couple of disgruntled soreheads who demanded an inquiry because Ruth' s stub had a crease in it."

The guys all booed again and the girls giggled.

"Well, I for one have great faith in Mike," Glenda said. "He's got my vote."

"Mine too," said Bev

"Put Kathleen and myself in the Stern column for Lotto Master," Carrie said.

"It's a veritable landslide!" Stern shouted. "And now would all of the entrants please place their unfolded, unspindled, unmutilated name placards into my Officer's cap."

We all put our cards into the hat.

"And now, I ask the lovely, above reproach, Miss Beverly Oglethorpe to mix up the tickets before I select the winner."

Bev swirled the eight placecards around. Mike closed his eyes and chose. from his hat.. Then as he pretended to read the name of the lucky person, he had the incredible chutzpah to use that old, worn out gag and announced, "The WINNER IS—Size 7 and 1/2."

Everybody groaned at this clumsy attempt to be witty, and Cal made an immediate motion to impeach Mike. But before anybody could second the motion, he read out," Correction, ladies and gentlemen. The actual WINNER IS—KATHLEEN O'MALLEY!"

Kathleen squealed with delight at her winning the $7.98 centerpiece. Then she took her place card and marked her prize. She inserted it in the middle of the flowers with her name showing. Sort of like Columbus planting his flag in the New World and claiming it for Spain.

We all went back to finishing our chowder. Then Malcolm announced that the buffet tables were open. Bev and I hustled to get a good position in line. After all, that little cup of soup was the only food that Bev had eaten since breakfast. And the last food I'd had, besides the clam chowder, was a salami on rye that I wolfed down at the wheel around ten AM.

There were only a dozen people ahead of us. The buffet was purposely arranged in that economically shrewd pattern that all caterers use to show the greatest profit. The table was about twenty-five feet long. It began with the inexpensive bread and rolls; then the guest could choose from different salad selections—lettuce, beets, coleslaw, sliced onions, *crudite*, and dressings. Items that filled up the plate, but didn't cut into the caterer's budget. Next on the buffet table were the pasta dishes. Very tasty and filling, but still fairly cheap. Macaroni and cheese, Lasagna, Stuffed Shells, and Parsley Noodles. Up until now, it was all *serve yourself* style. *Mickey Logan's Catering Service* didn't care how high you piled your plate with greens and macaroni that sold for ten cents a pound. But after you got past the Parsley Noodles, there were suddenly waiters to actually dole out the portions of meat and fish that retailed at twenty times that much.

At the beginning of the line, I helped myself to one small roll and a pat of butter. Then I told Bev that I'd see her next to the toothpicks at the end of the table. I skipped the salad, vegetable, and pasta offerings and headed for the meat and fish. I guess that I must've looked like some kind of authority figure in that blue uniform, because the servers in charge of the costlier entrees gave me two slabs of the fillet of bluefish in butter sauce, three fried chicken breasts, and five thick slices of that succulent corned beef. I dolloped a tablespoon of mustard on the corned beef, and waited for Bev, who had filled her plate with some low caloried salads, and a piece of bluefish, with most of the butter sauce scraped off.

Bev and I returned to Table 36 long before Mike Cal and the rest started straggling back. We'd already finished most of our dinner before everybody took their seats again.

"So where'd you guys disappear to this afternoon anyway?" Glenda asked as she sat down." We looked around for you but you were gone."

"We decided to do some sightseeing around Faneuil Hall," I said. "You know, to soak up all of the Bostonian Revolutionary War stuff. After all, it is the Fourth of July next week."

"Did you look at the neat weather vane on top of the building and go inside to see the paintings?" Kathleen asked.

"Yep, we saw the big copper grasshopper on the roof that's been showing the way the wind's blowing for two hundred years, and we saw the huge painting of Daniel Webster in the gallery. Afterwards we walked over to the *Durgin Park* for a glass of beer," I said.

Before coming to Boston I had looked over a couple of sightseeing brochures covering the old city points of interest, so my description of the make believe tour that Bev and I took sounded plausible. No need for the rest of the table to know about our matinee lovemaking.

"Yes, it was great seeing everything that Boston has to offer," Bev said as she squeezed my hand under the table.

I decided to change the conversation. I'd already told absolutely everything I knew about Faneuil Hall.

"By the way, whatever happened to those four other Lieutenants that formed the other half of the crossed sword canopy?" I asked.

"They headed back to Fort Devens right after the church," Turner said. "They only came to help out for those couple of minutes. Nice guys. Brian said that they wouldn't even take the travel expenses that he offered them."

"Well I think that you men were the most attractive, classiest part of the entire ceremony. Next to Emily and Brian of course," Carrie said.

"As far as good looks and elegance are concerned," Jim said," I don't believe that there's a more lovely group of young ladies than the four charming females, representing both the North and the South, that are gracing our presence right here at this table. Including of course my own delightful escort for the evening, Miss Carrie Terhune."

That Turner. He really knew how to shovel the crap when it came to flattering women. Carrie blushed. So did Bev, Glenda, and Kathleen.

The waiters placed two large pitchers of ale on our table. Cal poured us each a foamy mug. For the next half-hour we gabbed and got silly as we finished the first pitcher.

Then Malcolm announced from the bandstand, "Would everybody please encircle the dance floor counter-clockwise, put both hands on the hips of the person in front of you 'Conga Line Fashion' and join us as we play the BUNNY HOP!"

About fifty women and maybe a dozen men filed onto the floor.

"C'mon, c'mon Guys!" Malcolm shouted. "The women outnumber you by four to one. Let's try to even out the gender participation."

The band began playing that familiar theme. *Dun Da Da Da Da Da - Hop-Hop-Hop!* Over and over. Bev dragged me out to the dance floor, and we cut in the line behind Sean Terhune and Rachel Walker. *Hop-Hop-Hop.* If I hadn't had those three or four mugs of ale, I don't think that even a threat of facing a firing squad without a blindfold and cigarette could have forced me out onto that floor. *Hop-Hop-Hop!* When I broke ranks and "volunteered", Cal, Mike, and Jim lost any excuse that they might've had not to join the line.

Suddenly the band doubled the tempo, then quadrupled it. Everybody bumped into everybody else's rear end. The line collapsed, and bodies were laughing and tumbling to the floor. Then the drums and the accordion sounded an end to the dance and we all returned to our tables. The air conditioning was having trouble battling all of that body heat, and it must've been eighty degrees in the hall. I poured myself another cold mug of ale.

Later the band began the obligatory ethnic music, and some senior citizens in the crowd showed off the dances from the old country. Naturally Irish Jigs predominated for the first fifteen minutes. Then the band struck up a Tarantella, while the Espositos and the Contis, neighborhood friends of the Terhunes, locked elbows and whirled around the room. In the spirit of my Italian Mom, I joined them and spun Bev over the floor for a while. Then the band switched in mid-Tarantella, to a sudden Hora, piping out *Ha Va Na Ge La.*. The guy on saxophone even switched to playing clarinet, so the music would have a more *Klezmer-*like quality. Jewish dancers replaced the Italians. Dr. and Mrs. Levy, Sheldon and Etta Goldstein, and a couple of others made an effort to do the basic steps. Mike Stern, who was not about to see the younger generation of Jews shut out of the festivities, jumped onto the dance floor with Kathleen, and hopped around to the catchy beat. But it was a funny coincidence. The steps to the Jig, Tarantella, and Hora all seemed exactly the same. Different people hopping and spinning around in the same way to different tunes. After a Polka and a Mexican Hat Dance the band took a break.

Time for dessert. Malcolm officiated as the Bride cut the wedding cake and fed the Groom. *And the Bride feeds the Gro-oo-m!* Feeding a good portion up Brian's nose. Then Brian got his revenge during *the Grooo-m feeds the Brii-ii-de!* When he spooned a great big scoop of whipped cream on Emily's cheeks. Then she kissed his nose, and he licked her cheeks.

We all went up to the buffet table for our piece of wedding cake. I managed to grab Bev a corner piece, with a chocolate cherry on top. She bragged to the other girls at my success at finagling such a prize slice, like I'd captured the broom of the Wicked Witch of the West or some-thing. So for a few seconds I was a hero.

Then the band struck up the second humiliating dance of the evening –the Hokey Pokey! A lot of the men in the crowd- including Mike, Cal, Jim, and myself- had been considerably lubricated by the numerous pitchers of ale that we downed to ward off the heat in that hall, so we were a bit more conducive to embarrassing ourselves than we were for the Bunny Hop.

"*Ya put yer left hand in ! Ya put yer left hand out!....*" Malcolm began, as the co-operative crowd obeyed his musical instructions, gyrating their arms"...*and ya shake it all around! That's what it's all about!!*"

Then as Malcolm rattled off the rest of the body parts to put in, put out and shake, he eventually reached the rear end of the anatomy. In the middle of his direction to *"Shake it all around!"* Brian's Uncle Leroy dropped his trousers, revealing his revoltingly hairy legs, and the purple polka dot boxer shorts which mercifully covered his ass. His wife slapped him playfully on the behind, and wagged her finger at him as he rebuckled his pants. *"Thaat's what it's aaall abouut!"*

It was time for Brian to fling the bright red garter of his new bride to the crowd of bachelors gathered in the middle of the dance floor. A drum roll; a wild toss; and the elastic lingerie hit his brother Patrick smack in the nose. Patrick was barely seventeen, and would have gladly deferred the honor to an older man, but tradition is tradition. And to back out would have lost him too much face in the eyes of his other brothers.

For the women's half of the ritual, Emily stood on top of a wooden chair, with her back facing the single girls assembled with their arms outstretched. Emily was supposed to toss the bridal bouquet high into the air, where it would be "randomly" snatched by some lucky maiden. But the fix was in! Emily peeked from the corner of her eye and spotted Mindy in her sights. She hurled a backward line drive straight into Mindy's bosom where she clutched the bouquet and held it high.

The cast of characters for the "garter ceremony" was now set. Mindy, seated with dress uplifted; and poor embarrassed Patrick, kneeling and clutching the garter. The band started playing the theme song to *The Stripper*, as Patrick placed it over her ankle. As the ribald crowd yelled "Higher! Higher!", Patrick slipped it around her calf! "Much, much Higher!" roared the crowd. Then he slipped it above her knee." Higher! Higher!" Mindy had sensational legs. As *The Stripper* crescendoed in the background, and the males in the crowd encouraged him, Patrick placed it around her upper thigh. I think he was starting to enjoy it. Mindy kissed him on the forehead signaling that he'd reached the point of no return. He turned beet red, and smiled at Brian and the other onlookers. The guy on drums gave out a rim shot, and the accordion squeezed a Ta!Da! ending the ceremony.

Brian and Emily circulated among the guests, thanking everybody for coming. Emily had her big purse to collect the cash and cash equivalent donations. Bev and I had decided to pool our resources and make a mutual gift. We thought that a hundred bucks was too much; but fifty dollars was too little. Finally we settled on the perfect present. God bless those US Savings Bonds! We bought a $100 bond. It only cost us $75 cash, but at least it looked like a hundred bucks.

It was getting late. Not really all that late, but I had a marathon drive ahead of me in the morning. If I woke up at eight o'clock, I could have breakfast and leave by nine. Then I'd have to drive Bev back to New Haven, and ride non-stop, with a quick lunch break; take the Jersey Turnpike to Delaware; then circumnavigate Baltimore; finally reaching the D.C. area about five o'clock. I needed to wake up Monday morning at two-thirty AM, so bedtime could be no later than six PM Sunday.

And so we said Goodbye to everybody at Table 36, and headed back to the Marriot. I said Good Night to Bev, and went straight to bed. I think that I heard Cal come in about one-thirty, but I wasn't sure.

Anyway I got up about eight the next morning with an "Ale Hangover", something that I hadn't known since a late evening celebration at *McSorely's Tavern* in Downtown New York. I tiptoed around the room, so as not to wake Cal, and went to pick up Bev. She looked like she was exhausted too.

We were on our way to New Haven. When we arrived at Bev's place, I carried her bags upstairs; walked her inside; and kissed her on the lips. I said that we'd see each other soon, but I doubted seriously that it was to be. Five hundred miles is a long distance to sustain a romance, even though we were crazy about each other. No, this was goodbye.

I got back to my two bedroom apartment that I was sharing with Don Santini. You remember, my partner from *Operation Overnight*. I rang the doorbell and he let me in. He was just about to have supper.

"Bob, how are ya?" he asked. "How was the wedding? How's Brian, and Cal, and Mike and Jim? You look like shit! I don't think that I've ever seen eyes that bloodshot before. Don't blink too hard or you'll rupture a vessel and bleed to death. How's about a game of Gin Rummy to settle your nerves?"

"No thanks," I said. "I think that I'll just have a quick dinner and go to bed. What's on the menu?"

"Turkey Sandwich *a la Santini*," he replied. "I toasted the bread myself. *And* there's chocolate milk,' *stirred*, not shaken', and barbecue flavored *Wise Potato Chips.*"

"Fine! Just nothing with any alcohol in it!"

I ate dinner; we shot the breeze for a half-hour; and I sacked out in my new bedroom in the place that would be my home for the next two years

# Chapter Twenty-three

# The Russians Are Coming!

The morning of my first official day at the Pentagon, I took Cachuk's advice and showed up at 0330 hours. I displayed my shiny new laminated pass to the civilian security guard at the South Entrance, and headed for Room B 425 D in the basement. Probably the most remote place in the entire building. Down the second corridor past the steps; two hallways, make a left; another fifty feet, a quick right and smack into a Staff Sergeant guarding the door with a 45 automatic. The sign in front of the door read *Restricted Area-Authorized Personnel Only*. I showed the guard my ISB pass; he pushed a few buttons on the door keyboard and swung the door open for me. I walked ahead to an eight foot counter. Behind the counter was a gigantic filing area about the size of an auto warehouse. Between it and the counter was another Sergeant named Stempel, in a short sleeved khaki shirt, standing up and reading the morning newspaper. He took a sip of coffee from the paper cup in his left hand.

"Morning, Sir!" he said looking up. "You must be the new officer from ISB. Welcome aboard sir!"

I asked him what my next step was. He told me that I just had to pick up the few reports that he'd received over the *red wire* fifteen minutes before, and carry 'em upstairs. He then handed me about four sheets from the teletype machine. I signed his receipt book, and left to go back to ISB. Ten minutes later, Sergeant Lopes was letting me in the ISB door.

He told me that the place wasn't *always* guarded, particularly after 6:00 A.M. But I could always get in with the security code on the combination door lock—-007. Cute!

The office was like a morgue inside. Naturally there were no windows, and Sergeant Haskell was the only soul around besides myself.

"G' morning sir!" he said." All set for your first day?"

I nodded, said good morning, and thanked him for his concern.

"Well sir, I've already spread out the morning reports from CIA, DIA. DIPSUM, and the other spy guys. Half are on your desk, and I put the other half on Major Cachuk's. Did you pick up the post 0300 hours documents from Sergeant Stempel downstairs, sir?"

"Yes I did Sergeant. Thanks.

"Then the place is all yours, sir. Major Cachuk should be here in about a half hour. I've got some things to do for Colonel Black before he comes in at 0600 hours. There's plenty of coffee. Cream and sugar too. It's over by Marilyn's desk. She's the Colonel's secretary, Good luck sir!"

I went into the Oral Briefers' room, shed my jacket, and began to read over the reports that I'd just picked up from downstairs. They all seemed pretty innocuous. Changing of the guard at the Sino-Soviet border; Israeli patrols reconnoitering possible Syrian positions. Yada.Yada.Yada. But then I came across something that made my palms start to sweat. A squadron of Soviet MIG 1 aircraft (fifteen in all) had been dispatched from Potrov Air Force Base near Minsk USSR, and were heading for the West German border (0300 hours EDT). I skimmed over the rest of the pages. All crap.

But this Minsk thing could be important. Was I going to be like that little Dutch boy at the hole in the dike? You know, was it up to me to report this Russian assault on NATO? I kept calm and went over to Cachuk's desk. On it were taped the SOP steps to take in case of a possible emergency like this. It said:

## UNDER ALL CIRCUMSTANCES- USE RED PHONE

Step one: Call source of report and ascertain whether anything new has been received.

So I called Sergeant Stempel downstairs. No new reports from anywhere.

Step two: Call DIA Alert Section. Number 0346. Report matter. Await instructions.

So I pushed the numbered buttons with my shaky finger, sat down in the small swivel chair, and lay down the ominous report in front of me. Someone on the other end picked up.

"Hello, this is Captain Philip Meister, DIA Alert Section. Who's speaking please?" he asked.

"Hello Captain, this is First Lieutenant Robert Woolsey, ISB. (pause) I've just picked up a Top Secret Umbra Report from our sources outside Hannover, West Germany. It says that a squadron of Soviet MIG aircraft were dispatched from Potrov Air Base at 0300 hours our time—I mean Eastern Daylight Time. And they're headed for West Germany!"

"OK Lieutenant. Keep calm. Just read me the numbers and letters *preceding* the report- and the place of transmission."

"Yessir, Captain!" I said. "It reads 163Z59M. Hannover, Federal Republic of Germany."

"Fine Lieutenant. We're aware of that report over here. No need to panic. The Soviets send a squadron of MIG's from Minsk every morning at that time. They buzz over Poland for a while. I guess to impress the locals how good they look in formation. Then they fly over East Germany, reach Leipzig and head back home. We appreciate your concern, but it's a false alarm. When you start getting reports that our little squadron from Minsk is staying home—-then *panic!* But you didn't do anything wrong Lieutenant. *By the book* , all assault aircraft heading towards NATO should be reported.

"Y'know we do the same thing with the Russians every day as well. Each morning *we* send a squadron of our fighter aircraft from Ankara

Turkey towards their testing site at Alma Atta, Kazakhstan. Then when our guys spot Mt. Ararat at the Soviet border looming about 100 miles away, they turn back and head home.

"Anything else to report? If not, have a nice day."

I don't think I ever felt like such a dope. I thought the whole situation over in retrospect. Why would the Russian Air Force pick the very morning of my first day on the job to decide to attack NATO? I carried the morning reports, the evidence of my humiliation, to the Out Box at Sergeant Haskell's desk. At the end of the day, he'd shove them into the paper shredder where they belonged. Sergeant Stempel downstairs in the belly of the Pentagon would have already filed the original copy of the report somewhere in his warehouse.

But my morning bonehead move wouldn't go unnoticed. *Every* call to #0346 on the *red phone* was automatically logged. By 8:00 A.M. Captain Dobson , the Officer of the Day would confirm every one, note the disposition of it, and forward the results to Colonel Black. Except for *real* crisis situations that phone number was rarely used. Maybe it saw action in something like the *Pueblo* Incident or the Tet offensive.

I went back to review the raw data for this morning's briefing. I got out my scissors and started cutting out the obvious trash. *Special Army parade celebrates Franco's 32nd year in power in Madrid.* Snip, snip. *Kristjan Eldjan elected President of Iceland.* Snip, snip, and double snip.

Cachuk walked in the room.

"Anything going on this morning?" he asked.

"Not really," I said. *Then* I realized that the bastard had set me up. He knew all about the phantom aircraft from Minsk. *Take the appropriate action!* Damn his ass! That little son of a bitch had planned my mortification in advance. But I said nothing. I just kept cutting and pasting. Occasionally I'd ask him if he thought an item was significant. But he was so full of himself that he'd usually reply with a condescending "no". As though to even *think so* was a ridiculous idea on my part. I thought to myself. Beware of dishing out humiliation, my dear Major. Life has a way of turning tables.

We went out for our morning briefings. Cachuk did his usual piss poor performance, and we got back a little before 8:00 A.M. I carried the briefcase containing Cachuk's "world news", as well as the transparencies we used to *fancy* it up. As we passed through the gauntlet of busy desk officers, all went well until I got to Captain Dobson.

"Hey Bob! I hear that you prevented World War III this morning!" he chuckled.

Ouch!

Randy Dobson wasn't really such a bad guy. But he figured that my little boner was worth at least *one* tiny dig. After that small zinger, he gave me a big grin and a friendly wink. No malice intended.

I put down the briefcase on top of my desk. There was a note from Colonel Black to see him after the 7:30 A.M. courtesy briefing that we gave to General Stillwell's staff. He was the Army Chief of Operations. Cachuk was about to say something. I spoke first.

"Colonel Black wants to see me right now," I said.

"I'll see ya when ya get back," Cachuk said.

I knocked on Black's door, and he said to come in. There was a standing order that nobody saluted anybody or stood at attention to fellow workers inside the office. Black asked me to sit down.

"I spoke with Captain Phil Meister a little while ago. You *did* make us look a little silly with the Minsk attack. But it *is* your *first* day here. I understand that. There wasn't anybody around to ask. But maybe you *could've* compared *today's* reports with those from yesterday or Friday to see if there might have been some duplications and such false alarms. Maybe Major Cachuk could've clued you in a little better. I'm a little surprised because the *same thing* happened to *him* on *his first day here*.

"He called Captain Meister about the very same *attack*. Phil explained to him the facts of life—so to speak—and Major Cachuk got a little upset when Phil refused to take any further action. Phil finally hung up on him. But that's all water under the bridge. Just be *very* cautious when calling DIA Alert. OK? That's all. You can go. Oh, by the way, how'd this morning's briefings go?"

"Fine sir," I said, relieved to hear of the similar fuck up of my illustrious boss only eight months before. I returned to the Oral Briefers' office. Cachuk had his Kindergarten sarcasm and crude insults all ready for me. Unlike Randy Dobson , Cachuk was a malicious prick.

"Well, well, Lieutenant Woolsey,"he cackled, "I hear that you were acting like a regular *Paul Revere* this morning. Do you think that NATO's shot down those planes yet?"

"They may very well have, Sir," I replied. "They must've had a lot of practice firing at 'em when *you* reported them heading for Munich last September yourself. Oh, by the way Sir, Captain Meister sends his regards."

Cachuk was speechless. He'd probably memorized a whole list of one-liners that he planned to use on me. You know, to put the hot shot lawyer in his place and all. He didn't anticipate that Colonel Black would spill everything about his foolishness last year. When he didn't admit *his* mistake to Phil Meister, he *really* made ISB look like a bunch of clowns. They should've kicked him out of ISB then. But with every available man heading for Vietnam, there was a manpower shortage at the Pentagon. Nobody let anybody go.

Cachuk turned his flushed face back to reading the Sports Section of his newspaper.

# CHAPTER TWENTY-FOUR
# Poor Man's Walter Cronkite

For more than eight months Cachuk had been getting away with producing editing, directing and starring in a disaster called a morning briefing. If the spectacle had been an automobile, it would have been an American *Yugo*.

I had just seen Mel Brooks' funniest masterpiece, a farce called *The Producers*. In it the heroes, Zero Mostel and Gene Wilder, must find the world's worst play, destined to fail, so that the money that they bilked from their investors would be lost in the morass of financial ruin of the flop. They miraculously produce a hit and wind up in prison.

Unlike Brooks' *Springtime for Hitler*, a Cachuk presentation was a *guaranteed* disaster. Fortunately for the good Major, nobody important showed up, except for some Lieutenant Colonel who was cursed with being "War Room" duty officer that morning. He usually dragged along a couple of lower ranking cronies to keep him company. Three or four hungover Majors that he'd spent the previous night with, barhopping at some D.C. pubs. Nobody would voluntarily spend 7:00 A.M. listening to some mumbling misplaced, military, misfit Major from Artillery giving a half-assed *oral* briefing, when they could *read* a competent, professionally assembled black book prepared by Intelligence experts.

During the one week countdown before McChristian's arrival, Cachuk was feeling a sort of guilty embarrassment over his practical joke about *Operation Minsk*-and the way it *backfired* on him, that he actually accepted some of my Intelligence recommendations for his morning production. He even went so far as to take me under his wing with his helpful hints on the *Art of a Successful Briefing*. For example— No Smoking until after the performance; suck on a couple of Luden's cough drops before the speech; and his *greatest* trick—assuring that he would never mispronounce a foreign name or place.

He armed himself with a fine tipped red felt pen, and would phonetically re-create every single non-English name and place—even those he had already pronounced a couple of dozen times. He was determined not to let some barbarian tongue twister ruin his twelve minutes of glory. *Take that* Yasir Arafat! You are now become yet another victim of my merciless pen. You have become *Yah-seer Ahr- ah-faht`*. He pored over his copy, a crazed look in his eyes, scratching and redacting with his bloody red tipped sword. Take that, new Premier of Greece! You are castrated to a phonetic wimp with the name—*Gay-org Pah-Pah-Dah-Poo-Lahs!*

One final rehearsal before entering the Briefing Arena. A final cough drop. He was ready. *Mow-Tsay-Tung, Fee-dell Kass-troh,* and *Layohneed Brezz-nee-eff* might threaten world domination through Communism, but they would never make it past the fearful felt tip pen of Major Donald Cachuk, Oral Briefer *par excellence* and inventor of the "Hooked on Phonics Program."

# CHAPTER TWENTY-FIVE

# Keeping the Old Man Happy

Fortunately for me our very first briefing to General McChristian was a disaster. The *old man* was none too pleased with Cachuk's sincere but bumbling performance. He wasn't too pleased with our 1913 photo of Golda Meir graduating either. He asked Colonel Black why we were producing two briefings—a written one and an oral one. And why wasn't the oral briefing team being given the support of our twenty *expert* desk officers. His predecessor obviously never came to an oral presentation. All that was about to change. The map transparencies were sub par; so were most of the other slides. From now on the Oral Briefers reported *verbatim* the contents of the black book. I smiled to myself when I heard this good news. No more getting up at 3:00 A.M. Coming in at the practically human hour of 0600. Hallelujah!

Now that the new boss actually wanted to see a morning performance that wasn't put together with paste and troglodytic visual affects, Colonel Black called an emergency meeting with Major Cachuk, Mr. Johnson and myself. Since my experience in General Staff apple polishing was *nil*, and since I had spent less than 10 days of active duty at ISB, my principle role was to take copious notes and to make coffee. As the three others ranted and raved about how to keep the General Mac happy and prevent the mortifying debacle of this morning's briefing from happening again, I thought of Kipling's advice in times of crisis. "*If you can keep your head when all about you are losing theirs.... Yours is the Earth and everything that's in it!"* Black and Cachuk both lost their cool. So, to my surprise, did Mr. Johnson. Maybe he'd been at the Pentagon too long. He probably had done his best thinking during World War II in a little cubby hole, up to his nose with a stack of papers, occasionally bouncing an idea off a colleague next to him. *That's* how he helped cracked that Japanese code. If he'd behaved like this in those days, we might all be eating *Sushi,* and honoring the Emperor today.

But they did make at least *one* rational decision. They decided to hire a full time visual arts professional. Somebody who could spruce up the daily presentation with fancy red arrows and graphics on our transparency maps. We hired Ed Cogan, a former Army Sergeant, who had been in the graphic arts business for a couple of years, but was still struggling to make a living. He jumped at the chance to earn some steady income and make contacts for his future. After he passed our security clearance, he was given the big dusty storeroom next to the Oral Briefer's Office as his exclusive workshop. Sergeant Haskell, Sergeant Vickers, and Corporal Finster took two whole days cleaning out the place. Some of the stuff they transferred to Sergeant Stempel's warehouse in the basement. Other "top secret" documents, probably like records detailing George Washington's undercover attack on the Hessians across the Delaware River, were stuffed into burn bags for incineration downstairs. File cabinets that we *might* need access to were shifted around to unoccupied nooks and crannies all over the office. Cogan was in business. A couple of days later the place was something that even Walt Disney could be proud of. Sophisticated cameras and projection equipment, stacks of stencils and graph paper, closets of inks and chemicals—and a *carte blanche* requisition slip from Colonel Black, if Ed needed anything else. What McChristian wanted, McChristian was going to get!

Cachuk was assigned to get some new slides. I eavesdropped as he telephoned and asked the Map Service to have transparencies made of

every country in the world. Blow-ups of every province in South
Vietnam. Emergency. Stat. Then he called CIA. He needed recently
taken slides of every prominent personality on Earth—and those whom
they thought were going to be prominent. And of every conceivable
aircraft and piece of ordnance. Now the CIA was ready and willing to
help out the US Army if it could, but those guys weren't about to take
any bullshit from some dumb hysterical Artillery Major playing like he
was something out of Ian Fleming. They asked him for a specific list of
items and they'd be glad to co-operate. When Cachuk continued
shouting , the guy from CIA hung up. Cachuk complained to me about
those pointy headed intellectuals at Langley bringing down this
country, and how they were probably half communists anyway. I didn't
bother to question this Cachukian form of Logic, whose basic princi-
ples were that (1) anyone who didn't drop everything they were doing
to help him out was a Communist sympathizer; (2) anyone with an IQ
of over 60 was an outright Communist.

But Major Cachuk was enough of a military man to realize that he
had a mission to accomplish. Black told him to get that morning
briefing up to the General's standards—or else.

Cachuk was forced to ask for help from the desk officers. He would
rather have eaten ground glass. Hell, he almost had an anxiety attack
from his inferiority complex when he had to ask them for a name or
place pronunciation.You see, most of these officers were everything that
he wasn't. They spoke foreign languages. Many had attended prestigious Universities. They could leave the Army and get a decent job elsewhere. Cachuk had barely graduated from someplace like Central
Indiana A&M Community College. The faculty there had received a lot
of their degrees from institutions that advertised on the back of matchbook covers. He majored in something like Fertilizer Science. He once
told me the title of his thesis—*The Future of the Cow Pie in Modern
Farming—Crops Still Love Crap!*

He knew down in his gut that the desk officers laughed at him. And unlike him, they weren't combat officers. Except for one or two of them at the Southeast Asia Desk, none of them had ever seen a battle. But he was forced to eat crow and ask about the military and political big shots , present and future, in places around the Globe. He didn't even ask me to help him out. I guess he figured that an intellectual like myself, in the Army less than four months, would certainly screw up the *astoundingly difficult* assignment of asking Jeff Pritchard who'd be in charge of Nigeria next year, or asking Stu Rutkowski what new Soviet tanks would appear in next year's May Day Parade.

Anyway, the maps we ordered came in within 48 hours. Boxes and boxes of them. Since neither Colonel Black nor Major Cachuk, for that matter, had *any* idea exactly what the General had in mind, McChristian turned both thumbs down, with yet another verbal put down of the morning briefing. The map slides weren't in color ; there was no indication of topography; He couldn't tell if the distance from our forces to suspected enemy positions was a hundred meters or ten miles. We'd have to do better.

Then disaster really struck. Cachuk completed his briefing (such as it was), and then asked the standard, "Do you have any questions , General?" McChristian asked something about a new piece of Russian artillery that the North Vietnamese were suspected of transporting down to the South. Cachuk made a valiant but flawed attempt to answer. After all, he'd read something about the ordnance in a couple of DIA reports about ten days ago when he was used to cutting and pasting his way to oral briefing glory. And he was getting pretty sick of being told that he had the crappiest presentation in the world. So he volunteered a couple of genuine facts mixed with some creative Cachuk bullshit. The big boss had asked a question. It just wasn't in Cachuk's make-up to admit that he didn't know. To do so might make him look even more incompetent in the General's eyes.

The next day it *all hit the fan!* The General had been informed by a colleague at CIA that the capability of the weapon that Cachuk had described was false. Sort of like giving a six-shooter eight bullets. Colonel Black went through the ISB ceiling when we got back to the office. Cachuk had to face a fifteen minute dressing down. Like he had committed perjury or something. I had no great love for the Major, but I felt pretty sorry for him as he just sat there in silence and took all of Black's tirade. Within the next hour, Black had posted a formal memorandum on the office bulletin board. He also had Marilyn, his secretary, deliver a copy to every person in the office. It said in no uncertain terms that any person either delivering the Black Book by hand, or giving an oral briefing *thereof* was not to answer any question posed by any recipient other than the presenter's name, rank, and serial number. We were to say politely that we weren't certain as to the information, but that we'd furnish the information requested within 24 hours. Of course, if the Secretary of the Army wanted to know the score of last Sunday's Redskins game, we *might* make an exception. But we did so *at our peril.* Since my mama didn't raise no stupid children, I followed that standing order to the letter for the next two years.

# CHAPTER TWENTY-SIX

# The Rookie Saddam

In the midst of the morning briefing metamorphosis, a coup had taken place in Iraq. General Abdul Rahman Arif was kicked out and replaced by General Ahmad Hassan al Bakr as chief of everything. He was President, Prime Minister, Head of the Revolutionary Command Council, called the Ba'ath Party and Commander of the Armed Forces. Maybe he ran the fast food concession down in the government lobby too.

Cachuk armed himself with his red felt tip pen, determined to do battle with these new windmills of Arabic pronunciation. But he continuously referred to "Bakr" as *Barker*, like the host of *The Price is Right*, and the "Ba'ath" Party as the *bath* Party—like when you get into the tub to wash yourself.

Since we needed some pictures of these new Iraqi butchers, the Major paged through the latest editions of the *Washington Post* and the *New York Times* for photos for Ed Cogan to make into transparencies, until the CIA "Rogues Gallery" could come up with something official. So Cachuk clipped out a bunch of barely discernible mug shots from the newspapers. Some of the newspaper photos were so poor that I couldn't tell al- Bakr from Porky Pig. But I had to give Cachuk credit. He did the best he could in the situation. Ed was able to enhance them with his graphic wizardry. Cachuk lent further dignity to them by asking Cogan to mark each slide with a bright red "Confidential" stamp.

I guess he figured that his mere touch gave them an aura of restricted sensitivity.

One of these new Iraqi strongmen, was a young ruthless thug named Saddam Hussein. His formal title was Deputy Chairman of the Revolutionary Command Council. CIA described him as dangerous and of concern to US interests in the Middle East. Gary Maggio at the Middle East Desk told me a little more about the guy. Saddam was a killer. Somebody who'd put a bullet in an enemy's -or perceived enemy's- ear as easy as saying "Good Morning". He was a fanatic who began his rise to Second in Command by killing his own brother -in-law, when he was twenty one years old. Then there was that attempted assassination of former Iraqi Prime Minister Hassem. From there he went on to become an accomplished expert in the art of torture during a previous Ba'ath Party regime. Like Adolf Hitler, Saddam spent time in prison, which gave him time for reflection, time to plan his future. Like Hitler he had established his own personal units within his political party who pledged him their uncompromised loyalty. He spoke, and they murdered at his whim. Then Gary got in his pathetic attempt at humor.

"But, Bob," he said, "the worst thing of all about the son of a bitch is that he's a *lawyer!*"

# CHAPTER TWENTY-SEVEN

# What's a Little Invasion Among Friends

During the next six weeks I'd become quite comfortable at ISB. Except for the hours, the work was a snap. I just read the Black Book, that the Desk Experts prepared, and tried not to let Cachuk bother me too much. The General liked me. He even went so far as to delay the opening of my first performance behind the podium at the War Room. Nothing elaborate, mind you. Just an informal. "Good Morning, Lieutenant. You're new here. I can't quite read your name tag. Whazzit say?" "Woolsey, General. First Lieutenant Robert Woolsey!" I made it a point to call him "General ", and not "Sir". A little ego inflation was sort of like chicken soup. It couldn't hurt. Black caught the obvious flattery. "Nice touch with the 'General' thing , Bob. I think I'll make it SOP around here to do that with all the Brass wearing stars on their epaulets."

The morning of August 21, 1968, the phone rang in my apartment that I was sharing with Don Santini. You know, my partner from *Operation Overnight*. I glanced at my alarm clock It was 2:30 A.M. I rolled over and covered my ears with my pillow hoping it would go away. Santini didn't answer it either. After twenty-one rings I got out of the sack, fumbled around for the light switch, and felt my way towards the living room phone. I picked it up.

"Bob, is that you?" said a familiar voice on the other end. I was still too groggy to make it out. "This is Major Cachuk."

"Yes sir, what is it?" I mumbled, while clearing my throat.

"Didn't you watch TV last night? The Soviets invaded Czechoslovakia. Caught us with our pants down CIA, DIA, Army Intelligence, everybody. Colonel Black's scheduled a special briefing for 0600 hours. General Mac requested that *you* give it. Stu Rutkowski's been working at the office since seven o'clock last night trying to prepare something. But things are changing every ten minutes. See ya at the office in an hour."

My head still wasn't clear. The only thing that I could think of was why he said that the briefing was at "0600" hours, and why he Said that Stu Rutkowski started working at "seven o'clock" last night. Maybe Cachuk was turning civilian on me.

"What was that all about?" Santini yawned, dressed in skivvies at his bedroom door.

"The Soviets and their goons invaded Czechoslovakia," I said. "I've got to give a special briefing to General Mac at six o'clock."

"Oh," Santini said, "I thought it was something important. At least a horny phone call from one of those stewardesses on the sixth floor, that we met at the swimming pool last Sunday. I'm going back to bed. And please disconnect the phone before you go. The next bell I want to hear is my alarm clock at eight ! G'night. "


Stu Rutkowski was a twenty-eight year old Captain—a fanatic on East European History, who spoke fluent Russian, Polish, and German. He was one of those geniuses that the Army tolerated, because he was probably the *best* damned Iron Curtain analyst that we had.

He had a walrus-like mustache, that may or may not have been regulation. He categorically denied that he wore it to make himself look like Joseph Stalin. His horn-rimmed eyeglasses must've been at least an inch thick. I figured that his eyesight should've kept him out of the Army. Like most of our Desk Officers he usually didn't wear a uniform. The Department of the Army encouraged this. They didn't want the Pentagon to look like a military base. After all, the people in charge were *civilians.*

I entered the office and saw Stu gulping down what I assumed was his tenth cup of coffee. He was wearing his uniform especially for his performance in front of McChristian in a couple of hours. It reeked of mothballs. Stu probably rummaged it from the very, very back of his clothes closet. I'd 've bet that he hadn't worn the thing since Intelligence School.

Rutkowski's desk was more of a mare's nest than usual. On any given morning it was covered with CIA reports on Warsaw Pact troop strength and positions, little toy-like models of the latest Soviet tanks and aircraft; and pictures of four of his heroes—Peter the Great, Prokoviev, Dostoyefsky, and Kafka. Today they were all blanketed by stacks of papers. He was talking on the unsecured phone. That meant that he wasn't exchanging classified information with anyone. He didn't say a word. He just scribbled down notes feverishly on a legal pad. Every so often he'd let out a grunt, to let the party on the other end know that he was still there. The telephone receiver was permanently cradled in the crook of his neck. In his non-writing hand he held a non-filter ciga- rette—probably a *Camel* or a *Gauloise.* He must've smoked between fifty and sixty of them a day. His soup bowl ashtray was already piled high with his smelly butts. To further fit in with his Russo-Slavic image, he held the disgusting things like one of those Eastern European Secret Agents, played by Peter Lorre in the movies. You know, with the thumb and forefinger *under* the cigarette.

Ten minutes later he put down the phone.

"Who was that?" I asked.

"The *New York Times* !" he said. "No need to pretend that the guys at CIA and DIA are calling the shots any more. They were *all* caught looking at the wrong end of the biggest invasion since Hitler attacked Poland in '39. All those spooks working with about fifty billion dollars in special equipment, caught bareassed and with their pants down. Even those expensive 'moles' that we have working undercover at the Kremlin, weren't any help to us this time. This briefing is not courtesy of military Intelligence. Most of the stuff I got was straight from the press. I was just on the phone for over an hour with a contact of mine from the *Times*. I already pumped all of the information I could from an East European correspondent I know at the *Washington Post,* at about ten o'clock last night. What a disgrace! Getting Intelligence from the *newspapers*. Oh, we did do something right. Our forces in West Germany have arranged for the safe evacuation from Prague of Shirley Temple Black. It seems that we rescued America's favorite kiddy movie star in time. She happened to be visiting the place on some publicity tour. The curly haired li'l moppet won't be languishing in some Soviet P. W. camp after all. Hooray for Hollywood!

"The Old Man is probably gonna kick the first ass that he sees at this morning's briefing. Looks like the immediate targets are you and me, Bob. Mainly *me*. Just read what I give you , after Colonel Black gives it the OK. Try to look like you know what you're talking about, and refer all questions to me. You'd better join Colonel Black and Major Cachuk back in the Briefing Office."

I went back to my two bosses. They were busy talking about how the entire Intelligence community had fucked up. LBJ *himself* had no inkling of any of this until Radio Prague announced it last night. Colonel Black said that General McChristian was concerned about Intelligence ineptitude concerning the Czechoslovakian business, but that South Vietnam was still priority number one.

"Let's face it," Black said," the Old Man is primarily interested in our putting on a good show this morning. A dozen Generals who didn't give a shit about Czechoslovakia two days ago are suddenly curious. So

McChristian's invited them to sit in. He wants to show his West Point buddies what a professional shop we're running here.

"Not to worry. Stu Rutkowski knows more about Eastern Europe than anybody in this building. Probably more than anybody in the *Kremlin*."

Colonel Black then left to confer with Stu on possible questions that might come up this morning. Cachuk was still disturbed that he, as senior officer, hadn't been chosen to do the reporting. But he was sure that I would do credit to our "team". Put the red tipped pen away, Major, I thought to myself , today's briefing will be given by someone who at least knew where Czechoslovakia *was* before the current crisis. Naturally, the Oral Briefing Section had been reporting on Alexander Dubcek's "Compassionate Communism" for a few months now, but before that , I doubted seriously if Cachuk could've located Czechoslovakia on a map. *Maybe* he'd had seen a picture of Prague once on a bottle of Pilsner beer. But that probably been the extent of his knowledge about the place.

Colonel Black returned with a coupe of things. First, the briefing had been extended to half an hour. New reports were coming in every few minutes. I'd most likely have to read from raw data received over the *red phone* teletype machine. Cachuk would be running back and forth with fresh info whenever he could. Unfortunately a lot of the script would be garbled with misspellings all over the place. I'd just have to do my best. But I should be prepared to receive a report something like "Sovut tunks rolled into th moin sectn of doentown Prage." which if neatly typed would read *Soviet tanks rolled into the main section of downtown Prague!* Good luck Bob.

But the gods had blessed me with an unusual talent. I couldn't climb a rope. or shoot a target; I couldn't swim under water; hell, I couldn't even *match my socks*. But I could unscramble a text while reading it at the same time. I was also able to peek ahead at the next couple of lines while I was performing this little trick as a kind of oratorical geek, who might somehow work it into a circus act after my Army discharge. So as I told of *trps* assembling in Stanislaus *sqre*, I was already deciphering that *Wrsaw* Pact forces from *Hngry* and *Plnd* were being held in *risrve*.

I marched up to the speaker's podium with my tentative script, that I knew was soon to be replaced. I noticed a lot of new faces in the audience as I slowly darkened the room lights with my dimmer switch, leaving the ten watt bulb at the podium, which was shining on my report, as the only light in the black soundproof War Room.

This was to be the first briefing that the visiting Generals had seen on a conventional war in a long time. Sure there was a war of sorts going on in Vietnam. But it was strictly at platoon or company level. In Vietnam we were facing a silent enemy uniformed in black pajamas, that fought from ambush, and only in limited skirmishes. An enemy that was willing to take another twenty years to win the war, just as it had taken more than twenty years to get this far. Maybe they'd begin standard warfare as soon as the US forces left. Then we would see that they could put up a pretty good fight with mechanized divisions against their ARVN adversaries.

But the Czech War was different. It brought out the boy soldier in most of the Generals in the room. After the briefing they all could gather around the "War Table" in the back, and slide their little tanks and artillery pieces around the board. A game of military *Monopoly. Park Place* and *Boardwalk* became Bratislava and Prague. They could all try to outguess each other on Soviet strategy, as they wielded their pointers and chomped on their fat cigars. This was a conflict that they'd been trained to fight since their youth. Divisions matched up against divisions. Soviet T-54 tanks *en masse*. Sophisticated artillery. *Civilized Warfare* at last!

I wished myself a silent "Break a leg, Kid!", as I glanced down at McChristian for his permission to begin. He nodded. Show Time!

"Good Morning General, The overall classification of this briefing is Top Secret Umbra. Should anyone present not be cleared at this level of security, I request that they leave the room," I said.

Two Colonels stood up and left. I continued.

"At 2220 hours Czechoslovakia time, on the evening of August 20th, Warsaw Pact forces invaded the sovereign nation of Czechoslovakia. Forces included Twenty-three Soviet mechanized divisions........."

As I droned through the prepared script, Major Cachuk, trying to appear as inconspicuous as possible handed me a couple of unedited sheets of teletype paper that I casually placed on the left side of the rostrum. I completed the paragraph that I was reading and turned to the new copy. I paused and said calmly.

"General, I have just received up to the minute material from our sources in Eastern Europe. The Soviet 13th tank division has captured the city of Bratislava, after encountering only token resistance. The Czech Army has, at this moment, apparently conceded victory to the forces of the Warsaw Pact. If the General will focus his attention to the screen showing recent confirmations of both the location and strength of these forces, I will announce their anticipated courses of action. Captain Stuart Rutkowski, our Eastern Europe Desk Analyst, will locate these areas on the slide projection map. At the conclusion of this briefing, or at any time there is a question, he will answer, or attempt to answer, whatever queries the General might have. Shall I continue, Sir?"

The General nodded. At that moment Cachuk handed me some new pages about Polish mechanized units sealing off the Czech northern border, while Hungarian forces were securing the southern half of the country. Or, as the new unedited copy read :"*Hungrian* forces were *scuring* the south, while *Plsh* troops were mopping up in the *noth.*"

The briefing went on like that for the next twenty five minutes. Then I concluded with the standard ,"That concludes this briefing, General. Do you have any questions or comments?" Major Cachuk turned up the other adjustable dimmer switch at the rear of the room as I clicked off my little podium lamp. I could see the audience now, and its attention was centered on Stu Rutkowski, mustache, crumpled uniform and all, standing, his pointer at the ready, in front of the giant map of Czechoslovakia, dominating the rear view projection screen. The first question was a toughie from McChristian himself.

"Captain Rutkowski, how were 200,000 Warsaw Pact troops able to invade the country, while our side, with all its sophisticated equipment, and covert sources, didn't know a thing about it until it was a *fait accompli*, and it was broadcast over Radio Prague last night."

Stu had done his homework. Our brilliant Rasputin raised the pointer stick with his nicotine stained fingers, and described the position of the invading forces just prior to the massive assault. The Soviets had been clever. They had arranged for Warsaw Pact forces to play "War Games" months in advance. We knew about all that. But they were able to convert these "games" into an actual invasion before the CIA knew what was going on. But Stu was tactful as hell. He wasn't about to start throwing blame around. Captains— even genius Captains—weren't high up enough on the Intelligence totem pole to level charges at anybody-except maybe Lieutenants.

McChristian's question opened the floodgate for a dozen more. But Stu fielded them all like Willie Mays. He made it a habit to read *every* report that came into the office on Russian and Eastern Europe forces. Even those from the most *schlock* of sources. I suspected that if there had been a "*National Enquirer on the Warsaw Pact*" published, old Stu would've read it cover to cover. So, for a guy who could recite the menu of K-rations available to the average Bulgarian Infantryman in the field, this friendly session of the *Try and Stump Stu Show* just left the questioners, who were mostly trying to impress McChristian with their *Reader's Digest* knowledge of Eastern Europe, looking pretty foolish. Stu Rutkowski had given an Academy Award performance. I was a hit too. My name would sparkle in Pentagon lights. Two stars were born.

Cachuk came up to congratulate me at the end of the briefing, with a big slap on the back and a "Great job, Lieutenant Woolsey! *We* make a great team."

I thought of the old punch line, "Who's we white man?" as we both marched quick time back to ISB. Stu Rutkowski was already acknowledging his accolades from all the desk officers, some of whom had witnessed his coup from the back of the War Room. I received a couple of laurel branches myself. I flashed back a big grin, while Cachuk thanked everybody on behalf of the briefing *team.* What an asshole.

Later that afternoon a Major Dickens from McChristian's office showed up with a memorandum of congratulations for Colonel Black. He was happy enough to tack it right up on the bulletin board. It meant that his job at ISB was secure—for a while at least. He could continue attending those Embassy Parties that he liked so much, and hustling those young stewardesses for the foreseeable future. The memo read:

*To Colonel Black, ISB:*

*Allow me to congratulate you and your entire staff for this morning's excellent briefing. Particular accolades go to Captain Rutkowski and First Lieutenant Woolsey for their competence regarding the relevant facts and circumstances surrounding the Czechoslovakian situation, as well as their credibility and professionalism.*

> *Major General Joseph McChristian*
> *Assistant Chief of Staff for Intelligence*

# CHAPTER TWENTY-EIGHT

# Biggest Flareup Since Mrs. O'Leary's Cow

The apartment that Santini and I shared was about equidistant between the Pentagon and the Army Map Service where Don worked. His job was to read data collected from those satellites circling Red China and the USSR to make precise maps. When he first arrived he had to take the standard lie detector test. He was nervous as hell about taking it. I would've been too. Would they find out about my notorious teen-age crime spree, when on a dare, I stole a fistful of *Almond Joys* from old man Klempner's candy store. Or the dozens of times I'd used a phony draft card to get into a bar on Staten Island. Not exactly putting me in the same league as Julius and Ethel Rosenberg, but maybe falling *juust* short of a top security clearance. Don's fears were ill- founded. He past with flying colors.

About a week after my own personal triumph with the Warsaw Pact invasion another one of those events that cursed the year 1968, took place. It was the Democratic National Party Convention in Chicago, hosted by its gruff party boss Mayor Richard Daley.

The death of Bobby Kennedy a couple of months earlier, had all but assured Hubert Humphrey of the nomination. But I got a kick out of watching the silly extravaganza with the balloons and dumb straw hats all the same. I was raised in a political household and my dad had even run for Congress only four years before. Of course as a Republican in the Democratic stronghold of Jersey City, New Jersey, he lost by about 10 to 1.

Because my job allowed me to get home by about 2:00 P.M. I was able to watch the whole thing, gavel to gavel. I had seen the "coronation" of Richard Nixon a couple of weeks ago, but Republican conventions were traditionally boring stuff.

The Democrats, on the other hand, usually managed to put on a pretty good donnybrook, even when there was a foregone conclusion, like there was in 1968. There always seemed to be some inebriated, obviously prosperous, real estate broker or something, serving as a delegate from someplace in Ohio, glorying in his thirty seconds of fame by seconding the nomination of Ohio's favorite son, with a name like Horatio Higgenbottom, for Vice- President. Then a few of his polluted fellow delegates would raise the State banner and throw confetti all over the place. On cue the orchestra would play *Beautiful Ohio* or whatever the hell their state song was, and some guy in the balcony would release about a million red, white, and blue balloons.

Then they would take the roll call, and some other drunken real estate broker , this time from Alabama would start by shouting, "*Misterrr Chairmannn*, the *Greaaat* State of Alabama, home of *Beaaar* Bryant and the Crimson *Tiiide*, casts its twenty four votes for....". Then everybody'd cheer and yell, while the band played *Alabama Jubilee* for a couple of minutes.

But that good time spirit was confined within the walls of the Convention Center. On August 27th about nine o'clock, Santini and I were watching the TV. I usually didn't stay up past that time, what with getting up at about quarter to five in the morning and all. But suddenly the scene switched to outside the hall. Evidently some cameras that had been denied entrance inside the convention, were busy shooting a confrontation between cops and hippies. Officers in riot gear were chasing the suspected troublemakers down State Street towards the park. Dan Rather was getting the feed from inside the Convention Center. This was undoubtedly more interesting than the congressman on stage presenting the platform speaker. The riot cops were swinging billy clubs like crazy. Kids were running and throwing bottles as they fled. The cameras fed off the frenzy of the police vs. the radicals. They focused on individual rioters that had been clubbed by seemingly overzealous police who were now dragging the bleeding bodies of protesters to awaiting vans to be booked downtown.

Then Don switched to another channel to see what was happening on NBC. Huntley and Brinkley were reporting the same thing. Cops were using nightsticks partly in self defense, and partly to inflict punishment.

I had mixed emotions. Don and I both did. We both hated the War, but a lot of leaders that were provoking the police were people that we despised. Bobby Seale and Abbie Hoffman were anti-American swine who probably reveled in seeing some of those poor kids getting their heads bashed in. But it was getting late. I went to bed. I could read about it in the papers the next morning.

The evening of August 28th was a disgusting continuation of the events of the previous night. Some of the demonstrators had evidently bandaged their wounds and were ready for Round Two.

The violence from the evening before played again for the poised TV cameras. More demonstrators being slammed over the head by police refueling their anger with every blow. Maybe they were just beating up on their frustration over the war that had no end. Beating up on Sirhan Sirhan, who had changed the course of World History. Some were beating up on perceived spoiled middle class white kids, that were deferred from fighting in Vietnam. Maybe they were beating up on 1968. Maybe they were beating up on the frustration in having to turn to somebody like Richard Nixon to lead them out of their desperation. And these bludgeoning troops were Chicago cops, whose fathers had voted for Franklin Roosevelt and his New Deal, and who had mourned when their Democratic Mayor Cernak took a bullet meant for FDR more than thirty- five years before.

Don and I cursed the demonstrators. Then we cursed the cops. Most of all we cursed the war.

# CHAPTER TWENTY-NINE

# Fun and Games

A couple of weeks later Colonel Black thought that it would be a morale booster for the office to have an informal get- together, a barbecue at Rock Creek Park before Autumn and the chilly weather. He "requested" that Major Cachuk tend to the logistics of the event. Shit flows down-hill, so Cachuk ordered me to carry out the details. He would supervise. That meant that I'd have to reserve the Picnic Area; post directions on Marilyn's bulletin board; buy the hamburgers, hot dogs, salads, rolls, beer, soda, napkins, charcoal, lighting fluid, matches, garbage bags, tablecloths, plastic utensils, plastic glasses, paper cups and plates, spat-ulas, coffee, sugar, milk, ice, serving spoons and sundries. Then I'd have to requisition the necessary basketballs, softballs, bats, volleyballs, nets, poles, Frisbees, and sports gear from the Pentagon Gym to accommo-date about forty people. Then I'd have to personally check out the site to make certain that it had enough recreation space for the whole gang, including a basketball court and a softball field; plenty of parking; barbecue pits, picnic tables and trash bins, plus a nearby fountain for the coffee pot; *and* a couple of nearby *Porta-Sans* for ISB picnickers to relieve themselves.

I packed all of the vittles and athletic equipment into my Bonneville about 9:00 A.M. I got to the park at about ten to set the whole thing up. Cachuk showed up with Mrs. Cachuk at about noon. He brought along the family's 16 cup, non- electric coffee maker as his contribution to the

124

team effort. He strolled about in his plaid Bermuda shorts, checking out my performance. He chided me a little for forgetting the coffee stirrers (plastic spoons weren't good enough ). Then all three of us waited for the rest of ISB to show up.

Shortly after 12:15 Colonel Black and his date arrived. She was a buxom young thing who was wearing a U.C.L.A. tee shirt that was a size too small, and caused the "C" and the "L" to bulge out sexily from under her D-Cup bra. The tee shirt was tucked into a pair of snug fitting blue denim shorts. The six eyeballs of Black, Cachuk, and myself followed her as she jiggled over to help Mrs. Cachuk make the coffee and set the tables.

After she'd gone, the Colonel congratulated Cachuk and me on a splendid job. Cachuk took full credit, of course; then the bastard apologized for my inadvertence in not providing the coffee stirrers. Black winked at us and said that we'd just have to "tough it out" by using our plastic knives and spoons like "common barbarians". *Nobody* ever used those plastic *knives* that the utensil makers put into their packages anyway.

Among the first people to show up were Lt. Colonel Quigley and Mrs. Quigley. He was carrying on his shoulder, like a safari bearer, a huge twenty- five pound watermelon, probably the last one from the late summer crop. He was straining noticeably under its weight, until he eased the monster piece of fruit onto one of the picnic tables. It looked like a perfect dessert to top off the feast, as it took up the space of the whole table with its cool , deep green presence. I thanked Colonel Q for his generous donation. First, I wanted to cut off a few slices so that they could chill on the ice for a while. Then I discovered that the Colonel had forgotten to follow the Army's first *mnemonic*—PPPPPP. He didn't bring along a knife to cut the thing open. I made a pitiful attempt to perform watermelon surgery on the thick skin with one of those K-Mart plastic knives, but it proved to be more suited to a replacement coffee stirrer than a *machete*. So I stood on top of one of the picnic benches, and made an emergency plea to the crowd for anything that they might have that could cut open our dessert.

Major Whitfield from the Cambodia/Laos Desk motioned me over. Then he led me to the trunk of his *Buick*. He opened it up and produced the perfect kitchen gadget—a brand new, slightly stolen bayonet. We walked back to the defiant watermelon, and he unsheathed the bayonet from its scabbard. Then he plunged its virgin blade heartlessly into the abdomen of the defenseless melon, as though he was attacking some poor North Vietnamese Regular. He cut through, and it fell apart into two perfect halves. Then I borrowed the weapon long enough to slice the juicy red fruit into forty, half pound pieces, just enough for the picnickers. We went back to the festivities.

The weather was magnificent. A perfect mid- September afternoon. Just about everybody had arrived by a quarter to one. Then I made a little announcement to the crowd that *I'd start* the first half dozen hamburgers and wieners on the now white hot charcoal grill, but after that it was every spy for him or herself. I said that there were five pound vats of potato salad, macaroni salad, egg salad, cole slaw and baked beans, as well as several bags of assorted rolls to fit around the meat of their choice. The finest plastic cups, plates and cutlery that K- Mart could provide were located at the picnic table closest to the grill. Beer and soda were already chilling in fifty- pound bags of ice by the trash bin. Basketballs and sporting goods were next to my car, the white Bonneville with the red handkerchief on the antenna. I said that they could help themselves to anything, *but* they had to return the equipment to my car after they were finished, 'cause the Sergeant down at the Gymnasium swore that he'd report all unreturned items to Colonel Cavendish, the Lord High Guardian of Sporting Gear. Missing items meant that I'd be docked the *retail* value of the stuff from my pay; and ISB would be forever blacklisted from borrowing even a *Ping-Pong ball!*

Most of the group headed for the food. A couple of officers from the Southeast Asia Desk grabbed a basketball for a game of one-on-one. Around 3:00 P.M. Colonel Black passed the word around that a softball game would be starting in about half an hour. Mr. Johnson would be the plate umpire; Mrs. Johnson would serve as ump at first base; Mrs. Cachuk would be at third. Colonel Black would be pitcher and captain of his team; Lt. Colonel Quigley for his.

Mr. Johnson flipped his lucky Silver Dollar in the air, and sides were chosen just like back on the sandlot, when I was in the Fifth Grade. Randy Dobson and Carl Lebron were picked first. Stu Rutkowski and I were chosen last by Black and Quigley respectively. Cachuk was short-stop on Colonel Black's team. Black dubbed his squad the *Undercover Assassins* while Quigley named our team the less menacing *Double 0-Sevens*.

Seven innings. Slow pitch. No arguing with the umpires. I batted eighth, and played third base. A splendid choice by Lt. Colonel Quigley, if I must say so myself. One thing that I *could* do in my old Fort Benning days was *throw*. I could always hit my target with a hand grenade from about ninety feet, so lobbing a softball from third to first was a piece of cake. I didn't have to worry too much about anybody beating my accurate arm either. Most of Black's *Undercover Assassins* had been considerably slowed down by a heavy lunch of burgers, buns, baked beans, and *Budweiser*.

I actually got a single, and scored from first base on Len Roth's humongous triple that soared into the other end of the parking lot. Mr. Johnson should've called it a Ground Ruled double, because Major Carson had trouble retrieving it from under Quigley's old Chevy van. But Johnson allowed Len to remain at third, where he died after Matt Lehrer struck out.

Our side was leading 7 to 6 after our half of inning seven. Black's team had two out , and Cachuk was on First. Major Carson was at bat, and would be followed by Randy Dobson, who'd already hit two doubles and a home run, and was single-handedly responsible for five of the six *Assassin* tallies.

The count was even on Carson, when he lambasted a slow, fat pitch from the tiring Cy Young Quigley, and drove the thing past Carl Lebron in Center Field. But Carl had an M-16 for an arm. He picked up the softball, and fired it towards me at third base. Cachuk foolishly rounded second without even looking up. He wheezed and puffed as he churned those thirty-seven year old legs towards third. I just stood there as the ball from Carl flew over the struggling Cachuk's head on a fly, smack into my waiting hands, cupped at my chest. Cachuk was out by about ten feet. I could've stopped to light a cigarette before he even *started* his belly flop slide into the empty plastic vat of potato salad that was our improvised third base. I tagged him lightly on the shoulder.

Cachuk's wife was the ump at third. Her call was unchallengeable. The whole world was watching. The peace and harmony of the Cachuk household for weeks to come hung on her decision. But putting up with her husband for the past fifteen years had strengthened her character.

"Yer out, dear!" she said.

Cachuk turned beet red. He was about to argue the call. Then he sat up, smiled, and laughed at himself. He knew he'd pulled a boner. If he'd only stayed at Second, Randy Dobson, who'd hit nothing less than a double all day, would've no doubt pounded the softball from the exhausted Quigley halfway into the Potomac River. He and Carson would've scored easily.

He looked over at Colonel Black who was scowling, his hands on his hips at Home Plate. Cachuk got up and dusted himself off. Then he pointed to his chest with his left index finger, as he stuck out his right thumb giving himself the out sign. I threw the ball to Quigley on the mound. He raised both arms in triumph. Possibly his first taste of victory since that fateful day in China twenty years ago when he escaped from the Chinese Communists with Chiang Kai Chek.

By now Cachuk was laughing and cracking jokes with everybody in the playing field. He told how both of his legs felt like lead prostheses as he tried to make it to Third, not sure if he'd need CPR before the last thirty feet. Just then Mrs. Cachuk brought the would be Mickey Mantle an ice-cold beer, and vowed never to serve as umpire again.

# CHAPTER THIRTY

# Weekly Ball and Chain

Once a week both Cachuk and I would have to deliver a select summary of the Black Book to the Commander at Fort Holabird, about fifty miles North on Route 95. On our way back we'd deliver it to Major General Stevenson of Logistics and Supply, who for some strange reason had his offices in Northwest D.C.

In the Fall of 1968 Colonel Black determined that having *two* officers waste the better part of a day delivering the book was featherbedding that even Jimmy Hoffa couldn't have negotiated. The Generals only pretended to read the thing anyway. General Stevenson was in charge of procuring sufficient quantities of toilet paper, C- Rations, and other such staples from civilian suppliers at a price that was within reason. He couldn't give a damn about possible infiltration of North Vietnamese through Laos or the latest coup in the Middle East. As long as he could end his career without being called on the carpet for requisitioning a two thousand dollar toilet seat, he could retire a happy man. General Peck at Fort Holabird might have peeked at the Southeast Asia Section once or twice, but only if there was some really big crisis making newspaper headlines. But they *both* had to receive it and at least thumb through it as per the directive of the Secretary of the Army.

Black reduced the messenger service to one officer. So once a week Cachuk or I would put the book and a loaded 45-caliber pistol in a combination lock briefcase, handcuff the case to our left wrist, and meet Samuel Jefferson down at the Pentagon motor pool. Sam would be our driver for the day in one of those olive drab 1965 sedans with no air conditioning and crappy heating.

The first couple of times Sam drove me on my delivery, I sat in the back of the car reading a novel or doing the *Post* Crossword Puzzle. Then one day Sam and I got into a conversation about Washington D.C. He was born there the very same day that the *Titanic* sank. He told me of how he and his mother stood in line to see the opening of the Lincoln Memorial in 1922. How the next year everybody was talking about the big Teapot Dome scandal under President Harding whose Secretary of the Interior was cashing in on Government land sales , and pocketing moneys from ridiculously low bids. He remembered the *Bonus Army* of unemployed veterans, practically starving to death, that camped out in front of the Capitol during the early days of the Depression; and how Douglas MacArthur with his tanks and tear gas chased them away. In the true spirit of the cavalry, his horse soldiers galloped over their emaciated bodies in the process.

Most of all he told me about how he tried to join the Army after Pearl Harbor, and was turned down because he was a Negro. Then he went back home and tore up that happy photo of himself taken by his mother in front of the Lincoln Memorial. Two weeks later, after he cooled down a little, he pasted back the picture from the pieces he kept in his drawer.

Then he told me about how the whole city, blacks and even a lot of the white folks in Northwest D.C. cried when Martin Luther King was shot. Some of the black folks rioted, breaking windows and looting stores the night of the assassination. Sam was a regular Almanac on Washington D.C.

We didn't talk about it, but Sam and I both knew that the reason I had that briefcase handcuffed to my wrist, with a loaded gun inside, was to defend the top secret material inside from being seized by my Black fellow citizens during another riot.

But I thought that the whole cloak and dagger operation was silly. I was surprised that Colonel Black didn't give me a cyanide pill. I figured that if some D.C. residents suddenly decided to riot and attack the car, I'd have to fumble around with the combination lock, open the case, take out the 45, release the safety and shoot the unwieldy piece. By that time any self-respecting rioter would have broken into my side of the car, and knocked me unconscious, leaving me unarmed and handcuffed to an empty briefcase.

The business with the handcuffs is a story all by itself. When I left the ISB office either Black or Cachuk shackled my wrist to the briefcase handle. The key *stayed* at ISB. I was literally a one armed man, slave to a 1' x 18" x 4" tan leather ball and chain. I had to eat with it , and I had to go to the *bathroom* with it. It was at those times I felt like taking out that damned 45 and blowing away the handle that was keeping me captive. I'd report that some novice looter had misfired and shot off the handle by mistake. Then I'd tell how I managed to chase him away, saving my country's secrets by my bravery. Another letter of commendation from General McChristian.

But I knew that I'd never get away with it. So I learned the step by step method of responding to nature's call while handicapped. Unbutton jacket; wriggle out of right jacket sleeve; dangle left jacket sleeve from left arm over briefcase; unbuckle belt; drop trousers and shorts; complete my mission; redress myself; wash hands; and cross fingers that the washroom attendant had remembered to place soap and fresh paper towels in the dispenser.

This routine was always guaranteed a lot of laughs on TV, when Lucy *accidentally* handcuffs herself to Ricky and can't find the key; or when Gilligan does the same slapstick *schtick* to the Skipper. But in real life it's no fun. When Colonel Black released the manacles back at ISB, it was like I'd grown a new arm. I felt like buying him and his latest stewardess girlfriend dinner at the *Mayflower*.

# CHAPTER THIRTY-ONE

# Nixon's the One

November. The country was about to choose a new leader. I found it difficult to be enthusiastic. *My* candidate had been assassinated five months ago. There were two options. Vote for Nixon , and wait for him to unveil his "secret" plan to end the war. A plan that somehow had mysteriously eluded Lyndon Johnson for five years. Vote for Humphrey and take a chance on four more years of being mired in that senseless conflict, based on the principle of either keeping a friendly government in Vietnam, or seeing the North Vietnamese and their Chinese allies topple every domino from Thailand to Australia. Oh, there was a third alternative. Elect George Wallace—and defect to Sweden.

I had sent in my absentee ballot in mid October. I was a different person than that naive student who'd cast his first ballot for Barry Goldwater four years ago. The war and the Republican hawks that yelled for escalation had turned me around. I held my nose and put an "X" next to Humphrey's name.

The polls were getting tight. Nixon, who started with a comfortable lead, had blown most of it by just being Nixon. The paranoid anti hero with the five o'clock shadow, who lost to a clean shaven John Kennedy, dressed in a custom made suit was still around. Dick was a survivor. He made it through the "Checkers" speech; he made it past the JFK defeat; he made it past the embarrassing loss for Governor in California, when he whined that the press "wouldn't have Nixon to kick around any more". But he was persistent. For the past six years he'd campaigned for every Republican candidate from town clerk to dogcatcher, because he *knew* that those "losers" would be delegates in 1968. The Party Elite didn't stand a chance against him. Dick Nixon was like a political salamander too. Cut him in half and leave him for dead, and he'd grow another tail, ready to start life over.

The officers at ISB were split along predictable lines. I tried not to talk politics at the office, but the election of 1968 was like Bill Clinton's sex life. You just couldn't avoid it without joining a Trappist monastery. So I discovered that Roth, Maggio, Pritchard, and Lebron were in Humphrey's corner. Black, Carson, Oakley and Burton favored Nixon. Cachuk was casting his protest vote for George Wallace. He would've probably sent his write in for Senator Joseph Mc Carthy, but cirrhosis of the liver had taken Tailgunner Joe from us twelve years earlier.

Don, myself, and a couple of his cronies from the Map Service started watching TV about eight o'clock election night. We both kept our fingers crossed hoping for a Humphrey miracle. The Harris poll actually showed him on the lead, but I knew deep down that a lot of disheartened voters would just stay home. I feared that my prediction after the Bobby Kennedy assassination was inevitable.

Walter Cronkite was at his desk in front of the big colorless map, that would change into a blue and red crazy quilt before the night was over. When a state went for Nixon it turned blue; when one went for Humphrey it became red. The same colors on all three networks. Humphrey should have called in to protest. Like "red" meant that the Democrats were some kind of closet communists or something. Wallace carried a few states too. I forget what *his* designated color was. *Lily white* would have been appropriate.

At midnight the results still weren't official. But it looked like Nixon was a sure thing, unless Mayor Daley could "discover" some lost ballot boxes in Chicago's South Side Cemetery. Dawn came up and still no winner. Then it becomes clear that Humphrey has lost. He concedes. Nixon and Agnew raise their hands in a victory pose on TV. Life goes on.

# CHAPTER THIRTY-TWO

# Party Time at the Pentagon

It was Christmastime at the *Pentagon*. The *actual* holiday fell smack in the middle of the week that year, so I wasn't able to take a long weekend and go home. Colonel Black had requested that the entire staff meet at one o'clock in the afternoon on Friday the 20th of December. He wanted to have a little toast, and to congratulate everybody on the great job we all did that year. He even asked Marilyn to pick up a half a dozen bottles of *Cold Duck* to celebrate the occasion. She most likely returned about eight dollars change to him from the twenty dollar bill that he'd given her.

That afternoon the whole building was preparing for one big office party. It would be mind-boggling. Almost *25,000* men and women anxious to let off steam and forget about Vietnam, and the assassinations, and the downright depression of that year that enveloped the whole country. A lot of employees in the place were half loaded by lunchtime.

At about quarter past one, Colonel Black was raising his Styrofoam cup, filled with the pink, incredibly sweet *ersatz* Champagne, and thanking everybody for a job well done. Even the office teetotalers like Major Carson of the Vietnam Desk, were practically ordered to take a glass of the stuff. Imagine—*one* drink a year and it had to be from a two dollar bottle of *Cold Duck*.

I hung around the place for about a half-hour after that. I had arranged to meet Don Santini in the corridor outside ISB. There we could sortie out to locate a nice, respectable orgy, where the slightly looped secretaries were busy Xeroxing their asses on the office copying machine, and getting drunk on real Champagne.

I changed into civilian clothes, and could've passed for your average civil servant crunching out numbers for the Army Pension Office. I met Don in the hall and we headed for someplace more promising. But it would have been madness to leave our destination purely up to chance. Christ, we might have to cover twenty-five acres of space before hitting the right party. And most of the offices had more men than women. So I needed at least *some* clue as to where Don and I should start. Carl Lebron, of our Latin America Desk, usually knew about that sort of thing. He recommended one of the Air Force procurement offices on the second floor.

As we walked past the other noisy offices reverberating with party laughter, we doggedly headed for Room B 216 -Air Force Supplies, American Forces in NATO. After our quarter mile trek we finally made it. The revelers were already spilling out into the small waiting room. A friendly guy in civvies glanced at our ID badges, and welcomed us to the office that "kept our planes flying" in Europe. Then he put his arms around Don's Shoulder and mine, as he escorted us into the "main ball-room" where an enormous fest was under way. I saw Carl Lebron sitting in one corner, bullshitting with some babe.

Carl had called it right. There were dozens of real lookers all over the place. It seemed as though the General in charge of Air Force Supply, wouldn't trust the appropriation of life rafts and oxygen masks to anybody but well built females under the age of thirty—most of them tall and blond.

And did these flyboys know how to toss a party! I hadn't seen such a set-up since that day in Vic Stimmon's room back at Benning. *Glenlivet* Scotch, *Absolut* Vodka, Imported Champagne. A whole table filled with scrumptious *hors d'oeuvres*- bowls of shrimp, Camembert cheese, Iranian caviar, and the finest lox. A gourmet's Nirvana.

It didn't take all that much thought on my part to figure out why these supply guys were drinking *Piper Heidseck*, while their impoverished Army cousins at ISB were forced to consume lukewarm *Cold Duck* and stale potato chips. Our Air Force friends here at Supply probably handed out about fifty billion bucks in contracts each year. The grateful suppliers of everything from pressurizers to parachutes could easily afford ten or twenty pounds of caviar and a few wedges of imported cheeses to show their gratitude.

I was smearing my melba toast with a tablespoon of crabmeat, when I met a cute young secretary named Patricia De Fazio, a real knockout with curly black hair and bedroom blue eyes, She gave me a big dimpled smile, and I had thoughts of asking Colonel Black for a permanent transfer to Air Force Supply for the balance of my military tour.

Maybe Patty felt a little insecure among all the 5'9" Swedish type young ladies that she worked with, but she was five feet three inches of Italian sex appeal. She lived with her folks in Arlington, Virginia, and she'd come to the Pentagon straight out of Business school. We gabbed and giggled over a few more glasses of Champagne. I told her all about what I did, and what I expected to do after the Army; and she made me feel like some kind of Douglas MacArthur and Clarence Darrow combined. I looked around the room. It was a little past four o'clock. Don Santini was talking to a blonde in high heels that was twice his size. I went over and told him not to wait for me Then I asked Patty if she wanted to take a walk. I took her hand. We stood up and she brushed something or other from the shoulder of my sports jacket. I closed my eyes and breathed in the marvelous fragrance of her *Charlie* perfume.

We both were a little high from the *Piper Heidseck* as we began sauntering over the Pentagon's shiny terrazzo floors. My heart was simultaneously pumping alcohol and infatuation throughout my body. Suddenly we were in front of the ISB office. I peeked into the small vestibule, where Sergeant Lopes or one of his cohorts, should have been manning the entrance door. Meanwhile the champagne had a delayed affect. I was suddenly plastered.

"Wanna see where *I* work?" I said. "I think that all the spies have gone (hic) home."

She stood on tiptoe and gave me a big buss on the cheek. With that I pressed the 007 combination. The tumblers in the lock fell, and I pushed open the door. It was pitch black inside. Sergeant Vickers, who usually tidied up the place and was the last one to leave, was no doubt already at the PX raising a pint of beer with his pals.

I flicked on the main light switch that revealed Marilyn's desk, Sergeant Haskell's, the *Xerox* copier, the long table with the coffee urn, and a couple of file cabinets. Nothing really hush-hush about this room. We continued on past the second doorway and made a quick left. A few steps more and we were in the Oral Briefers' office. It wasn't as though we were walking through stacks of Top Secret documents or anything. Besides Patty was more tipsy than I was. By morning she probably wouldn't even remember that we'd been there.

She tickled my neck; and I kissed her hands, her ears, and her dimples. Then I

sat on Cachuk's desk and kissed her fully on the lips. Her tongue darted out Suddenly every male hormone in my body sped towards my erect penis. Patty's little nibbling of my ear inflamed my passion all the more. Where to make love? On the floor? No! Ed Cogan's office? Of course. The chamber of visual effects. Ed had that immense seven foot table that he used to draft symbols of enemy troop strengths and positions, that he'd shrink down to 8" x 11" transparency size. I opened the door to Ed's room and we both headed for the big table. Patty was rubbing her unbelievably sexy body all over me. My jacket was now on the floor and my pants were unbuckled. I fumbled with her blouse and removed her brassiere with my trembling left hand. Our lips were still joined in a prolonged French kiss. I lifted her onto Cogan's table and we made love. We finished and made love again. And once more after that. I'd never felt more like making love with a woman in my life. All the tension and anxiety pent up inside me for that whole year sought release in that passionate embrace with Patty. I was ecstatic.

Then she stood up and walked toward her clothes that were strewn all over the Graphics Room floor. As I followed her rhythmic hips with my eyes, I couldn't help but notice strange markings on her behind. Her rear end had been resting on Ed Cogan's artwork depicting the location of the Fourth North Vietnamese Army Regiment in III Corps. Her *tusch* was literally covered with sensitive information.

"Wait Patty!" I shouted. "Don't touch those panties, Honey. I've got to declassify your ass."

With that I took some grain alcohol and a cotton ball, and lovingly began to remove the top-secret graphics. I took my time. After all I wanted to make absolutely sure that all the stuff was totally eradicated. It was the most pleasant job that I'd ever performed at the Pentagon.

Patty just giggled and wondered we might have accidentally stumbled across the most innovative method of passing top secret information since the microdot hidden in the hollow false tooth. I said that I'd pass the new discovery onto Colonel Black

We dressed quietly. Then as she rested her head on my shoulder, I opened the door that led from Ed Cogan's room to the Oral Briefers' office. Then, as I gave her a loving peck on the forehead, I opened the second door leading to the officers' desk area. I pushed it forward and—
-I spotted Stu Rutkowski shuffling some papers in his file drawer. Then I pulled back the door and gave Patty a panicky *sshhh* sign. I was starting to sober up by then. I knew damn well that Patty had no authorization to be there. At Air Force Supply her security clearance probably didn't exceed "Confidential". Her office didn't care if you were feeding information to the Russians about how many tee shirts, or ball-point pens Frankfurt Air Base needed before the Spring. Actually they only had three concerns. That you could read an Inventory List; that

you paid the Department's bills on time; and that you didn't *squeal* to the Inspector General about your boss's kickbacks.

I didn't think that Stu would report my little indiscretion, but I couldn't take the chance. Instead I hustled Patty *very* gently back into Ed's office. I had to think. Stu might only be at his desk for a few minutes more. Then again he might stay for an hour. I glanced over at Ed Cogan's new *red phone*. Word had spread quickly throughout the Intelligence Community of his visual affects magic. Navy, Air Force, and Marine spooks were willing to pay for his help with their briefing presentations. Of course he asked Colonel Black for permission. Ed was one of our hardest workers. He had helped to improve the morning report by about 300%. Black said that as long as he did the outside work on his own time, sure! He was more than glad to help him make a few extra bucks as long as ISB didn't suffer.

So Ed exchanged calls on the *red phone* all the time. I looked up Stu's number in the classified *red pages* of the tiny directory next to the telephone. I told Patty of my brainstorm and wrote what she would say *verbatim* to Stu. Then I dialed his number. He picked up the phone.

"Hello, this is Captain Stu Rutkowski, ISB," he said.

"Hi, this is Mary McCarthy for General Berelli over at ACSI," she began. "You're in charge of the Soviet Desk I believe. Well, the General has an important meeting at CIA Headquarters in Langley on Monday morning. He'll need the latest information on Soviet Forces in the Warsaw Pact Nations ASAP. Otherwise he'll have to make a special trip back here at 0630 hours on the 23rd. Could you make a special delivery here with that info right away? You'll be doing me a big favor?"

"Ten minutes quick enough?" he asked.

Patty felt the ingenue's urge to pad her script. "Could you make it five?" she said.

"Done!" Stu replied like a good soldier.

I left Patty alone in the visual effects room, while I peeked out the door of the Oral Briefers' office. Stu was just yanking a couple of pages from his files to make a copy on the machine in the outer office. He was about forty feet away from me when he donned his jacket and hat, and rushed out the door to meet "Ms. McCarthy". When he took his hat I knew he wouldn't be back. The coast seemed clear. I fetched Patty from Cogan's room, and we both made our escape past Sergeant Lopes' unmanned desk outside.

I could only guess what Stu would think when he discovered that Ms. McCarthy was somebody's idea of a joke. I sort of figured that he'd blame it all on some half-tanked Field Grade type at an office party someplace. Maybe one of General McChristian's lackeys that asked an imbecilic question at the Czechoslovakia briefing, which Stu artfully dodged because it was so dumb. "Captain Rutkowski, since the French have been making so much trouble in NATO, do you think *they* might have served as accomplices in the invasion." *Reeaally now!*

Patty had to get home right away. Her two sisters from Florida were coming up for the holidays, and she had to help her mother with dinner and stuff. We both kissed again. Then we headed for the parking lot. She had come to work by bus, so I drove her home.

Monday morning Colonel Black had tacked up one of his memos on the bulletin board. He wanted to discuss an urgent matter with the entire staff at 1400 hours.

"I've called this meeting," he began, "because it has come to my attention that there was a possible breach of security in this office last Friday. Sergeant Rivera, one of our new guards, reported to me that he saw an officer entering the premises with a woman late that day."

I tried to gulp down my suddenly very dry throat. Black continued.

"I didn't ask the Sergeant who it was. I wanted to give the guilty party an opportunity to step forth voluntarily and confess. This shameful conduct will not be tolerated. I can't confine you to quarters. After all this is the Pentagon. But you will write an extended letter of apology to this entire unit, which I will post on the bulletin board. Of course the girl in question will have to be contacted and debriefed. It wasn't really *her* fault. Now will the offending party stand up for the whole office to see."

Well it was like that scene in *Spartacus*. You know when Lawrence Olivier, asks Spartacus to stand up in the huge Army of slaves, so that he might be identified and hanged. Kirk Douglas and Tony Curtis rise simultaneously; so does every other guy in the slave Army shouting "*I am Spartacus!*"

As I stood up, so did Len Roth, *and* Major Donald ( Don Juan with two kids) Cachuk. My lovemaking just might have taken place during the first romantic shift. Roth and Cachuk must've taken their turns later on. Kind of like three horny ships passing in the night. Black hadn't anticipated a trio of fornicators. He blushed, dismissed the meeting, and retired to his office.

All three of us wrote our letters asking forgiveness. Patty and the other two *Mata Hari's* were taken into Black's office that afternoon and debriefed by him and Mr. Johnson. Like a military confession by a couple of ISB priests that removes all traces of sin. Anyway, Patty and the rest left the office in tears. I felt like an overtestosteroned Benedict Arnold, as I saw her leave.

I later found out through Mr. Johnson that she wouldn't get into any trouble. He had arranged for a harmless ruse. A CIA friend of his had contacted the immediate superiors of all three young ladies, with a trumped up story about how the Agency needed some bright young secretaries for an extended project. If selected they would receive a twenty five dollar a week increase in pay, but the interview would have to take place that afternoon. It was nice of Mr. Johnson to go to all that trouble to cover up the incident. I thanked him in a personal letter to his home address.

I telephoned Patty at least a half dozen times after that, but she wouldn't take any of my calls.

# CHAPTER THIRTY-THREE

# I Guarantee It!

Santini and I couldn't wait for Super Bowl III to take place. Both of us were from New York, and were inspired by a brash young Quarterback named Joe Willie Namath, who guided the destiny of the Jets. Lined up against the loudmouth Galahad and his troops were the Baltimore Colts, a bunch of veteran tough guys, with cracked front teeth, who threatened to send our heroes back to Shea Stadium in intensive care. The oddsmakers had fixed the chances of the Jets beating Baltimore to a rough equivalent of *my* winning the Nobel Prize for Physics that year.

But we'd have a good time anyway. Charlie Winter, an old friend from Fort Benning, knew somebody with a 21" *Color TV*. Every *big* event was broadcast in color then, but most folks still just owned a Black and White. Having a color set in 1969 was something like being the only kid on the block with a VCR in the early '80's.

Eight of us guys chipped in six bucks apiece. That gave our host, Eddie Kramer, about fifty dollars to stock up an ample supply of beer, soda, munchies, Velveeta, and Ritz Crackers. For half-time he'd already reserved a couple of pizzas for us (cheese topping only) at the joint down the block. Two slices per man ! Anyone wishing something different, like Chop Suey or Egg Foo Yung could order it at the half from the local Chinese place. This was not included in the cover charge.

Charlie Winter was from Scranton, Pennsylvania, and had been a Colt fan ever since they broke every New York Giant's fan's heart by capturing the NFL championship eleven years back, in the snow at Yankee Stadium. Charlie was hoping to retire comfortably from the winnings he would make from Santini, myself, and another New Yorker at Kramer's apartment. *Well* maybe not *retire*; but I had no doubt that he had spread around about a hundred dollars in bets. Thirty bucks alone from Don, Me and Ernie—the third Jet fan. Not exactly a fortune, but still a lot on a Second Lieutenant's pay thirty years ago.

The crowd for our Super Bowl Party began to trickle in about 2:00 P.M. NBC had already presented an hour of all the pre-game bullshit. An interview with the Colt's Place -Kicker's Uncle in Romania; stats on how many fumbles the Jets had on artificial turf as opposed to grass; fumbles in November; fumbles in the rain; and on and on and on. All of this mindless garbage became intolerable after a while, so Santini and three other guys began a game of Poker with a deck of cards he just *happened* to bring along. At the request of the remaining fans, Eddie Kramer mercifully changed the channel every so often from NBC to an old movie on CBS or a show about trout fishing on ABC.

We didn't want to miss the opening kick-off, so at 4:00 P.M. Eddie set his kitchen timer for one hour. Five o'clock would give us a little less than ten minutes to endure Curt Gowdy and Al De Rogatis comparing Namath and Unitas; or making another endless tribute to the Great Vince Lombardi, whose Green Bay Super Bowl teams had totally annihilated their AFL patsies over the last two years. A pause for a commercial before the opening whistle. A clever ad for Alka Seltzer by a guy sitting in front of an empty plate of spaghetti , and moaning that he couldn't believe he ate the *whole thing!*

The game began as expected. Baltimore began doing to the Jets what the U.S. should have been doing to the Viet Cong. They played like hitmen. But the breaks kept the game even. The Colts would move the ball effectively. Interception. Long drive. Interception. But when Joe Willie got his hands on the ball he was brilliant. No sixty yard passes.

Just enough to keep the ball moving. Enough to score. The Jets were in the lead. Mother of Mercy! Is this the end of Baltimore?

Meanwhile Charlie Winter was starting to perspire. Half-time was over. He hadn't even touched his pizza. Don and I helped ourselves to his abandoned slices. Spoils of war. This wasn't turning out to be the football coronation that Charlie had expected. He was looking down into the arena, and the Christians were *devouring* the lions. Every so often a Baltimore comeback seemed imminent, and old Charlie'd shout "the momentum of the game is changing!" Then the Colts would make a stupid high school mistake, and the Jets would have the ball again. Don and I shouted back, "the momentum of the game *was* changing!" We shouted it at least ten times during that second half. Then the legendary Johnny Unitas comes in to create a Colt miracle. He leads them to a score. A last gasp plea about momentum from Charlie but it's apparent that the day is lost. Say it ain't so Joe! But the inexorable gun sounds, ending the contest. Ernie, Don and I raise our cans of beer for a victory toast. It's Miller Time! Charlie opens his wallet, drops three ten dollar bills next to our cold slices of pizza, and slinks out of the room.

[Adapted from *Casey at the Bat* by Ernest Lawrence Thayer]
*Oh somewhere in this favored land the sun is shining bright*
*The band is playing somewhere, and somewhere hearts are light*
*And somewhere men are laughing, and somewhere children shout*
*But there is no joy in **Coltland**, 'cause **Joe Willie's psyched them out!***

# CHAPTER THIRTY-FOUR

# Gettin' Down-G.O.P. Style

Nixon was to be sworn in later that January. Major Carson, a good Republican, had been given , or rather had the option to purchase, ten tickets to one of the many Inaugural Balls sprinkled throughout the city. A hundred bucks a couple. All you could eat and drink.

I would've liked to have taken Patty De Fazio, the temptress from the Christmas Party, but she was still too pissed off to speak to me. So I asked Debra Wickham, a Kindergarten schoolteacher, who lived on the twelfth floor of my Falls Church high rise building. I had met her a couple of times down in the Laundry Room. She used *Tide* and *Clorox*. Dependable but unexciting. Probably voted for Nixon herself. She was thrilled at my invitation, and accepted it during her "Rinse Cycle". Since we both had to work the morning after the January 20th Ball, I promised to bring her back from the cotillion by the Cinderella hour of midnight.

I winced as I forked over the hundred bucks to Major Carson. I knew that this money would probably be used to support the campaigns of Strom Thurmond and other reactionaries that I despised. But you only get a chance like this once in a lifetime. So I dropped the five twenty dollar bills in Carson's hand. Had it been Cachuk, I would've asked for a receipt. But Carson was Bible Belt honest. I 'd 've trusted him with my last dime. Two days later I got the tickets. Inaugural Ball D, Hotel Buchanan, 7:30 P.M. EST. Nice to see something official that told time in good old fashioned numbers, and not something like 1930 hours.

I could've attended the affair in my dark blue uniform, that made me look like a fancy hotel doorman, but I decided to rent a tuxedo instead. This way I wouldn't have to keep looking over my shoulder every ten seconds to see whether I was about to talk to some Chicken Colonel that would make me feel like I was back at work. Even considering the twenty five dollar rental fee, a tux was the best move.

I picked Debra Up just before seven o'clock. She looked sexy as hell. I'd been used to seeing her in messed up blue jeans and a sweatshirt, smelling of soapsuds and bleach down at the Laundry Room. She was a different person now. Her gown had probably set her back a couple of month's pay. No cruise to the Bahamas this summer. And it must've taken her two hours to get her hair to look that perfect. I couldn't help but stare at her décolleté. That sloppy *Georgetown* sweatshirt had been hiding a gorgeous pair of breasts all this time. My male hormones came to attention and began streaming towards my private parts. I was getting aroused. I told her how beautiful she looked and we headed downstairs to my Bonneville.

When we arrived at the Hotel Buchanan, I handed the keys for my beloved car to the valet, who incidentally *did* look like he was wearing my dress blue uniform. Then we went inside.

Waiters were floating all over the place, carrying trays of champagne glasses and fancy canapés. I grabbed two glasses of *Dom Perignon* for Debra and myself. But I had to shout to get her attention. She was mesmerized by the stunning dresses and dazzling jewelry worn by the wives of wealthy campaign contributors, some of whom had spent ten times more than a hundred dollars a couple, to be seated at a front table next to the dais, where the President and Mrs. Nixon would be seated— if only for a half hour.

I looked at *our* ticket stubs. Table 87. Probably somewhere inside the *kitchen*, next to the dirty dishes. The orchestra was playing the expected *California Here I Come* in Nixon's honor, and every ten minutes they'd break into *Happy Days Are Here Again*. But I swear I didn't really understand why they felt compelled to play the theme song of Democrat Franklin Roosevelt's campaign against Herbert Hoover.

I was getting a bit nervous about leading Debra toward our banquet table. I was afraid that Major Carson had seated us with folks from ISB. I wasn't all that thrilled at being seated with Major Beecham, Captain Porter and their spouses. Then there was bound to be the embarrassing question as to why I wasn't wearing my dress blue uniform.

But Carson had been tactful. He'd obviously spread his ticket choices for different tables around the room. No need to fidget at a table with my ISB comrades. No need to keep the conversation moving with shop talk. In fact no military types whatsoever at Table 87. Just successful civilians that had flown in from Pittsburgh, St. Louis and Miami to celebrate the victory of their political hero. I took their expected Republicanisms in stride. "About time we got back to fiscal responsibility and lowered taxes. Too much coddling of criminals. Not enough moral values anymore. Since Ike was President, we've had to put up with that skirt chasing Romeo, Kennedy; and then that dumb cowboy LBJ, that *stole* his first election. It's good to have an honest man in the White House again."

Yeah! A real *honest* man!

Then after they got the political soundbites out of the way, they talked about how exciting the Inaugural Parade had been; about how they'd almost cried at the release of the *Pueblo* prisoners a couple of weeks ago; and about how proud they were that *American* astronauts had just circled the Moon.

Byron, the manager of a meat packing plant in Pittsburgh, asked me my line of work. I didn't want to get into the spy thing, so I said was a Department of the Army procurer of Office Equipment and Material. I told him that I dealt mostly with Graphics Supplies—inks, paper and boring crap like that. Ed Cogan had taught me enough about the stuff so I could easily bullshit a meat packer into falling for what I was talking about. Debra went along with my harmless deception.

The *Prime Ribs au Jus* seemed to be favorite at Table 87, except for Byron and his wife Marion, who both ordered the *Grilled Sole Almondine*, a funny choice for a couple that earned their living from dead cows. But I supposed Byron had seen enough beef on the hoof, feeding on chemically treated oats and barley to fatten them up. And then he must've witnessed the hapless cattle being shipped to his company's abattoir where they were slaughtered *en masse*. Then their carcasses were treated with more chemicals, additives, preservatives, and tenderizers, before they finally ended up at neighborhood butcher shops across America. But Debra and I were both blissfully ignorant of the biographies of our particular medium rare specimens. We just knew that they were tender enough to cut with a butter knife—and oh so tasty.

All the couples at the table were nice folks really, and we were having a good time. A few more glasses of Champagne, and we were toasting America, and Nixon, and our astronauts. Byron, Casper, and Lyle were laughing and calling us Bob-*by* and Deb-*bie* as they fumbled through their wallets to pass around their business cards and make with the invitations to their homes in Pittsburgh, St. Louis, and Miami before dessert was served.

And what a dessert it was! For the final course we all pigged out on three scoops of ice cream banana splits, with whipped cream, chopped walnuts, chocolate syrup, and a couple of maraschino cherries on top. This mega caloried example of GOP decadence was listed as Pat Nixon's favorite dessert on the menu. How the hell did she manage to stay so *skinny?*

About 11:15, the orchestra interrupted itself right in the middle of *Some Enchanted Evening* with a sudden drumroll followed by a fanfare. Ta da! Then the trumpets blared out *Hail to the Chief,* and the Nixons marched into the hall, surrounded by a couple of dozen Secret Service

Agents. They were about fifty yards from our table, but we could see them pretty well.

Dick had his left arm raised in that trademark victory sign of his, and he flashed that pasted on smile, perfected over twenty years of campaigning. His right hand was clutching Pat's. She smiled and nodded to the cheering crowd. We all acknowledged the Nation's new President by standing and applauding. I felt a little hypocritical. I couldn't really *stand* the phony son of a bitch, but he *was* the country's leader, and he held the office once occupied by Jefferson and Lincoln and Teddy Roosevelt. That alone deserved my applause. Debbie and I even toasted to his success. Then Nixon took his place at the center of the dais, and thanked the crowd in a thirty second speech. Again the victory sign and forced smile. He sat down. The middle age groupies followed his lead, and the band resumed playing *Some Enchanted Evening.*

I whispered to Debra that now would be a good time to leave, because when the President decided to go, in about half an hour, the Secret Service would start securing the exits. Given their paranoia since the recent assassinations, they might subject the both of us to a strip search in the rest rooms for our coincidental departure. Leaving now would just barely get us home by midnight. She agreed. We said our good-byes to Byron and everybody. I told them all how memorable the evening had been, but that we had to leave. I regretted not bringing any business cards, but I scribbled my name and phone number on a couple of cocktail napkins. "Bob *Vukov*, 6060 Ryerson Drive, Falls Church Va., Tel. No. (202) 555- 1639. This was the phone number of Wong Loo's Tea Garden, my favorite take-out Chinese Kitchen. I was sure that Byron, Casper, and Lyle and their wives would enjoy Mr. Loo's Cantonese Lobster.

We got past the stern looking Secret Service Men in their tell tale black Oxfords and portable phones. We didn't look threatening enough to be stopped on our way out. I gave the valet in the familiar blue uniform a tip, and drove Debra home.

# CHAPTER THIRTY-FIVE

# The Inscrutable Captain Roth

Captain Len Roth was an academic Hercules. Harvard undergrad, *Summa cum laude*. Rhodes Scholar. Yale Law Review. He was the junior officer at our Far East Desk, under Lt. Colonel Horace Quigley.

By mid-1967, it looked as though Len's talents were doomed to be wasted at some remote outpost called Song Trinh in II Corps South Vietnam. He would probably be using his considerable smarts to discover the whereabouts of a couple of AK-47s stashed in a local village.

But Len had a couple of allies at ISB in the person of Jeff Pritchard and Matt Lehrer from the South Asia Desk. They had met Len at cocktail party in New York two summers ago. While Jeff and Matt were undoubtedly blabbing away their nation's most hush-hush secrets to some young ladies over Harvey Wallbangers, Len happened to mention to them his upcoming assignment as an Intelligence Officer at Song Trinh.

This waste of brainpower was outrageous- even by Army standards. Len's IQ was needed at the Pentagon-at ISB. But Jeff and Matt had to cook up some Sergeant Bilko-ish scheme, and make the Army do the *smart* thing -in spite of itself.

Step 1. There was a slot available for a China expert to work under Quigley. They were certain that they could convince Colonel Black that Len Roth was the man for the job- the Greatest Caucasian maven on things Chinese since Marco Polo.

151

But Len wasn't so sure. Once at Harvard , he'd taken a course on Confusian Philosophy, but that would hardly qualify him as even a half-assed expert on China. Not to worry. Leave it to Doctor Jeff. Pritchard poured Len another Single Malt Scotch, and in fifteen minutes Operation Mao was in effect.

Step 2. The team of Pritchard and Lehrer had to get Colonel Black to use his influence to transfer our new China whiz kid to ISB. Black finally agreed that if Quigley gave Len high marks, he'd go all out for the transfer. He pulled a couple of strings with some Generals upstairs and the wheels were set in motion.

Len still had three weeks of Intelligence training left at Fort Holabird. He devoted every spare second to Far East studies, borrowing every book he could lay his hands on concerning Chinese thought, Mao Tse Tung's military philosophy, and Chinese History and Culture, particularly since the fall of Chaing Kai Chek. Len had a photographic memory and a steel trap for a brain. After he had mentally devoured every book on China at the Fort Holabird Library, he borrowed every book he could in the City of Baltimore. The Intelligence Course was over; Len took some leave back in New York City.

Only two weeks left before the Quigley interrogation. Len got down to some serious cramming. Subsisting on a diet of *No-Doz* and black coffee, he spent eighteen hours a day in intensive study of China. He got carried away in his passion and branched out into Korean History. The day before his oral exam with *Herr Professor* Quigley he zonked out for twenty hours straight. He took the early morning train to Washington D.C.

Lt. Colonel Horace Quigley was one smart guy himself. He was a West Point graduate at the end of World War II that had studied Chinese. He had mastered considerable fluency in the language—something highly unusual for a Westerner at that time. As a young lieutenant he was assigned to the staff of Douglas MacArthur in Tokyo, after the general had been appointed "King" of Japan by Harry Truman. Horace spent a year there , before being transferred to the staff of American advisors to Chiang Kai Shek in China.

From 1946-1949 Quigley was one of Chiang's right hand men. In those three years he mastered Chinese. Then he watched helplessly as the disoriented( no pun intended) Kuomintang were run out of China. He was a fugitive in Shanghai during the summer of 1949, and left on the very same plane with Chiang and Madame Chiang, as they all headed towards Formosa and the new government in exile. They could hear the Communist artillery on the other side of the Yangtse River pounding away at the few token Nationalist troops left in the city.

Quigley loved Chinese food. One afternoon he invited a few of us younger officers to the recently opened *Golden Dragon* in D.C. Real Mandarin cuisine. No chop suey or fortune cookies here. Since Quigley was paying for the meals, he insisted on ordering for the whole bunch of us. The waiter just about fell on his ass when he heard this freckled faced Irishman with balding red hair read aloud from the *Chinese* menu, laughing and joking in the sing-song dialect. He became an instant celebrity. But we all had to plead with him not to start telling the stuff about the good old days with Chiang, or we wouldn't get out of the place until midnight. Everybody from the owner on down was a refugee from Mao's "Paradise", so there was no doubt as to where their political sympathies lay. Quigley was their honored guest.

When we finally left, Colonel Q. had to *literally* beg the owner to take his money for the check. He ended up sneaking back in, and leaving three twenty dollar bills under the teapot.

Anyway Quigley bought Len's credentials hook, line and egg roll. Pritchard and Lehrer shared in his glory. This had to be the sweetest con job since Henry Higgins passed Eliza Doolittle off as the Princess of Hungary. It would have been perfect if only Len hadn't hated Chinese food, and couldn't share in Quigley's monthly dinner search for the best Peking Duck in Washington D.C.

# CHAPTER THIRTY-SIX

# 007's Little Black Book

Our office lothario was Carl Lebron, a young Lieutenant from USC who sat at our Latin American desk. While at Southern Cal he played running back, who didn't attract much notice as a second stringer behind a new rookie sensation named Orenthal James Simpson. Carl was raised in Guatemala where his dad served in the Diplomatic Corps. Hazardous duty, considering that the insurgent forces seemed to attempt an assassination or kidnapping of a US Ambassador just about every month.

Lebron was tall and swarthy, a Latin James Bond type. I pictured him as being this real cool guy, who'd meet a devastatingly beautiful girl playing *Baccarat* at the Soviet Embassy. He'd flip out his *DuMaurier* cigarette, Light it with his gold lighter, and say to her, "Hello, the name's Lebron, *Carl* Lebron."

Then she'd try to seduce him to get all of ISB's top secret information for the Russians that were paying her. Carl would take her to bed for an evening of lovemaking, but would keep his honor intact, and not reveal his country's secrets. He'd leave her sexually exhausted in bed, get dressed, light up another cigarette and place a gardenia from his lapel on her dressing table or do something cool like that.

Since Carl was leaving ISB, I thought it would be a good idea to discuss with him the destiny of his own "little black book" and its female listings in the D.C. area. He handed it over to me without much ceremony. He said he'd be heading back to L.A. in two weeks, so he'd have no further need of it. The 2"x3" treasure was all mine. I thumbed through it to find a list of about twenty names.

That evening I sat myself by the phone next to my sofa bed, opened up the compact *white pages* and began to call. My *spiel* was simply to introduce myself, "Hi, my name is Bob Woolsey." Then I'd explain how Carl had mentioned the young lady's name, and thought that we just might hit it off together. How about dinner?

Carl's little directory was a disappointment. Some of the names were almost two years old. I suspected that our Latin James Bond had gotten some of them the same way I did, and not at some soiree in the Soviet Embassy. About half of the women were engaged or had moved. Two were *married*. But I kept on dialing with the zeal of an Amway salesman making his pitch. Without any orderly procedure , I just kept on dialing. Dial. No answer. Dial. A short conversation. No interest. Dial. A little *schmoozing*. A couple of laughs, and then acceptance. Helen Montrose. Pick her up Friday night at seven. Success.

I went down the rest of Carl's confidential directory. Then I made a date with Carol Crawford from Fall's Church for Sunday afternoon. I gave the phone survey a rest and went out for an hour. Then I came back and started all over again. I had already scratched off the names of the married, affianced, and otherwise disinterested, as well as those who had just moved away. Still a few names left. Bridget Moore, (202) 555-3397. I began my intro with my standard "Hi Bridget, this is Bob Woolsey...", when a shrill, pissed off voice on the other end yelled back

"Bridget? This is Helen-Helen Montrose. You called me before. You're telephoning from some kind of *list*! You horny son of a bitch! What is this? Some kind of perverted *Dial-a-Date*? You can forget about Friday night, Buster! If only I had a copy of that bastard Lebron's little book of names, I'd call every prospective number and warn them of this Junior High School stunt. Don't ever call me again!" Click.

I was humiliated. Something like that panicked phone call that I had made to Captain Meister at DIA Headquarters. But *this* time I had nobody to blame but myself. I had glanced at Bridget Moore's name, but my treacherous eyes betrayed me, and directed my dumb finger to dial the number of Helen Montrose.

I tried to assuage my feelings of guilt by reasoning everything out. After all, I was just trying to make some social contacts, wasn't I? So I made a little mistake. Why did I feel like such a jerk? I knew why. It was because other people have feelings too. Especially women. When I *first* called Helen, she probably felt pretty special. I bet she thought that Carl had singled her out as a unique match for a friend. She might've even had a fantasy of him printing her name and number on some kind of gold embossed calling card or something. Instead she was just an entry scribbled in a notebook, like one of Carl's favorite take out Pizza Parlors.

Next afternoon after work, I hunted down a special card to send to Helen, to apologize for behaving like an idiot. The Hallmark Company came through for me. It showed some poor guy up to his chin in quicksand. Perfect. I drew a voice balloon above the poor *schlemiel's* mouth with the words, "Hi, My name is Bob Woolsey, glub, glub, glub..." Underneath I signed it,"I'm sorry. If it's OK, I'll call you next week. Mortifiedly yours——-Bob.

I called her a couple of days after the card and we actually went out. But it didn't work out. Helen spent most of the evening talking about her dates with Washington politicians and journalists, when she wasn't talking about herself of course. Heaven had decreed its own punishment for my sin with Carl's book of names. Dinner with Helen. The Hallmark card wasn't enough.

# CHAPTER THIRTY-SEVEN

# Major Donald Cachuk, I Presume

It was early 1969. Nixon had been in office a couple of months, and the World situation was changing. American casualties in Vietnam were dropping slightly. The Russians had successfully doused the flickering Czech hope for freedom. A brand new Field Grade officer had been assigned to ISB, and in the spirit of Spring cleaning, Colonel Black had decided to sweep Major Cachuk out of the Oral Briefers' office. McChristian had no doubt had enough of his bumbling, phonetic pronunciations of *Check-oh-sloh-vahk—ee-ya* and General *Soo-hahr-toe*. Major George Loomis had formally taken his place. But Black wasn't sure of where to put Cachuk exactly. Probably the best slot manpowerwise would have been making coffee or shredding classified papers into the burn bag. Sergeant Haskell, who kept the whole place running smoothly and knew where every file and CIA report was located, could have put the time he spent on such *household* chores to more efficient use.

But after all, Cachuk was an Officer and a Gentleman. Anyway that's what it said on his ID card. Black finally decided to put him with Jeff Pritchard at the African desk. Jeff's Army service was over in about four months so he would need a replacement there. Until Army Personnel could locate a competent substitute, Cachuk could learn enough to get by. Africa was still the *Sleeping Continent*, at least the Sub Saharan part, and nobody really paid too much attention to it. But it was an area that the Military knew would be very critical in years to come. And so the decree came forth. Major Donald Cachuk was to be the new African guru. It was laughable. The closest that the little twerp had been to anything African, was watching Katherine Hepburn and Humphrey Bogart on screen, riding the rapids to Lake Victoria in *The African Queen*. But what the hell! I mean if old Cachuk fucked up in reporting about *Tan-gan-yee-kah*, the World wouldn't be set on the brink of war. It made me a little mad though, to see Jeff Pritchard who had spent more than five years. mastering the History and Politics of Africa, being subordinated to an intellectual lightweight like Cachuk.

With the transfer of Major Cachuk to the Africa Desk, Colonel Black had created a desk analyst *Frankenstein*. As an Oral Briefer, he wasn't expected to know anything. But now his nameplate read "Major Donald Cachuk, Chief African Desk Analyst". The Army had given him the new title. It must be so. So he read all the books and articles that Jeff gave him, and after a few weeks he began flaunting his new found knowledge all over the office. I avoided going to the coffee machine out of fear that he'd buttonhole me there. He caught me once. Then he went on to tell me some esoteric, irrelevant piece of bullshit, like whether I knew that General Ojukwu of Biafra was a chain smoker that liked American folk music.

# CHAPTER THIRTY-EIGHT
# Bolshevik Squabble

The Russians and Chinese turned their own private cold war into a hot one in early March 1969. The two super powers had been moving further and further apart for years. It started around the time when Nikita Kruschev drew the world's nervous laughter as a tough guy/court jester by pounding his shoe on his desk in the UN Assembly Hall

The Chinese and Soviets have the world's longest common border. A good piece of it runs along the Ussuri River in frigid Siberia. For months each side had been leveling charges and counter charges against each other about provocations there. For instance, the Russians thought that it would be a lot of laughs to steal fish from the nets of Chinese fishermen, and then douse the defenseless peasants with water from fire hoses as they shook their fists in futile protest. The Chinese also accused their Russian "allies" of committing more serious violations, such as assaults on frontier guards, and armored penetration over the frozen river. The Russian excuse to the World Court of Public Opinion was akin to that of the young twin caught scuffling with his sibling, and reprimanded by his exasperated mother." It's not *my* fault. *He* started it!"

Anyway the Chinese thought that they had taken just about enough if this Russian harassment. So before dawn on March 2nd, some of their soldiers, camouflaged in snow-white uniforms, crawled halfway across the Ussuri ice in the cold darkness to Chen Pao Island in mid river. The Soviets spotted this clumsy ambush right away, and confronted them around 10:00 A.M. While both sides were slipping and sliding all over the ice, some trigger happy Chinese opened fire on the small Russian detachment, killing several guards. All hell broke loose. Machine gun and artillery fire from both camps shattered the silence. ISB's Intelligence sources reported the incident.

Lt. Colonel Quigley and Captain Len Roth assembled their report for the March 2nd Black Book. So did Stu Rutkowski, who'd been promoted to the rank of Major in January, and his new junior Eastern European maven, Captain Brewster. The articles from each desk differed ever so slightly from one another that day; but they weren't exactly contradictory, so Colonel Black allowed them both in.

For the next two weeks ISB received daily follow ups and messages from our covert radio intercepts along the Sino-Soviet border, particularly around Chen Pao Island. The reports from our Soviet and Far East Desks differed more and more each day. Our guys were actually *rooting* for their respective commies.

Stu would refer to the Chinese forces as fanatical, Mao spouting, lunatics, who were trying to export their insane "Cultural Revolution" to their innocent Siberian neighbors. Quigley and Roth, on the other hand, claimed that those Vodka swilling Russians had been picking on those poor Sinkiang fishermen, who were barely struggling to eke out a living. They had no doubts that some drunken border guards, probably fresh from a cosmopolitan city like Moscow or Leningrad, became bored, got shitfaced, and thought that it would be fun to use some Chinese folks for target practice.

Day by day the formerly cordial Soviet and Chinese Desks split up into two distinct camps. Each *in support* of their sworn Marxist enemies. Horace and Len were literally taking the side of Mao Tse Tung and the bloodthirsty forces that had all but exterminated their nationalist Chinese opposition in 1949. The USA didn't even have *diplomatic relations* with Peking, and suddenly the Far East Desk was making them out to be some kind of heroes. This was *somewhat* of a surprise from

Len, who up until 1967, had thought that "China" was the porcelain that his mother set the table with, to impress his big shot Uncle Leon and his new *shiksa* wife, when they came for dinner during the High Holy Days.

But I was even *more* shocked at the behavior of Lt. Colonel Horace Quigley, a veteran of the Kuomintang Campaign, a former military advisor to the Honorable Chiang Kai Chek twenty years ago. I guess Quigley forgot that his rescue plane had been just minutes away from being shot down by Mao's relentless anti-aircraft batteries outside Shanghai. Would his conscience ever allow him to set foot inside the *Golden Dragon* again?

As for Stu Rutkowski, I couldn't believe that he was siding with the disciples of Joe Stalin. Troops obeying the orders of a bastard like Leonid Brezshnev who had shown no mercy as he crushed poor little Czechoslovakia just seven months earlier. How could he forget the evening news reports in August of 1968, showing Russian tanks rolling over the screaming men, women, and children of Prague. Captain Brewster, who practically worshipped Stu, followed his pro-Soviet bias straight down the line.

Of course, Colonel Black noticed these reporting discrepancies between the two ISB desks after the first couple of days. But General McChristian had expressed considerable interest in the border clashes, so Black couldn't just eliminate them from the briefing. He got an idea. *He* would become the editor-in chief of his own private *Sino- Soviet* desk—for the time being anyway.

He and Mr. Johnson used their combined Intelligence expertise and literary talents to produce ISB reports that *favored* both sides , or alternatively condemned them. For example, an article might begin with something like, "Beleaguered Soviet forces along the Ussuri River were fired upon by their long suffering Chinese counterparts late last night. Although no reports of casualties have been confirmed, it is estimated that the ill-equipped but valiant Chinese lost more men than their better trained Russian adversaries, with their more sophisticated weaponry."

For a change of pace, the next report might start something like, "Red Chinese barbarians mounted a sneak artillery barrage on their treacherous Russian enemy, who, Intelligence sources confirm, will soon be reinforced by advanced ordnance capable of inflicting savage destruction."

And so it went. Balanced articles were issued on a daily basis. But the Soviet and Chinese teams at ISB, both convinced of the justice of their newly formed causes, sought allies among the other desk officers. Different area experts began lining up on one side or the other. Usually it was along personality lines, or even degree of physical proximity to the Sino or Soviet desk. Rod Burton, who'd been sitting next to Stu for more than a year, sympathized with the Russians; while Matt Lehrer at South Asia, who shared the morning paper with his buddy Len Roth, hoped for a Chinese victory.

The Southeast Asia desk initially remained aloof. As a rule they were a more sober, conscientious bunch, diligently carrying out their duty to report on a bloody war, where American boys were still being shipped home in body bags. They had no time for intra-office squabbles. But after a few days, even *they* became involved. They probably took a voice vote on an informal proposition. Namely: "Who's making life more miserable for American troops in Vietnam? Those stinking Russian commie bastards who were manufacturing the weapons for the North Vietnamese, or those damned Red Chinese S.O.B.'s that were building the roads to haul them over? Was a puzzlement!

Finally their consensus seemed to come down for the support of the Communist Chinese. I figured that last year's Summer Olympics in Mexico City had a lot to do with that decision. You see, sports was one thing those guys at the Southeast Asia Desk really took seriously. Our American athletes had literally beaten the crap out of the Soviet team last year—in track and field, swimming, basketball, and boxing. The day after George Foreman pounded the shit out his clumsy Russian opponent, winning the Gold Medal; and then paraded around the ring with his little American flag, the Southeast Asia guys couldn't talk about anything else. Of course they conceded that the Russians won a few medals in that faggot sport of Gymnastics, but other than that, it was an American show. American pole vaulter Bob Seagren beats *Russian*; Dick Fosbury with his unorthodox "flop" beats *Russian* in high jump. Hell, those guys at the SEA desk probably didn't know whether a Chinese Olympic team even existed. So chalk up five more ballots for the Red Chinese cause.

Normally the Oral Briefing team wasn't even consulted on such matters of substance. After all, we were just a couple of talking heads. Now that Cachuk had been transferred to "Darkest Africa" to work alongside Jeff Pritchard my new boss, Major Loomis was in charge.

Shortly after six o'clock on the morning of the fourteenth, Stu Rutkowski came into the Oral Briefers' office, a cup of black coffee in his left hand and a half smoked *Gauloise* in his right. His visit during the "panic" hour, when the Black Book was painstakingly taking shape for its 0715 hours deadline was unusual.

"I've submitted a piece for this morning's book on the Red Chinese sniping and harassment along the Sino-Soviet border ," he began," I wonder if you guys have some slides showing Red Chinese brutalization of civilians in Tibet a few years back, or maybe the CIA has sent you some more recent stuff showing the slaughter of Commander Strelnikov and his Russian guards at Chen Pao Island last week. The gorier the better. Or maybe you could have Ed Cogan whip up a special transparency for the border area map, depicting a menacing looking Chinese soldier wielding a machine gun, and you could kind of super-impose that over the slide. Maybe Ed could show some smoke coming out of the gun barrel?"

Loomis was new to this sort of office politics. Frankly so was I. Loomis thanked Stu for his suggestion to add zest to the morning pres-entation, but said that he'd have to clear it with Colonel Black first. Stu flicked his cigarette ashes into our burn bag, mumbled a weak thank you, sipped his coffee and headed back for his desk.

Major Loomis gave the oral briefing that morning. *Stepped Up Activity in South Vietnam; Egypt and Israel Exchange Artillery Fire; Unrest in Chile and Peru; and Sino-Soviet Clash Imminent.* And *no* slide of brutal Red Chinese soldier, or slaughtered Russian guards.

Later that afternoon, Lt. Colonel Quigley paid his respects to our suddenly popular office, carrying some tiny home made slides, and an antique portable viewfinder.

"You fellas got a minute?" he asked.

We both nodded yes.

"I've got a couple of things to show you," he said." Snapshots that I took more than twenty years ago. It was back in 1946, in Sinkiang Province, before that bastard Mao took complete control of the place. Beautiful country. Nice friendly people. Here take a look through the viewfinder."

Loomis and I took an embarrassingly uncomfortable peek at the things. It was like when some guy on Social Security shows you pictures of his grandchildren.

"Well," he continued, "those Russian sons a' bitches were causing trouble for the Chinese even then. Nothing like last week of course, but they've always been prejudiced against the yellow race to the South. Probably jealous of the Chinese for inventing printing and gunpowder—the magnet too. You can keep the slides. Their only copies. I just thought that you might be interested. I'll leave them here, just in case Ed Cogan wants to convert them into transparencies."

Next day the imminent clash along the border became a reality. The Russians suckered the Chinese into making the first move. Then they threw everything they had against them while their flanks were vulnerable. The Chinese lost several hundred troops; the Russians about fifty. The battle was finally over, and both sides went back to lick their wounds. Intelligence reports about skirmishes subsided; and ISB returned to normal.

# CHAPTER THIRTY-NINE

# Dinner with the New Boss

With Major Cachuk assuming his new role as the *Bwana* at Jeff Pritchard's desk, Major George Finley Loomis of Waterloo, Iowa, was now presiding as the new chief of Oral Briefers'. And our section had become so important that Personnel was going to send us yet *another* body to serve as the third member of the team, Second Lieutenant Pete Gilmore. At long last somebody would have to call me *Sir*!

Loomis was an Infantry officer who had already done three tours in South Vietnam. He had a slight gimp and two Purple Hearts to prove it. This cushy job at ISB just might have been the Army's way of saying "thanks" to a guy who'd put his life on the line for Uncle Sam for three whole years, toughing it out and being separated from his wife and two small boys all that time.

Loomis was a literate change from my former boss. I got used to seeing a copy of the latest novel by William Styron or Philip Roth on his desk. The only time I ever saw Cachuk with a book was when he had to look something up in the *Yellow Pages*. Once in the Pentagon Coffee Shop, George and I were munching a Danish and watching *Jeopardy* on TV, the ancient version hosted by Art Fleming. Well, Loomis impressed the hell out of me, when he blurted out that Aristophanes wrote *The Birds* and that Ulan Bator was the Capital of Mongolia—in the form of a question, of course. Major Loomis was a pleasant surprise.

The good Major wasted no time inviting me to his home in Falls Church. Major Cachuk had never even taken me out for coffee at the Pentagon cafeteria. I rang the doorbell of the modest Cape Cod residence, and was greeted by Mrs. Loomis. Since I wasn't sure whether the Loomis household was alcohol free or not, I handed Mrs. Loomis a dozen carnations as my meal ticket. She asked me to come in. The house was just big enough for a family of four, provided the children didn't grow at all. But for the time being their two boys of seven and nine had adequate space. Both Larry and Matthew were the image of their father. That was partly due to the ultra GI haircut they each sported. Daddy also had a shaved head. I guess Loomis figured that the kids'd probably be bald in forty years or so anyway, so they might as well get used to it now.

Protocol at a superior officer's house is ticklish, so I waited for my hosts to make the first move. Sally, Loomis' wife, had been through this awkward situation before.

"Now, Bob," she said ," you can just call me Sally. The boys are Larry and Matt. And for tonight Major Loomis is George. But come Monday morning, it's back to the formality of rank. But I would just feel funny hearing you say something like, 'Would you mind passing the rolls, Major Loomis?' in my own home. Don't you agree dear ?"

Loomis smiled and nodded his predetermined approval.

We sat around and chatted for about half an hour while the roast beef was just becoming medium rare. I couldn't help but notice the highly polished Baldwin piano that crowded the rest of the living room furniture into unsymmetrical positions left and right. Naturally I asked if she was the musician of the family. She blushed a little, and said that playing her grandmother's heirloom was one of her greatest joys. She hoped that the two boys would have an ear for it.

Dinner was just what I expected. Roast Beef, mashed potatoes, corn, fresh baked rolls and gravy, served with a huge salad, lightly flavored with oil and vinegar. Nothing exotic, but she had put a lot of love into the meal, and it was delicious. The peach pie with pistachio ice cream was exactly the right dessert.

I told Sally that I was holding her to her promise to perform. She feigned a rehearsed reluctance, but I began some polite applause, and she sat herself down at the keyboard. I looked over at Major Loomis. He loved her.

She started with some Chopin, maybe just to show me that she could do the good stuff. Then she played a random selection of Irving Berlin and, my personal favorite, Cole Porter. When she started his catchy *Anything Goes*, I started singing in my best Glee Club Tenor to the music. She joined me; and so did George after a few bars. *The World has gone mad today/ and good's bad today/ and black's white today/ and day's night today/ and most guys today / that women prize today/ are just gigoloooos....*

I was having the time of my life. The *Cherry Kijafa* that the Major kept filling my glass with, made the off key singalong all that much more fun. One more chorus of *'Swonderful, 'Smarvelous,* a last sip of *Maxwell House,* and I was thanking them both for a great time, and calling him "Major" again. I found myself humming *I Get a Kick Out of You* over and over, all the way home.

# CHAPTER FORTY

# Look Ma I'm a Captain

On March 11,1969, exactly one year after my Army induction, I was made Captain. The promotion from First Lieutenant was automatic for everybody. All you had to do was show up at the job, not punch out your superior, and not reveal the strength and location of every US military installation to the enemy, and you made it.

But Colonel Black and Mr. Johnson made a big fuss about it, and they scheduled a formal pinning on of my two silver Captain's bars , followed by some polite applause from the intimate gathering, along with their congratulatory handshakes. And General McChristian himself showed up at the conclusion of the ceremony to wish me luck. Now that was a big deal. Sort of like the Archbishop of New York City showing up at the installation of a neighborhood parish priest. Black and Johnson beamed as the old man congratulated ISB on the fine job that I had done over the past year.

Because I had no wife to adore me in my moment of glory, Mrs. Loomis volunteered her services as a sort of token spouse for the afternoon. As such, she smiled as the new symbols of my rank were fastened to my olive green jacket, and she even gave me a peck on the cheek on behalf of the women of America.

But all these accolades and the extra $98.62 on my monthly paycheck had at least one drawback. You see, it was customary for the newly promoted sucker to throw a costly party for his colleagues at work. If the officer in question didn't have space at home to accommodate everybody and their spouses or dates, he was expected to rent a private room at the local joint of his choice for some Saturday afternoon, and foot the bill for the festivities. These usually took place within a month or so of the promotion.

When I returned to the office after the presentation, Major Jerry Porter was waiting for me on the Oral Briefers' room with a suggestion. He'd been promoted to Major from Captain about two weeks earlier, and proposed that we combine our two parties into one Saturday afternoon bash at his house. Share expenses 50/50. If the weather was nice enough, we might even use the barbecue in his backyard. All the moochers at ISB would get their free food and suds, and we'd save ourselves a couple of bucks in the process. Made sense.

But if there had been a graceful way out of Jerry's idea, I would've taken it. Jerry Porter was a racist and a bigot. A die-hard Confederate apologist that represented everything that I despised. When he first came to ISB, his vile references to Martin Luther Coon and those darkies that were takin' over the country, turned me and just about everybody else off. Unlike Major Cachuk, whom I wasn't very fond of either, Jerry Porter was not just a dumb, incompetent, little son of a bitch. Jerry was clever ; he was able; he was dangerous. However, about a week after his introduction to the Southeast Asia Desk, his "niggers this" and "niggers that" talk caused the very conservative Major Carson, head of the section, to read him the riot act. He explained to him in no uncertain terms that the United States Army of 1969 was integrated, with no room for prejudice from anyone. And if he couldn't accept that, then Carson would transfer Jerry's ass out of ISB before the month was out. Captain Porter kept his mouth discreetly shut after that.

Jerry Porter, and officers like him posed a greater danger to the American military than all the traitors and cowards we had—combined. His Ku Klux Klan attitude of an Aryan society, free of niggers, spics, and kikes, was not only inherently detestable, but threatened the cohesion and morale of the entire Army. Any unit where the individual member refuses to sacrifice his own well being for the good of the whole, because the other guy is black, or prays in a mosque or synagogue would self destruct. There'd be no need for a Soviet or Chinese Division to destroy it.

But I had to admit it. Jerry's idea was a good one. Of course if he'd extended me an invite to a private party at his place, a party filled with John Birchers and neo Nazis, I'd have R.S.V.P'd with a resounding "No Thanks!" But this crowd would be exclusively ISB folks. Major Porter would be held in check. I could mingle with Gary, Jeff, Loomis, Colonel Quigley, Len, and even Colonel Black. So I said yes.

The word went forth that a promotion party would be held for Captain Woolsey and Major Porter, at the latter's residence at 3 Calvert Road, Chevy Chase, Maryland on Saturday, April 11, 1969, at 1400 hours. Casual attire. Bring only a hearty appetite and a healthy thirst.

I showed up about noon to help Mrs. Porter with the food and stuff. Jerry was out picking up the charcoal, refreshments, and party decorations. She met me at the door.

"Hi Bob," she said. "I'm Kimberly. C'mon in !"

We exchanged a little chit-chat as she led me to the kitchen. Jerry had met his wife at Mississippi State Something or Other College. He was the head of his R.O.T.C troop, and she was the Magnolia Queen. She was still gorgeous. She was probably thirty years old now, but wouldn't have had any trouble winning that Magnolia thing again—even competing against those nineteen year old Southern Belles. She had the bluest eyes, and the smoothest alabaster skin. And was she stacked! A marvelous bosom, and a body that tapered down to the tiniest waist, with long shapely legs that seemed to begin at her armpits. She really didn't need that bleached platinum blond hair, or that overapplication of Enjoli perfume to make her sexy. Kimberly could have turned any guy's head, wearing just a prison dress and no make-up. That afternoon she had on cut off blue jeans, a tank top, and sandals. She told me she'd change clothes in about an hour or so, before the guests arrived.

Then she assigned me to the details of making the tossed salad, spooning the melon balls, and preparing the universal snack dip of Lipton Onion Soup mix and sour cream.

I donned one of her aprons to protect my new sports shirt from the splattering of snack dip and salad dressing. Kimberly was glad to have my company, and I made her laugh as we joked around in the kitchen. She'd already had a few sips of Sauterne before my arrival, so I guess that my little quips seemed a bit funnier than they actually were. For instance I told her that at a party like this in New York, we'd first have to make sure to hide the silverware and the TV set, before the guests arrived. I also mentioned that I'd trade my new promotion to Captain in a second for an immediate discharge from the Army.

When she came over to inspect my salad, she made sure to touch my right shoulder with her ample breasts; and the earlobe drenched in the Enjoli perfume was only a couple of inches from my nostrils. What the hell was keeping Jerry Porter and those refreshments?

Kimberly was an incorrigible flirt. And the Good Lord had blessed her with more than her share of feminine charms. That's why I was surprised that the Porter's had no kids. They must've used a truckload of condoms and birth control pills a month. As I peeked over at her humming and struggling to make little finger sandwiches with those three inch long, bright red fingernails, I wondered she'd ever strayed from her fidelity to Jerry over the last ten years. Particularly when he was in Vietnam. It was a good thing that Carl Lebron had departed ISB a month ago. With their combined overactive libidos, they would no doubt have been humping each other before sundown in the upstairs bathroom, while Jerry and the rest of us were playing parlor games downstairs. Then I suddenly pictured Jerry about a hundred years or so before, in ante bellum Mississippi, dueling a scoundrel a week for attempting to violate his sweet young bride.

At last he came through the back door loaded down with boxes of cold cuts, jars of pickles, packages of hot dogs, chopped meat, and chicken parts, bottles of soda, and some party decorations.

"Hi, Honey!" he said to Kimberly, and then, "Hi, Bob!" glancing over at me. "Say, could you bring in the cases of beer and soda, and the bag of charcoal that I left in the back seat of the car. Thanks!"

Then he put the party stuff on the kitchen table. I lugged in the cases and the charcoal just in time to see them getting playful over the sink. He was just then kissing her neck.

"Have you been successfully defending yo' honor 'gainst this hyeer no 'count Yankee carpetbagger, mah sweet thing?" Jerry wisecracked in a mock Southern drawl, while nibbling her *Enjoli* laced earlobe.

Then she joined in the improvised scene. "Why Beauregard, Honey, what makes yo' thaynk that li'l ole me would even *look* at another man?" she asked, while batting her eyelashes.

I decided to add my two melodramatic cents to our *ad lib* matinee of *Gone with the Windbags.* "Captain Butler Sir, Miss O'Hara Ma'am," I said while bowing formally. "I am greatly offended that *either* of you would dare to malign the character and integrity of a New York Barrister. It's the most insulting thing I've ever hoid—er, heard. *Sir,* my seconds will call upon you at dawn tomorrow morning, so that I might have the satisfaction of avenging your slanderous remarks with pistols at twenty paces."

Then I decided to abruptly end the performance.

"Should I start the charcoal fire in the backyard grill? I've completed my duties at K.P. by making a huge chef's salad, assorted melon balls with cherry syrup, and a mouth watering snack dip, made from a secret recipe, that has been in my family since we landed at Plymouth Rock," I said.

With that, I went outside to get the charcoal started. Jerry put up some decorations. Just a few strips of red crepe paper in the dining room and parlor, and two gold colored banners hung at either end that read, "Congratulations Major Porter," and "Congratulations Captain Woolsey." Kimberly spread the cold cuts and salads on large serving platters, chilled the beer and soda, put out the chips and dip; then she went upstairs to change clothes, and returned to wait for the guests with Jerry and me.

Lt. Colonel and Mrs. Quigley showed up promptly at 2:00 P.M. Then during the next half- hour, the rest of the mob trickled in after congesting all of Calvert Road with their parked cars. The few coats and hats that they wore were piled onto the Porters' King—Size Bed upstairs.

When the crowd started to outgrow the kitchen, living room, and dining room, it spilled out into the backyard, where Jerry had earlier placed a few beach chairs. The first five or six "spiller outers" got the flimsy aluminum seats. The rest had to sit on the grass. But the "grass people" had a lot easier time eating and drinking than the seated few. They just lay their paper plates and plastic glasses on the ground, sprawled out like ancient Romans, and ate while lying down. Meanwhile, those seated had to perform a balancing act of paper plates on their knees, and beverage containers precariously perched on the wobbly arm rests of the beach chairs. More than a couple of cans and plastic glasses flipped over, splashing *Cokes* and *Budweiser* onto the lawn.

But the only major catastrophe occurred when Stu Rutkowski, while attempting to light up a cigarette, knocked over a heaping plate of heavily mustarded wieners, and equally heavily mayonnaised potato salad, together with greasy chicken wings, dill pickles, and assorted relishes onto his tan slacks.

"Jerry! Kimberly!" Stu pleaded. "Do you guys have any club soda?"

Kimberly remained the calm hostess, went to the kitchen and fetched a siphon seltzer bottle. Then like a Barnum & Bailey clown, she began spritzing Stu all over, from his crotch to his cuffs. He kept yelling, "Stop, Kimberly ! It's OK, it's OK!" But like a fireman at a four alarm blaze she kept dousing him. I think that she was getting a kick out of drenching the intellectual Major Rutkowski, whose political philosophy differed so greatly from that of hers and her husband's. Stu's lower torso was now dripping with carbonated water. Then he wiped off his pants with a dry Turkish towel that Kimberly provided. A few moments later she gave him a nice dry pair of Jerry's *Levi's*. Then he waited in the backyard after he had changed into them, and let his soaked slacks tumble dry in the *Maytag* down in the laundry room.

By sunset the crowd had dwindled down to just a handful of us; and by eight o'clock, only Jerry, Kimberly, and I were left. Then we cleaned up the place for about an hour. Jerry brought out his receipts and totaled them up. The tab ran about a hundred and twenty dollars; but there were a lot of leftovers, including soda and beer. Then I wrote him a check for sixty bucks. We both calculated that if *he* kept the rest of the food, and *I* took the unconsumed beer, wine and soda, we'd break out about even. And since we *did* use his place as the banquet hall, I came out a little ahead. I brought my stuff out to my car and went back to say Good Night.

All day long, everybody from Captain on up had been calling him Jerry. ""Where's the ice, Jerry?" and "Is there a bathroom in the basement, Jerry?" or "Great chicken, Jerry!" After all we *weren't* at the office; and most of us were still used to him being *Captain* Porter. But when we were alone, and I shook hands with him , I said "G'night Jerry!" His eyes flared up with indignation at my informality, and he returned to his old misanthropic self. He didn't say it in so many words, but I got his message which was, "The name's *Major* Porter to you, *Captain* ! And don't you forget it!"

# CHAPTER FORTY-ONE
# Dining Around the Globe

Colonel Black came up with a splendid idea to foster *Espirit de Corps* among troop ISB. A very palatable idea. He assigned each desk the task of holding a luncheon at a moderately priced restaurant that served the cuisine of their desk area. These were to take place on the third Friday afternoon of each month. Quigley could choose Chinese or Japanese; Stu Rutkowski got the chance to show off his favorite Goulash Emporium or Russian Tea Room; and Rod Burton probably had the easiest selection of all; he had the *Frugal Gourmet Guide,* listing hundreds of French, Italian, and Greek *bistros* that saturated the D.C. area.

Black encountered a minor snag as to what to do with Pritchard and Cachuk at the Africa desk. There were really no sub-Sahara restaurants to speak of. Then there was the problem of what to do with the Oral Briefing section. We were men without a country. So we were stuck with hosting the annual barbecue again. Then Black allowed Gary Maggio to split his Middle East culinary assignment into Arabic and Israeli eating establishments. *Gary* took command of Arabic restaurants, while Cachuk and Pritchard were in charge of the Israeli selection. Most of the Middle East places were Egyptian and Turkish. There were a couple of Israeli eateries, but they served mostly the same stuff. You know falafel, baba ganoosh, couscous, stuffed grape leaves, roast lamb and so forth.

Finally the African desk came up with the perfect solution for variety. They chose a kosher deli on 14th Street in the Northwest. Israeli, no. *Jewish* definitely yes! The bill of fare at *Sol's Pastrami Palace* was more reminiscent of the Lower East Side than Jerusalem. The house specialties included Chicken Soup with *Kreplach*; Stuffed Cabbage; Roast Chicken; gigantic Pastrami and Corned Beef sandwiches; potato pancakes; pickled herring; and *Cel-ray* tonic to wash it down. Len Roth volunteered his expert knowledge of the menu to Majors Carson and Loomis, as well as others from the U.S. Corn Belt, who were totally unfamiliar with the Joys of Kosher Cooking, and some of whom undoubtedly thought that *Matzoh Balls* were the testicle delicacies of the domesticated male *Matzoh* beast!

The proprietor himself , Sol Kronegold, took a special pride in tutoring the Pentagon's *finest* about the best in *Kashruth* that his establishment had to offer. For dessert he particularly recommended the Apple Blintzes and macaroons that Mama Kronegold had baked fresh. And for our men in uniform a special treat- a helping of his world renowned apricot compote for everybody—*on the house!* There was a minor flak when Cachuk balked at not getting cream for his coffee. But Sol tactfully explained to him that the mixing of dairy and meat was taboo in any kosher restaurant.

"Major Cupcake, my good friend," he said, "By a kosher restaurant, cream and a pastrami sandwich are a no-no. Cream you can get by my brother Marvin's *Dairy Delicacies* establishment over on Pennsylvania Avenue. But with my Esther's coffee you don' need no cream anyhow. Like nectar from Mount Olympus it tastes, just black and strong. But if you like it light and sweet, for you I got the solution.

"Myron !" he yelled to one of his waiters, "For Major Cupcake, bring 'coupla non-dairy creamers and a jar *Golden Blossom* from the pantry." Then he said to Cacuk," You'll see, Major from Indiana. A big tablespoon nice honey can make you forget about the cream." Then he looked around the room and asked, "*Nu*, did everybody enjoy Mama's cooking?"

"Hey, Solly!" Len Roth said from the table next to Cachuk's, "I think that maybe we should send the M.P.'s around tomorrow to close this place down for cholesterol poisoning. Don't you serve anything with vitamins in it? Except for the cole slaw and pickles, I haven't seen anything resembling a vegetable. By midnight we all could be dead from acute hardening of the arteries."

"Chp, chp, chp!" Sol said. "Look at the big shot ' Dining Out Critic' from the *New York Times* already. Well, for your info, Mr. Smart Alex, my food is probably the best meal you had since you left the Bronx. I know the kind crap that your blondie *shiksa* girlfriends, that you're *schtupping*, drag you out to eat. Raw tuna fish from one those fancy shmansy Japanese joints, where you take off the shoes to eat the seaweed and lumpy rice. And between the chopsticks and the bowels the food doesn't stop from the lips to the throat to say 'toodle-do' to the taste-buds. Pfui ! Styrofoam that don't deserve to be called food!

"And when Miss Blondie with the paradise legs is taking you to a picnic, what kind food is she bringing? Sliced cucumbers and tomatoes on *Wonder Bread* with the crusts cut off—and no-fat mayonnaise. Here I serve *real* food. Like a genuine Jewish missionary from my Mama's kitchen on Delancey Street. Look, Mr Weisenheimer, third generation know-it-all, for five thousand years *Glatt Kosher*'s been keeping our people alive. We don't need no new chefs from Harvard changing the menu. Eat! Enjoy!

"And you, Major Carson from Kansas, at the other table, you haven't even *touched* half the golden brown stuffed chicken on the plate. I don't give no rebates on leftovers. And don't pick at it with the fork! Emily Post doesn't show up with the etiquette lessons until next week. Meantime chew it straight from the bones like Henry the Eighth, starring Charles Laughton, with all the beautiful *schmaltz* dripping from the chin."

Sol was like a borscht belt comic, working the room, serving the one-liners with the skill of a Catskills pro, needling the weekend clientele. Then he smiled.

"All kidding aside," he said, "you guys are the greatest people in the world. Heroes ! *Hee-roes!* I don' care what people say about this damn *fakockte* War in Vietnam. If I could, I'd bring back all those lovely boys tomorrow. All I know is, without the American GIs to stop those Nazi bastards twenty five years ago, Hitler would now be swiveling in a big red leather chair in the Oval Office, and some other Nazi cock sucker would be serving pigs feet and red cabbage in this place. And mama and me would be long dead from the gas pellets in the make believe showers, like my Uncle David and Tante Rebecca, and all my *mish-puchah* in Krakow.

"But you guys stopped 'em ! You stopped those schmucks just like *I* stopped 'em in 1918. Practically a baby I was, a snotnose kid barely seventeen years old, still soaking behind the ears. In March I enlisted at Fort Dix, and by May I was toting a rifle across the Atlantic Ocean to fight the Hun. And then *schlepping* through the trenches of Northern France, freezing in the mud and scrounging whatever food I could find. Uncle Sam wasn't observing dietary laws.

"Then one day the Huns break through our defenses and totally cut off our supply line. No food for three days. I almost ate the bullets, so hungry I was. A slab of *bacon* I would've eaten yet! Then I spot this beautiful non-kosher rabbit that God must've sent into that slimy trench. So like the Elmer Fudd from the Lower East Side, I catch the plump little Bugs Bunny and skin him. Then me and Tommy Flaherty and Hank Borone, two *goyim* Buck Privates, cook the chubby little son of a bitch., almost eating the meal while it was still roasting over the fire. Two days later those two guys was blown to bits by an artillery shell while I was snoozing at the other end of the trench. Two days after that, the Krauts gave up, and the ' World's Last War' was over. They gathered up the pieces of Tommy and Hank and buried them side by side in a cemetery outside Chateau Thierry, with the plain white wooden crosses.

"Just young kids we all was. Patriotic, scared to death Yankee Doodle doughboys, that President Wilson sent off to keep the World safe for democracy."

Then a tear came to his eye. He raised his glass of seltzer for a toast.

"Fuck all wars!" he said. "But God bless the American soldier! God bless the USA! *L'chaim!* "

The next luncheon was hosted by Matt Lehrer of the South Asia Desk. His desk's responsibility ranged from Iran through India. He had spent most of his youth in New Delhi, the son of an American representative of a toy manufacturer. Matt was reciting the *Pledge of Allegiance* in class at the American School of New Delhi that tragic morning in 1948 when Mahatma Ghandi was assassinated.

As host it was Matt's prerogative to select either Pakistani or Indian food. He picked the *Ganges Grotto*, one of his favorite Indian places. This was a wise choice, because many of the Pakistani possibilities were Moslem Establishments, with a strict prohibition against serving alcohol. *And* since one of the goals of our Third Friday feast was to get pleasantly looped—if possible on the alcoholic beverage of the host country( Saki, Tequila, Ouzo etc. ), we all convened at the *Ganges* about 1300 hours. Major Loomis drove me and Lieutenant Gilmore there in his VW.

Matt had preceded the rest of us by about half an hour. He wanted to make sure that Mr. Prahat Ram had reserved the small private room with the pleasant fountain, and that we'd have two private waiters assigned exclusively to our tables. After we were all seated, Matt made a short announcement welcoming everybody to India. He said that all the entrees were good , but he gave four stars to the Lamb Curry, the Tandoori Duck, and the Pork Vindaloo. And the Cream Cheese Balls in

Syrup or the Banana Sweet Meats were the most delicious desserts in all of Washington D.C.

It was a great afternoon. Matt spent the better part of an hour recalling his days in India to Len Roth and myself. I felt as though I was listening to the ghost of Rudyard Kipling talking about *Gunga Din* and *Riki-Tiki-Tavi*. Loomis came over, said that he was heading back and wanted to know if I had a ride to the Pentagon. Matt said that there was no rush, and he'd be glad to chauffeur me back. For all practical purposes ISB was closed anyway. Len Roth accepted Loomis' offer. He said that he needed to do a job for Quigley by Monday morning, and that he might as well get it over with.

Lehrer got more and more nostalgic as he told of the early days living in the new Indian democracy; the split with the Moslems of Pakistan; and the death of Mahatma. He described the shock and disbelief that consumed the whole nation over the death of the twentieth century's most selfless humanitarian; the funeral procession bearing the slain leader that stretched for miles, silent except for the pounding of the ceremonial drum, and the clatter of the wheels of the horse drawn hearse over the cobblestones. The ten year old Matt knew that he wouldn't see such a sight again.

Everybody else had gone. Matt was in a good mood. He even gave Jamal and Krishna, our two waiters, a couple of twenties as a bonus gratuity, in addition to the other tips left by the rest of the crowd. We headed back to his car as he suggested we stop off at his apartment for a mid-afternoon "nightcap". Then he bragged a bit about the collection of Indian and Persian Art in his apartment that he and his family had gathered over the last forty years

Finally we arrived at his luxury Arlington high rise, and Matt parked his Mercedes. We walked through the ultra- modern lobby and into a waiting elevator. Matt pressed the button for the 23rd floor.

The elevator chimed, and its doors opened to a pleasant blue carpeted hallway. Matt led me to apartment 2315, facing Washington

D.C. He fumbled with the latchkey for a couple of seconds; then he swung the door open and flicked on the lights.

"Welcome to Taj Mahal West!" Matt announced.

He wasn't exaggerating all that much. True, it *was* only a two-bedroom version of the stately mausoleum, but it was a showplace of South Asian Art. Bronze statues of the god Vishna and the dancing goddess Shiva adorned the living room. Gipta Buddhas and Mughal Paintings decorated the halls. Then there were the exquisite Persian carpets on the floors and walls.

You couldn't help but be impressed. Matt's father had done very well for himself, manufacturing baby rattles and Mickey Mouse dolls. The Socialist lobe of my brain kept thinking how this magnificent collection was formed by the labor of underpaid Indian workers who produced these profitable playthings for spoiled American kiddies, at three cents an hour wages. Meanwhile Daddy Lehrer lived the life of a Maharajah on a six figure annual income. But I was a damned hypocrite. I would've traded places with him in a minute!

Matt directed my attention to the mobile cart carrying a dozen bottles of liqueur. It was next to the sliding glass door leading to the small balcony that overlooked the Capital.

"Help yourself, Bob!" he said. "There are glasses next to the booze. If you need ice, there's plenty in the kitchen freezer. If you want to smoke try not to get ashes on the rug—pardon me, on the *carpet*. After I leave this man's army, I plan to sell it and live off the proceeds for a year. I'll be back in a couple of minutes. I'm putting a record on the stereo. I hope you like Ravi Shankar." Then he left.

I poured myself a small glass of cognac, without ice, sat down on the long tan leather sofa behind the coffee table and relaxed. Ravi Shankar wasn't exactly my favorite recording artist, but the music did fit the setting. I lit up a cigarette and sipped the brandy.

Then Matt came out of the bedroom. He had a hashish pipe in his left hand and a glass of port in his right. And he was wearing a royal blue satin bathrobe and slippers. As Sol Kronegold might have aptly put it: this new development didn't seem exactly kosher. But maybe my big city paranoia and experiences in Greenwich Village were getting the better of me. Then Matt tendered me the hash pipe.

"Here, take a drag," he said. "There's nothing like quality hash and a cognac chaser."

I accepted the long porcelain bong, and took a good deep drag. After all, I didn't want to appear rude. A couple of moments passed and Ravi Shankar began sounding awfully good.

Then Matt sat down on the sofa beside me. I returned the glowing pipe to him. Then he put his hand on my knee. Suddenly this was not paranoia any more. Captain Matt Lehrer was indeed making a pass at me—on the 23rd floor of his fancy apartment overlooking the Capitol Building and the White House, with Ravi Shankar's sitar music in the background, and me sipping fifty dollar a bottle cognac between puffs of Hawaiian hash. I began sweating over Matt's preliminary seduction and wanted out of Taj Mahal West.

Maybe he'd mistaken my sensitivity somehow for a gay element of my sexuality; or maybe I'd inadvertently sent him a wrong signal. Maybe the recall of his boyhood days in India where he first felt these feelings set him off. But I was all at once nervous, guilty, and - goddammit- still high from the cognac and hash. Why hadn't Matt been considerate enough to make his pass at me in the Pentagon men's room, where I could've just elbowed him away, and told him to fuck off! Why did he have to wait until I was feeling so good.

Anyway I took the offensive. I took a sip of cognac and faked a cough, as though it had gone down the wrong pipe. Then I coughed again. It was as though I'd just swallowed a chicken bone.

Matt kept asking, "Are you OK? Are you OK?"

Then I raced from the couch and stumbled towards the bathroom, where I feigned coughing and throwing up for the next few minutes.

When I came out, my eyes were bloodshot red, and my body was still shaking from the coughing spasm.

"I'm sorry Matt," I said," but I'm sick as a dog. I'd better go home and drink a coupla' bottles of Pepto-Bismol and get to bed."

Matt seemed to buy the whole performance. God , it seemed had blessed me with a talent for lying convincingly. Like that time at Fort Benning with that idiot Lieutenant Vukov. But Matt was way at the other end of the intelligence spectrum. So it made me a little proud knowing that I could fool the likes of the dumbest imbecile to a sophisticated genius like Lehrer.

"Are you sure you're all right?" he repeated. "Should I drive you home?"

"No, No!" I insisted," I'll get a cab downstairs. I could use some fresh air too. Besides I still have to pick up my car at the Pentagon parking lot. I'm so sorry I got sick on you, but at least I didn't puke all over your Persian carpet."

"Nonsense, nonsense, "he said. "I'm just glad that you survived. Sometimes hash and brandy can be a deadly combination."

I alternated my apologies and thank yous as I walked towards the door. I even gave him a manly hug as I was about to leave. I don't know why exactly. Maybe I thought that it might make him feel a little less embarrassed. After all, Matt was a fine person, and I still liked him. I left.

He stood at the open door to make sure I made it to the elevator OK. I looked back at him as he smiled and lifted his wineglass in an imaginary toast. Then I must've pressed that damned elevator button a hundred times during the next two minutes that seemed like an hour, until the doors opened to carry me down to the lobby.

# CHAPTER FORTY-TWO

# Come Fly with Me

In May 1969, Santini and I decided to spend the bulk of our vacation time "hitching" our way out of country, courtesy of the US Air Force. You see , the military offered its servicemen "free flights" on Cargo Planes headed for bases near Rio de Janeiro, and Frankfurt, and Madrid. The junket to Brazil sounded like the most fun, until we learned that there was only *one* flight per week out of the Air Base at Fort Dix New Jersey. So *if* the flight was carrying hazardous cargo, or *if* twelve other guys were ahead of us for the dozen available spaces on the aircraft, then we'd be- to use that military mnemonic- SOL. We'd have to spend our time cooling our heels in the Fort Dix officers' lounge.

There are always some guys, who know some guys, who know about how to get the most out of the Army. Santini played poker every Friday night with a Master Sergeant that was familiar with the Army's system of living comfortably on wages below the poverty level. You know the kind of character. "Psst, hey buddy, ya wanna buy a *tank*—-real cheap—hardly ever used!"

Anyway we called up this "street smart" individual on how to proceed. He gave us a complete rundown on flight options and alternatives just like a *bona fide* Liberty Travel Agent. According to "Manny" the Air Force Base at Dover, Delaware was the smartest point of embarkation. Flights were taking off three—maybe four times a day for Europe. Frankfurt was the most frequent destination, but there were lots of flights to Spain and Italy too. Manny was a kind of "tout" like they have at the race track. Only he specialized in predicting Air Force flights. Because he owed Santini forty bucks in Poker IOU's, these flight tips were "on the house".

How could we miss? Even if we could only manage the Frankfurt run, we could take a cheap second class train ride south, and by morning we'd be sunning ourselves on the Costa del Sol, drinking ice cold Margaritas in the 85 degree weather watching bikini clad *senoritas* on the beach. With the money we'd save on airfare we could even afford a three star hotel.

Lieutenant Frank Stichter and Captain Fred Burns were two guys that lived down the hall from Don and me at our Falls Church, Virginia high rise. They both had more than a month of stored up vacation time, and jumped at the chance for complimentary air fare to Europe. Sipping inexpensive cocktails on some Mediterranean beach sounded just *fine*.

On Saturday morning, May 1st, we all piled into my big Bonneville, setting the compass for our two hour ride to Dover, Delaware. One last anal compulsive check upstairs to make sure that the door was locked and the water faucet shut off and we were shouting out the first chorus to "Ninety Nine Bottles of Beer on the Wall!" Stichter and Burns were in a particularly good mood. Just four months before they were attached to some forgettable post fifty miles west of Saigon.

First thing that we did on arrival was to sign in at the Flight to Europe Desk. We went down the list. There were ten guys ahead of us. But if the flights were frequent enough, that would pose no problem. We concocted a fair lottery system as to who signed up first. From our assorted change we selected four pennies with different dates. We'd pick. Most recent penny goes first. Oldest penny last. All the pennies went into Santini's hat. Stichter went first—1961. Burns—1965. Santini—1963—and the WINNER AGAIN IS—BOB WOOLSEY—1967! A procedure certainly as fair as the Fort Benning A-Z Russian

Roulette. But deep down, I wished that Santini had picked that 1965 penny. Who knew? Maybe we'd all be separated and I'd wind up with Fred Burns. I *knew* Don Santini. We'd lived in the same apartment together and got along well. I hadn't spent any time *solely* in the company of Fred Burns. But certain warnings about him should have tipped me off. His shoes were always shined. Not just his Army shoes, but the ones that he wore when we were all sitting around watching TV. That was another tip off. TV shows. Burns practically went into mourning when they took *Gomer Pyle* off the air. And he made it almost a religious sacrament to watch the *Porter Waggoner Country Music Show* every week. Although I must admit, I enjoyed ogling his busty blonde co-star Dolly Parton myself.

During the trip from Falls Church to Dover we each got a half hour to choose our favorite radio station. Burns chose this really redneck one, way at the end of the dial. Not Willie Nelson or Patsy Kline, but real caterwauling like you wouldn't believe. *Mayyh Daarlinn yooor guwwn, soo Ahyll jest strooke thiss hyeer Gitaar ayand preteyend its yooor haairrr!* I would've given ten bucks to listen to the farm report.

There were no flights to *anywhere*. We stayed around for five consecutive days at the Dover Delaware hellhole of monotony. We couldn't leave even to go into town to see a movie. You see all outgoing flights with places available were announced over the camp loudspeaker. Next folks in line had *one* hour to report to the plane, or you went to the bottom of the list. By Wednesday we were all crawling up the wall and getting on each other's nerves. It seemed like the whole time, we'd been playing bumper pool in the lounge, and listening to the *Fifth Dimension* sing *The Age of Aquarius* for the three hundredth time on the juke box. If I'd had a gun, I'd 've blasted that goddam box by Wednesday afternoon. Six P.M. Still no flights in sight. The information desk told us that *all* flights bound for Europe the last few days had "hazardous cargo" on board. Just about anything that was flammable was hazardous. wearing apparel, cigarettes, parachutes, paper towels. If it wasn't made of metal or sealed inside a can, it was combustible, and none of us "hitchhikers" was permitted to fly beside it. There was a small fire on board a plane two weeks ago, and regulations were being carried out to the letter. The Sergeant was a bit more optimistic than we were. We were bound to be called soon.

Then suddenly about 7:00 P.M. the loudspeaker announced a dozen names. Woolsey and Burns completed the list. Even a plane ride with Fred Burns was a welcome relief. We told Santini and Stichter that we'd wait for them two days in Frankfurt. After that they could call military information and pick up our message about where we'd be. Phone calls between bases were free. If they called Frankfurt from Madrid, we'd be able to reunite. "Last call for Flight 465 to Frankfurt." We shook hands. Burns and I grabbed our bags and ran for the plane.

The craft didn't seem all that bad. No stewardesses pouring cocktails from those two ounce bottles, but the non-com, Sergeant McCann, in charge of Cargo brought a case of fairly cold cans of Coke on board. He shared them with the guys. The Military's way of saying "Thanks". A couple of fifteen cent cans of Coke. Nothing was too good for our boys in uniform.

I brought a book along to read, in case Burns wasn't in the mood for conversation. But there were no windows on the Cargo area, and the light in the hold was so dim that I couldn't see anything. Fred was asleep an hour after we were airborne. That guy could fall asleep in the middle of a Rock Concert. So I spent about six hours staring at the cases of C-Rations and spare parts on their way to our boys in West Germany. I also managed to eavesdrop on a couple of Corporals gabbing away about their next two weeks, and giggling like a couple of schoolgirls. But I had to admit it. I was pretty excited myself.

Since this was a military flight, we all had to wear our uniforms. Word came from Sergeant McCann that we'd be landing in about half an hour. At least we wouldn't have to wait for our luggage. Our passenger accommodations held our suitcases as well as us. So after the plane taxied to the terminal, Fred and I just grabbed our bags and hopped down the portable staircase leading from the plane. We were directed towards customs, which we cleared in about two minutes. Then we took a cab to a hotel that I'd researched in *Europe on Five Dollars a Day* just before we left from Dover.

It was cheap; and our room *was* a little cramped. But it did have its own private shower. I just wanted to get out of that itchy smelly uniform, and fold it away in my suitcase for the next two weeks. A shower, some clean civilian clothes, and maybe a little nap, and I'd be ready for a late breakfast someplace.

After our jelly and rolls, Fred and I took a taxi back to the Frankfurt Army Base. We told the Desk Sergeant of our situation, and how Santini and Stichter were either still playing bumper pool in Delaware, or hopefully on a plane to meet us. He said that he'd contact Dover and would let us know in fifteen minutes. We walked around a bit and then returned to the disheartening news. No flights since *we* had left, and none expected for the next two days. He said he was sorry and recommended a couple of local brauhauses in town that were only moderate rip offs for servicemen.

I was starting to panic. I couldn't last more than twenty four hours more with Fred. It was bad enough that I was acting as his personal translator, but our personality conflicts were becoming more and more pronounced. Fred was a neat freak! Even on vacation. He objected to the way that I threw my socks on the floor, and didn't fold my towel tidily in the bathroom. Armythink had taken over the mind of Fred Burns. Like in the *Invasion of the Body Snatchers*. I made it through *one* night. When I awoke the next morning I discovered that he had actually made his bed—-*with Hospital Corners yet!*

If I wanted to crumple up my towel, that was my business. I was on vacation. If I wanted to stop shaving for a couple of days or drip mustard on my shirt, that was how it was going to be. I had a mother three thousand miles away, who had *some* privilege at calling me a slob.

I didn't need Fred Burns to take her place overseas. I made a concerted effort to avoid an argument. But I was developing a slight twitch in my lip. Fred and I had an early Lunch of Veal Cutlet, Dumplings and Red cabbage. The cold frosty beer tasted wonderful. We had Apple Cake for Dessert, and headed for the Army Base again. No word about any flights. No messages.

I was developing a compulsion to remove myself as far as possible from Fred. I wasn't exactly deserting Santini and Stichter, but I couldn't last another day alone with him. Compared to Burns, Fort Benning was a Furlough in Hawaii.

"Fred," I said, "it doesn't look like Don and Frank are going to be here any time soon. And, to be honest, I don't think that I can last another day of wiping the shower curtain after I use it, or putting back my toothpaste tube on the *second* shelf, that you set aside for my toiletries. I'm sure that you're equally annoyed with my pig like habits. So maybe it's best if we split up before I accidentally shove you in front of a Frankfurt streetcar, or you club me to death with one of those shoetrees that you brought along, so that your *Florsheims* don't curl up. But don't get me wrong. I'm not deserting you , Frank, and Don. I'll call up this Hotel every day as I head South. I'll call up the base in Frankfurt too! In a week or so, when the four of us are back together, we'll probably laugh our asses of about all of this. In any case, you can appreciate Santini's self control in having to put up with "Oscar Madison" all these months.

Fred took it well. Now he could fold and clean, and be finicky as much as he wanted without worrying about me. He even rode with me to the train station, where I bought a one way fare to Naples, Italy. I had some relatives to look up.

# CHAPTER FORTY-THREE

# Whatever Became of...?

But before I began to sponge off my Italian family, there was one stop in Germany that I just had to make. Cliff Tubman, the Ponce de Leon of the Fort Benning Map Reading Course, had been transferred to Stuttgart, bordering the Black Forest. Unlike his name might suggest, Cliff was a tall, gangly, Ichabod Crane lookalike, who was maybe even *more* physically uncoordinated than me. I was curious to see if he had got lost trying to locate Stuttgart.

He was a friendly enough guy, but I never got to know him all that well. Maybe he felt more comfortable with the good ol' boys like Vic Stimmons and Ollie Taylor. But he *did* receive the Company's best assignment, at far as I was concerned. Two years in the glorious countryside, only a couple of hours by car from France, Switzerland, and Austria. I would have sacrificed another year in uniform to get that job! I was dying to see how he was making out.

Why *Cliff* was sent there, I'll never know. He couldn't speak German. *Hell*, he had trouble communicating in English. Not that he was stupid or anything, but he had a prodigious Arkansas drawl, that was so unintelligible that I had to ask him to repeat everything twice. But after my map reading counseling, I figured that he owed me at least a drink and a sausage down at his local beer hall.

After the short train ride from Frankfurt, I took a cab to the small American Post on the edge of town. I walked inside and told the

Sergeant on duty that I was an old friend of Cliff's, who was abroad on holiday, and would like to see him for a few minutes. The Sergeant buzzed him on the intercom.

"Tell that Yankee son of a bitch that I'll be right out!" I heard him chuckle over the speaker.

As he opened his office door, I could barely recognize him. The rich diet of pigs' knuckles and home fried potatoes, not to mention the double portions of creamy Black Forest Chocolate Cake, had added about twenty pounds to his once spindly frame. He was delighted to see me.

He was a Captain now and was in charge of the place. He told the Sergeant that he was taking the afternoon off to discuss "Intelligence Matters" with a distinguished representative from the Pentagon. We walked to his Beetle just outside the door and he drove me to his two-story walk-up, a few blocks away, so he could change into his civilian clothes. We didn't get *lost once*.

He poured us each a bottle of cold beer, and we talked about our lives since Fort Benning. He bragged a bit about bargaining with his stodgy landlord to get this comfortable, three-room apartment for just under sixty bucks a month. He just had to supply the old geezer with an occasional pair of blue jeans, a few jars of peanut butter a month, and a steady supply of that nice, soft, Scott toilet paper from the PX. Some "luxury" items from the American marketplace still hadn't made it into West German stores.

Cliff also prided himself on being the mainstay of the finest brothel in Stuttgart. He'd even picked up some German vocabulary from his female "professors" down at the whorehouse. He tried to practice a little bit of it on me over our pretzels and beer, but most of the conversation centered around bedroom talk, like what type of sex I preferred, or whether I'd brought along enough prophylactics for my trip. Then he asked me if I had enough time for a *quickie* down at the "ladies lounge". He boasted that, although it was usually closed this time of day, he was sure he could use his influence to get one of the girls to open the place up, and to a special favor for a buddy of his.

I thanked him for his offer, but refused politely. So he took me to his favorite tavern, where he ordered me the specialty of the house—a big bowl of their spiciest Goulash with noodles. It took a whole liter of beer to revive my palate.

We talked shop a little in our private booth. Cliff admitted that his command was probable the easiest sinecure in Germany. He just had to review the Intelligence reports from Czechoslovakia and Hungary that came in every morning, and pass along the important stuff to Army Headquarters in Munich. He also had to discreetly monitor the activities of our French "allies" on the other side of the Rhine. This latter assignment was totally unofficial.

It was already about 4:00 P. M., too late to head over the Alps for Naples. I asked Cliff if I could crash for the night on that big, comfortable, beat-up sofa on his living room. He was happy to oblige. First he stopped by his office to check whether anything had come up since his "conference" with me. Nothing new.

Then he gave me the usual tour, driving me along the pleasant landscape of the Neckar River valley, and then through the lush Spring foliage of the Black Forest. It started to get dark, so we headed back to Stuttgart.

On the way back, Cliff stopped off to buy our supper. *Blutwurst,* Emmentaler Cheese, Ham, and Black Bread. He'd adopted the German custom of having a noon *hot* meal, and eating cold cuts in the evening. After dinner we sat around his place for a while, but we were starting to run out of things to talk about. And I was getting sleepy. So Cliff draped a sheet over the big couch, and borrowed an extra pillow from *Herr* Strassner, his landlord. He even managed to find a spare blanket for me. I studied my train schedule. There was an express leaving the main railroad station at 8:07 the following morning for Naples—arriving at 5:47

P. M. I hit the sack about 9: 30 and I guess Cliff struggled with German TV in his bedroom for an hour or so after that.

Next morning he was nice enough to prepare me a box lunch for the train trip- a couple of Black Bread sandwiches, thick with two inches of ham and Emmentaler Cheese. He even packed a cold bottle of beer. But that would probably turn warm by the time I had it for lunch. Then he dropped me off at the station, and told me to give his best to Don Santini if we ever caught up with each other. I boarded at eight o'clock sharp.

# CHAPTER FORTY-FOUR

# Strangers on a Train

I had bought a copy of Der Spiegel, the German version of Time magazine, to read on the trip. Then I wandered down the aisle of the train until I located a half-occupied smoking compartment. I entered and hoisted my suitcase onto the luggage rack. A couple of thirtyish men were sitting at the window seats. They looked like they might be foreign workers on holiday. They were conversing in Arabic. One of them offered me a cigarette.

Impromptu, I decided to assume the role of a Danish businessman, Bjorn Bjornson, from the House of Bjornson, exporters of Havarti cheese. Because of the Vietnam War, Americans were not exactly popular with some Third World countries. And because of the perceived US support of the State of Israel, we were looked upon as Imperialist Yankee bullies in much of the Arab World. To be Danish was better.

Omar and Ahmed, the two passengers in the second class compartment, politely interrupted their dialogue in Arabic to welcome me into their conversation. They told me in their broken German that they had recently been employed as construction workers on the stretch of *Autobahn* between Munich and Stuttgart, but when their well paying jobs had terminated, they were put on a forced vacation. But they did manage to save up a respectable sum of *Deutsch Marks* to send back home to their families in Syria. The rest they could squander on a two

194

week holiday in Naples, sunning themselves on the beach, drinking cheap wine( they left the Koran's prohibition on alcohol back in the Middle East), and trying to seduce the *signorine* of Southern Italy by posing as exchange students from Damascus. Then they asked me whether my trip was business or pleasure.

I made the mistake of embellishing the Danish cheese magnate fabrication a little too thick. I boasted that, because of my family's success in the Havarti business, they were sending me south to Benevento to explore the possibilities of opening a Gorgonzola plant down there. Suddenly Omar and Ahmed abandoned their careers as builders of the *Autobahn*, and bragged endlessly to me of their talents in the science of making cheese. On their familys' farms back in Al Qutayfah, a little town outside the Capital, they both woke up at dawn every morning to milk the goats, separate the curds from the whey, and make the best damned cheese in Syria. They didn't know the German words for curds and whey of course, but they got the idea across with graphic hand gestures , while mimicking the bleating of a nanny goat.

They were certain that they could be of help to me in my new Gorgonzola factory, and wrote down their names, addresses, and telephone numbers, both in Stuttgart and Al Qutayfah. When they asked for my business card, I pretended to fumble through my wallet in a futile search. I apologized at not being able to find one, and said that they were probably buried at the bottom of my suitcase. But I *did* write down a phony telephone number, just like at the Inaugural Ball, of the main cheese plant in Copenhagen, on a couple of matchbook covers. I told them that if I wasn't around, they should ask for my father , Victor Borge Bjornson, or my brother Hamlet. I felt a little guilty though, seeing them carefully fold the precious matchbook covers into their wallets, and dream of their future jobs as caretakers of the giant simmering vats of goat milk curds, working at a nice steady *indoor* job in Benevento, at two thousand *Lire* an hour, making Gorgonzola.

For a couple of tense moments however, Omar smelled a rat about my stories of cheese grandeur. He wondered why I wasn't traveling first class to Italy. I had to think fast. Then I told them about my great grand-father, Hans Christian Bjornson, who had once worked as a railroad porter on the Acheson, Topeka, and Stockholm line in the late eighteen hundreds. He worked for practically slave wages, and depended on tips to make a living. The snobs traveling first class were incredible cheap-skates, so it took him close to twenty years to build up a nest egg for his business. He and my great-grandmother, Ophelia, swore an oath that neither they nor their descendants would ever spend a single *kroner* to ride first class and mingle with those stingy phonies. Ahmed and Omar must have had some unpleasant experiences with greedy Western capi-talists themselves. They told me that they could understand how great-grandpa must've felt.

So I played my part as Bjorn Bjornson for an hour or so more as we talked. It was a challenge for me to see how long I could carry off my little charade. I'd always wanted to try this stunt back in the United States, but we Americans don't travel by train. I would've had to do it on a *plane*. Airplanes are awkward. If you get caught in a big fib, you can't change your seat in mid air. You've just got to spend the rest of the flight seated next to some stranger that thinks that you're an asshole.

I was really putting on a convincing act for my two traveling companions, when suddenly I heard—"Passport Control!" from the corridor. We had crossed the Swiss border. I was trapped. The two Arabs would notice my unmistakable American passport, and the show would be over. I blushed as I handed the greyish-blue document to the Swiss official. Omar and Ahmed stared as he stamped the inside. When he left the compartment, they were obviously furious, and went back to chat-tering in Arabic. They ignored me totally, convinced that I had made them both look like fools. I was going to make up some *coup de grace* of bullshit about having dual citizenship on my Brooklyn born mother's side, but I decided not to risk it. So I grabbed my suitcase from the luggage rack, and slithered away to a different compartment, where a group of Neapolitans, returning from big Soccer Match with Stuttgart, were drinking wine and celebrating their 3-2 victory. I abdicated as Bjorn Bjornson, King of Havarti Cheese, and resumed my role as just plain Bob, an American on vacation. I ate the lunch that Cliff had prepared. Then I read *Der Spiegel*, until the train pulled into Naples Station around a quarter to six.

# CHAPTER FORTY-FIVE

# Our American Cousin

My Grandparents on my mother's side were Neapolitan. Grandma came from some hic town about fifty miles north of Naples. But my Grandfather came from the fairly cosmopolitan city of Benevento. His brother and nephew still lived there. Now was *juust* the right time for a friendly family visit. I knew both their names. So after the ten-hour ride down "the Boot" of Italy, I made a call to Benevento Information for the number of Adolfo or Aniello Ferrara.

Despite the dumb incident on the train, traveling alone was ten times better than being saddled with Fred Burns. But as a social animal , I had to have somebody to talk to until Frank and Don showed up. It took a pretty big set of *cujones,* now that I think about it, but I assembled all my courage, and dialed my second cousin Aniello.

The conversation went better than I could've expected. I'd picked up a good deal from my mother, and I'd studied a bit on my own while living in Germany. Aniello couldn't' have been more delighted. Maybe it was his way of saying "Thanks" to his *American Family*, for helping out the Ferrara Clan during the bad times after the War, with money and food packages.

So he dropped whatever he was doing and canceled all his plans that evening just to come and pick me up. I told him that I'd be waiting in front of the railroad station looking like a "pazzo Americano" in front of a big gray suitcase. To make me stand out even more I'd be holding a copy of *Time* magazine. He showed up an hour later, with his two small boys, Carmine and Maurizio, who were both anxious to meet their "Cugino Roberto" who someday would invite them to Hollywood to meet Jerry *Lew-ees.*

I squeezed my bag in the trunk , and climbed into the front seat with Aniello. He knew about twenty words of English , mostly words that he'd learned as a young man from American GI's. However, mastering the phrases "Do you have chocolate?" and "Fuck Mussolini!" aren't enough of a basis for a conversation. But I was pretty good, If I must say so myself. I told them, in my best tourist Italian, that I was in the Army at the Pentagon, and had a couple of weeks leave before I had to get back.

I told him of my mother's brothers and sisters, and what little I knew about my Grandmother. The kids were fascinated by the first American they had probably ever met. They must've both wondered how a seemingly normal, twenty seven year old guy could manage to fracture the language that *they* spoke so effortlessly. But, they were polite enough not to correct me. They did, however, struggle to hold back a snicker, when I asked them in my disjointed Italian, "Are you much pleased for the eating of Pizza?"

They both turned out to be proficient teachers. Aniello set up a cot for me in their room, and for days I learned enough of the language of my ancestors to feel at ease at a train station or a restaurant. I could even understand most of those cartoon characters they watched on TV- Walt Disney's unintelligible *Donaldo Anatrino* and his little pal *Mikki Topolino.*

I learned that when Italian men walk down the street, they do it arm in arm. That a visit to an Italian Cafe takes about thirty seconds. At his favorite *Cafe Pirandello*, Aniello would order his usual *Campari*, gulp it down, and pay for it in the same motion. No long, drawn out nursing of beverages *a la* Starbuck's. I even learned to sleep in the afternoon between one and three P.M. Italian siesta time. "Neil" as I now called him, had his own small business, which he practically abandoned, during my stay, as he chauffeured me to Capri, Vesuvius, and the scenic Amalfi Drive. He took great pride in pointing out the beauty of the Bay of Naples coastline. But I spent half the trip clutching my seat, and closing my eyes in terror, as Neil barely negotiated the curves along the narrow road. As I took a frightened peek from the window of his *Fiat* over the two thousand foot drop to the sea below, I could have sworn that only three tires were touching gravel. I could picture the headlines in tomorrow's *Herald Tribune*. "*Army Captain on Leave Plunges to Death from Cliff*". Colonel Black would break the news to the office and there'd be a moment of silence. God forbid that Major Cachuk would read the eulogy. " *Untimely death on **Ah-mahl-fee** Drive, just North of Sohr-ren-toh*.

During my stay with Neil, I called Fred Burns every day from the pay phone at the Cafe. Finally, *two weeks* after we arrived at Dover Air Force Base, Fred had some good news. It seemed that Don and Frank had boarded the first available flight *anywhere*. And that was three days after *our* flight to Frankfurt. It was to the Azores. Then they had to stay *there* for another three days, playing bumper pool, and listening to the *Fifth Dimension* on the officers' lounge jukebox.

But finally, two weeks after our planned "No Cost Flight to Europe", we were all on the same Continent again. Burns had remained the whole time at that same *Blue Orchid Hotel*. He rented a car and took a few day trips to Cologne, Mainz, and Wiesbaden, but mostly he just stayed in Frankfurt. The hotel staff was probably heartbroken to see him go, what with his making his own bed and all, and cleaning up after the maid.

But we'd be together again tomorrow afternoon. If the guys left early in the morning they could make it to Benevento in ten hours. I gave Don the directions to Neil's house, and spent my last night with my Italian family.

The fellows showed up at 6:00 P.M. the next day. Santini joked that the Azores was not all that it was cracked up to be. He said that the Army Office of Supply must've finagled a special discount on bumper pool tables, 'cause the Puerta del Gata Officers' lounge had a duplicate of the one back in Dover. He'd played enough pool to last him fifty years. But it wasn't such a total loss. He'd played a lot of Poker with a bunch of guys too bored to care about losing money, and they'd lost enough to pay his rent back home for a few months. Don was a big hit with Neil and the family. At last an American who could speak Italian without embarrassing himself.

We still had about a week left before we all had to report back to our jobs in D.C. It felt good to be speaking English again. I was even a little happy to see Fred Burns. With Don and Frank back in the group, I'd only be one of three people that had to put up with him.

We squeezed ourselves into the *Volvo* that Burns rented in Frankfurt. Thank Goodness for that luggage rack. Even with two suitcases strapped to the roof of the car, there wasn't quite enough room in the trunk for all our stuff. Don and I wound up sharing the back seat with Fred's canvas bag.

We were off to visit Don's relatives in Reggio de Calabria, on the toe of the Italian boot, just across from Sicily. After about an hour Burns started getting tired. Who could blame him. All three had taken turns driving, since they had Breakfast in Frankfurt. So I volunteered to take the wheel for the 250-mile trip ahead. When we pulled into the *Jolly Motel* around midnight, my three partners could've sacked out right there in the parking lot. But we *all* mustered one last shred of endurance, dragged our luggage into the lobby, and checked in. Two double rooms with twin beds. This time Frank Stichter had the pleasure of Burns' company, and I bunked with Santini.

Next morning we called up the chief *Goombah* of the Santini family in Reggio, and drove over to meet all Don's aunts, uncles, and cousins, who seemed to comprise half the city's population. Don had visited these same folks a couple of times in the last ten years, so he knew everybody by their first name. He even was re- introduced to Adrianna, a five foot, one hundred and fifty pound *signorina* that his Aunt Carmella had tried to matchmake with him only three years before. Don proved to be a skillful liar, as he explained to Adrianna that he had a fiancée back in Queens. The nuptials were set for the summer of 1970, after his Army discharge. We all backed him up on his little fib. Donaldo's fiancée? Lovely girl. Schoolteacher. Her father's a Doctor. Sure, everybody in Reggio would be invited to the ceremony! Poor Adrianna was crushed at this unexpected news. She was already twenty years old. Two more years and she'd be an old maid.

And now time for the feast to begin. Out came the buckets of macaroni, drenched with thick Calabrese Sauce, that reeked gloriously of garlic. Sausages and peppers, calamari and mussels. A two day celebration. We all ate and enjoyed. I stifled my urge to practice my Italian conversation with any of Don's *paesani*. They all spoke such an indecipherable dialect that I couldn't understand much more than Stichter and Burns could. But Don's cousin Ernesto did speak a little English that he learned as a waiter in a London hotel three years before. I almost fell on my ass when I heard him come out in Calabrian flavored Cockney, "Attsa bloomin' shame, you gotta go! You chapsa shoulda stay wit us another fortanighta!"

But we had to start heading back home on Thursday. We all had to be in uniform and ready for duty next Monday morning. We couldn't take any chances. Colonel Black was a nice enough guy, but after that business with security last Christmas I couldn't take any chances. After all, they did still have a thing called AWOL. The Air force Base at Torrejon, Spain, seemed like the best bet to catch a flight back to Dover or even Fort Dix

Before booking a fairly cheap civilian flight from Rome to Madrid, we returned Fred's *Rent-a Volvo* to the *Hertz* office at Rome Airport. Splitting the car rental fee four ways came to less than eighty bucks apiece. I wasn't about to nickel and dime Fred Burns, who had the exclusive use of the *Volvo* for a week. After all, I had the best vacation of the four of us—by far.

Don was all excited about this brief stop in Madrid. He'd spent a year at the University there, studying Spanish after college. But we only had at most a day in the Capital. We just didn't have the time for another fiasco like the one at Dover air Force Base.

We arrived in Madrid about 10:00 P.M. , just in time for dinner. Don took us to the *Student Prince*, an astoundingly cheap *taverna* near the University, where *Arroz con Pollo* for *four* and a couple of pitchers of *Sangria* cost only about fifteen bucks—total. The food was adequate and the portions huge, but I'd been spoiled by Neapolitan and Calabrese home cooking for more than a week, so I didn't feast with my usual *gusto*. I was still tasting that garlic bread sopping up all that wonderful sauce. In two days I'd be home. Nothing to look forward to but my staple recipes of meatloaf, chili, hamburgers with fries, and franks 'n beans. An unexciting menu of carbohydrates and cholesterol, that would be a disappointing change.

Bad news from the Air Force. Flights taking passengers were slow and there was a waiting line of fifteen people ahead of us. AWOL time, unless we moved fast. As long as they didn't stick me in the same cell as Fred Burns.

By Saturday morning we'd already given up on getting a free air lift home. We took a taxi to Madrid Airport, and headed for Iberian Airlines. Last minute booking. No Washington D.C. flights available. Wait a minute. Four passengers. Some space left. Flight 434 to JFK. Departing 6:00 P.M. Spanish time. ETA New York- 8:00 P.M. EDT. Cost one way $300. We had no choice. So we put everything on Fred Burns credit card. He was the only one of us to bring his along. So much for Air Force "courtesy" flights. *Operation Free Flight* was a flop.

But we'd be in New York by 8:00 P.M. Two A.M. to our exhausted bodies. Then we'd have to rent a car at JFK. With luck we might catch some sleep on the plane. Pray that there wouldn't be any crying babies on board. Arrive in Dover at 11:00 P.M. Pick up my Bonneville at the Base. Split into two teams. Drive both cars to Washington D.C., the closest city with a 24-hour Hertz drop off. Then we'd all transfer to my car, and head for our apartment in Falls Church. Without any hitches we'd be able to collapse into bed at 2:00 A.M.— 7:00 A.M. Madrid time.

Then we all could relax a little, and sleep all day Sunday. As for me, I'd make it into ISB by 0600 hours Monday morning, fighting off a dozen kinds of jet lag. Maybe I could drink a half-gallon of coffee, and survive the day. By Wednesday everything might be normal again.

There were no snags in the Saturday night plan. Don and I got back about Two-thirty in the morning. We paid no attention to that horrible musty smell of non-use that pervaded our apartment after a few weeks of vacation. I opened the window, and stripped down to my underwear. I kicked of my shoes and flopped onto the bed. There's no place like home.

# CHAPTER FORTY-SIX

# The Drowning of Camelot

While the country was being consumed by *Moon Fever* in that summer of 1969, an incident on a rickety bridge in Massachusetts, was to change the course of American politics. Teddy Kennedy had been involved in a tragic accident with a young campaign volunteer named Mary Jo Kopechne at some island called Chappaquidick. It didn't look good. A married man alone with a pretty young girl. Late at night. Liquor. But this paled in comparison to the aftermath. After Ted had run his car off the bridge, he apparently abandoned the drowning Kennedy groupie, and swam back to shore. Then he told the police a story full of holes, which he revised a few days later.

The nation was running out of Kennedys. The pick of the litter (Joe Jr., John, and Bobby) were already gone. Teddy was the least accomplished of the clan. He had graduated from U. Va. Law School eight years before I did. He was next to last in his class, beating out only John Tunney, U.S. Senator from California, son of the former heavyweight champ. It was rumored that Ted was such a campus Casanova that on any given Friday night, he could call up *Mary Baldwin College* for girls, down the road, speak with the dormitory counselor for a moment and announce his arrival. In a couple of hours he'd show up to meet a line of adoring females waiting to make with the sexual favors.

Nixon and Agnew couldn't have been more ecstatic at this turn of events. Ted had not only shot himself in the foot; he had *blown it off!*

There weren't too many Democrats around with name recognition to put up much of a struggle with them in 1972. Humphrey was through. Eugene McCarthy was perceived as a radical hippie lover. Not much left to choose from. In America the voter has two realistic choices for President, Republican or Democrat; vanilla or chocolate; meat or dairy. Of course in 1968 he had a third choice —*arsenic*, if he decided to choose George Wallace.

Washington was buzzing about the incident for days. It almost replaced the *Apollo Project* over morning coffee. The Pentagon is the biggest civilian employer in Washington D.C. I used to say that it was perfectly designed so that gossip could travel from the front entrance to the most remote parking space in the unreserved lot in the shortest time imaginable.

And it was a Mecca for visitors. Business and tourist alike. They came in droves. Guys from ISB were always meeting CIA personnel, people from DIA and other agencies. And they knew guys from the FBI, who knew guys, who knew other guys…who knew all about Chappaquiddick.

Summertime at the Pentagon was when rumor could really run rampant. You see, the dead center of the complex was a pleasant two-acre outdoor courtyard. We called it Ground Zero. The exact prime target for the first Soviet missile to be launched at the United States. It was dotted with kiosks selling hamburgers, hot dogs, French fries, and salads that you could eat at cozy tables next to flower bushes. At lunchtime hordes of miniskirted secretaries crossed their shapely legs at these tables. So naturally most of the male employees followed along to ogle the girls while they ate. Generals and corporals; sailors and marines; all took advantage of the pleasant atrium at one time or other.

Rod Burton and I met there a couple of days after the "incident" at Martha's Vineyard. He ran into a fellow named Brian Curtis, who used to be with the Defense Department. Brian saw no harm in using his D.O.D. contacts to make a little profit for himself now that he was a civilian. A phone call here; a handshake there; and suddenly he'd negotiated the

XYZ Widget Company a five million dollar contract to furnish the Department with dog tags. As agent for XYZ he made a tidy commission, as well as a reputation as a guy who got things done.

Maybe he wanted to impress Rod and me. Most likely he wanted his voice to carry and be heard by the two incredibly stacked secretaries sitting at the next table. Maybe he'd approach them later with some line of bullshit.

Brian began yakking like an old washerwoman about Chappaquiddick. It was mind boggling how he managed to interweave every possible rumor, from the barely plausible to the absolutely ridiculous during our hour lunch. Everything from cocaine use to involvement of the Red Chinese Government—all unsubstantiated. But I listened attentively as he rambled on and fed off our obvious curiosity, when we asked "Is that a fact?" or "You really think so?"

I tried to separate the totally absurd from the possibly truthful allegations he was making but I soon gave up. I just filed them all in my memory bank under *Tabloid Trash*. Maybe I'd get a chance to use them in the next few weeks when trying to impress a secretary of my own.

# CHAPTER FORTY-SEVEN

# The "Other Kind" of Football

"Captain Woolsey, do you know anything about Soccer?" General McChristian asked me, right after my briefing, out of the blue, one mid-July morning.

His query was occasioned by the mini war that had broken out between Honduras and El Salvador, the direct result of a violent Soccer Match in Tegucigalpa.

The war was a satirist's dream. Comics like the Monty Python troop could have milked laughs out of the thing for days. A 1960's battle being fought with World War I equipment. The "attack" planes were F-51's, a model only marginally more advanced than *Snoopy's* Sopwith Camel in his dogfights against the Red Baron. Half the aircraft barely flew, and the other half were used mainly for spare parts.

The rusty guns didn't fire, and when they did, the chances of the bullet coming out the front end of the barrel to exploding in the rifleman's hand were about 50-50. This unpredictable adventure with a carbine caused a good number of Honduran and Salvadoran *campesinos* to throw away their weapons, and beat a hasty retreat *a casa*. The rest of the brave and foolhardy were awarded chestfuls of the Central American version of our *Purple Heart* for their missing thumbs and forefingers.

But it *was* the only war we'd had in the Western Hemisphere for about 40 years, so the *old man* had some concern. I wondered what he was up to.

"No, General, "I answered." Except that I find the sport pretty boring, being raised watching *American* football on TV."

"Me too," he said. "But El Salvador and Honduras thought the game thrilling enough to go to war over. So maybe you can give me a two-minute briefing about it tomorrow morning, Nothing too elaborate. Just a summary of the rules, and what the final score was that set this whole conflagration off."

"Yes General," I said, as I folded my script, and exited the War Room.

Even the most minor request of a Major General is like a something etched on a tablet on Mount Sinai. So Colonel Black gave me the whole day away from my desk to come up with something. I was to call up the *Washington Post* Sports Department, get my ass down there, and take notes on everything they could tell me about Soccer. I had to be back by three o'clock to work with Mr. Johnson on a two-minute draft for tomorrow morning. See if there was a book at their library diagramming a Soccer field that maybe had a picture of Pele or somebody. Ed Hogan was to give me all the visual effects help I needed.

I called the *Post*, and told them all about my assignment. They were glad to help out. After all, another contact at the Pentagon, any contact, was always a good thing for a newspaper to have.

Sam Jefferson drove me down to D.C.'s most prestigious daily, the future oracle of Messrs. Woodward and Bernstein only three years hence. I walked inside and was directed to the cubicle of Marty Pelligrino, Assistant Sports Editor.

"Delighted to help you out, Captain," he said, "But you'd probably get the real skinny at any Italian delicatessen or Mexican Taco Joint downtown. However, I *did* dig up the only book we have on the game, which you're welcome to borrow, if you promise to bring it back next week. Like yourself, I'm just a junior grade officer around here. The librarian downstairs'll probably charge me an additional ten cents a day, if I keep the thing more than a week."

Then he took a piece of foolscap paper from his desk. He drew a rough sketch of a soccer field, and noted down its dimensions, the number and positions of the different players, the goal area and so forth. Then he went on to explain the basic "hands off the ball" policy that applied to everybody but the goalkeeper; a brief definition of "offsides" that I still don't quite understand (Try not to be closer to the other guys' goal than the ball ); the length of the game; and the almost divine authority of the sole referee, who could, by awarding a penalty kick, determine the outcome of the whole contest. He also had an opinion why the damned sport was so popular everywhere but the United States. Americans like to see their gladiators *huge*. Heavyweight boxers. Jumbo linemen. Seven foot Centers. In Soccer, size doesn't count. A little fella has as much chance to score as a Goliath.

Soccer was inexpensive to play too! No equipment other than the ball was necessary. No bat; no helmet; no net; no shoulder pads; no gloves; and no fancy field or court to play on. So a few kids in Brazil could chip in a couple of *cruzieros* apiece to buy a beat up ball, and—Presto! Twenty two boys have a game. For ninety minutes the cops down in Rio don't have to worry about some juvenile delinquents picking pockets or swiping fruit. Finally he gave me the little blurb that the newspaper had published on the Honduras-El Salvador game. I thanked him and had to head back to Sam's awaiting sedan, before I dozed off at Marty's desk. His explanation of Soccer was almost as boring as the game itself.

While Sam was driving me back, I made a short outline of tomorrow's script. Then we stopped at a *McDonald's*, and I bought both of us some hamburgers and coffee. ISB generously funded its personnel, that left the office on business, a *whole five dollars* as reimbursement for "eats" in town.

I got back around three o'clock to confer with Mr. Johnson, who thought that this Soccer research project was just a silly waste of time. But, if it kept the General happy—?

We worked up a presentation that Howard Cosell himself would've been proud of. Ed made a special slide with detailed over laps depicting miniature halfbacks, forwards, and goalkeepers strategically placed to score and defend. Colonel Black approved. GOOOOAAAAALLLL!

So while US astronauts were heading for the moon, and Teddy Kennedy was swerving his car off some bridge in Martha's Vineyard, I was busy explaining the subtleties of the world's favorite sport to the Head of Army Intelligence, who thanked me for a job well done.

By the way, the score was El Salvador 1-Honduras 0.

# CHAPTER FORTY-EIGHT

# Good News for a Change

That third week of July 1969, while the country was still reeling from the Chappaquiddick incident, we finally got something to cheer about. For the last few years , Americans just seemed to suffer blow, after blow, after blow. JFK assassinated; the endless war in Southeast Asia; King murdered; Bobby Kennedy killed; riots at the Chicago Convention; hard-hats clashing with students. Finally we got a break.

At 6:00 P.M. Eastern Daylight Time, July 27th, 1969, Neil Armstrong set his foot on the surface of the Moon. It couldn't compensate for the lives of 45,000 dead soldiers, but it brought a smile even to the lips of those America Hating bastards like Abby Hoffman and Eldridge Cleaver. US scientists using US equipment had finally overcome the *Sputnik Complex* that loomed over the nation since the Soviets launched that dinky satellite into outer space.

And we made History without having to blow anything up; we didn't have to invade anybody; and it was probably just as much of a triumph for *all* mankind as it was for the United States. For Gallileo, Newton, Copernicus, and Einstein, as well as a couple of thousand scientists working twenty hours a day at a lab in Houston. The scientific equivalent of shooting a dime dead center with a pistol at five hundred yards.

We all just sat silently in front of our TV sets, watching the Apollo resting on the *Sea of Tranquillity*. The newscasters didn't even have to speak. Every so often Brinkley or Cronkite would interject some inane

212

filler about Buzz Aldren's mom and dad, or the design of the spacesuit. But mostly we just watched, content to see the camera beaming back a picture of the Earth from a quarter of a million miles away.

Back in the War Room the General Staff was curious about this incredible event. At one briefing General McChristian, just in passing, wondered out loud about the possibility of some biological threat to mankind by a bacteria or microscopic life form brought back to Earth by a contaminated spacecraft. Maybe some *supergerm* that stubbornly burrowed into Armstrong's boot and miraculously survived the return voyage. I don't think he really expected an answer.

But Colonel Black went bonkers. Since this wasn't the province of any particular ISB desk, he picked three officers at random to research the project. Major Carson of the Vietnam Desk, Rod Burton at West Europe, and I were granted a two day sabbatical from our daily duties to come up with a twenty page report, that could be further distilled down to one summary page. Comprehensive, yet simple enough for even a two star general to understand.

Carson gave Rod and me an hour to list fifty possible sources that might even have *data* concerning the *old man's* request. NASA, the Surgeon General, Walter Reed Hospital, the Smithsonian and Georgetown were just a few of the temples of science that we came up with. For the next thirty six hours we all were on the phone with , or personally interviewing guys and women with lab jackets, and coke bottle glasses, or reading articles that touched on our inquiry. Finally the three of us divided the project into (1) the possibility of *any* kind of life on the moon; (2) whether it could be transported to earth by accident; and (3) the *Twilight Zone* question, would this lunar virus spread and obliterate mankind. Rod Burton was assigned this Science Fiction portion of the Paper. Unfortunately he was a big *Star Trek* fan and fantasy poisoned his reason. Scientific Analysis went out the window, and at one point I thought that he was going to list footnotes on *Klingons, Tribbles,* and *Scotty's Transport Beam.*

But Carson did a good job of organization, and we got out a twenty-page paper with valid documentation and reference cites. Then we boiled it down to a single page. I could've boiled it down to a single sentence. E.g. *The scientific community hasn't got the foggiest goddam idea about an answer to your question, General!*

Colonel Black told me to present the one page answer at the morning briefing two days after the question had been posed. General McChristian thanked our office for its painstaking research. He asked me to leave all of our findings with Lt. Colonel Brewer of his staff, and he'd try to take a look at them. He never brought up the subject again.

# CHAPTER FORTY-NINE

# All Quiet on the Western Front

I had begun my tour of duty at ISB the same time as Captain Rodney Burton. Rod was a career officer that took over the Western European Desk that I'd been sort of promised. He'd served one year at a post just outside of Munich. So much for his expertise in West European affairs. He'd also served for a year in Vietnam and later had taken the Army's Language Saturation Course in *Serbo-Croatian!* Rod , unlike Major Cachuk , at least had some borderline qualifications for ISB. He *was* an Intelligence Officer and possessed an IQ of more than two digits. But , dammit , he took my *job* away. Colonel Black and Mr. Johnson were both pretty smart guys, so I suppose they had their reasons for giving him that position, but I thought that they made a mistake.

Rod had a plum assignment. Like Jeff Pritchard and Gary Maggio had told me back at Fort Holabird, the West Europe slot was a cinch. It was like one of those airplane spotters in Nebraska during World War II, whose mission was to look for Nazi aircraft over Omaha. And boy did they do a *terrific* job. Not one German plane got west of the Mississippi River during the *entire war.*

The purpose of our office was to report on matters that might affect US Army strategy around the World. Some conflict or possible future conflict that might have consequences for our forces. Some diplomatic blockbuster, like President DeGaulle resigning was undeniably important, but it had no real bearing on the mission of our little unit. Every so

215

often, we'd get a report about the French Air Force developing a new plane or tank, and Colonel Black would OK a twenty second blurb about the thing. Then the Oral Briefing team would show a picture of the Eiffel Tower just to have something up on the screen for a few moments to make the presentation look a little professional.

I asked the Colonel why we just didn't show a picture of any old French aircraft or tank that would seem to reflect the gist of the report more accurately. He said in no uncertain terms that any attempt to do that was *verboten*. Joe McChristian prided himself on knowing just about every NATO and Warsaw Pact aircraft and piece of ordnance like the back of his hand. He'd spot any attempt to try and pass off the substitute in about two seconds. Then he'd chew out Black's ass for five minutes at the post briefing conference for trying to put one over on the *old man*.

No! If the British were developing some new military hardware , we'd show our standard slide of Buckingham Palace. If the Italians invented something new, we'd use the Tower of Pisa slide. And on the remote chance that the Dutch came up with something, then we'd show that stupid slide of a *Windmill* that was gathering dust in our files.

Meanwhile Rod was itching to make some kind of contribution to ISB. Even a token article. In August of 1969 he finally got his chance. British troops moved into Northern Ireland, and there was actually the possibility of a limited war. No extended conflict between Great Britain and Eire, of course, but a deployment of British Armored Units on the streets of Belfast. Maybe a sniper war. British regulars being killed. Shades of 1921 and the Black and Tans. So for about a week Rod felt useful. He'd research his files, and I'd see him running back and forth to check the reports from our Intelligence Services. During that brief time, if anybody in the office even *attempted* to engage him in a routine fifteen second conversation about the weather, he'd continue staring down at his papers, and tell the offending party that he was too busy to discuss any irrelevant bullshit. And *this* from a guy who was used to doing Crossword Puzzles, and loitering around the coffee urn, waiting for somebody to talk to.

But by the end of August, the Northern Irish situation calmed down a bit. The prospects of escalation became remote, and Rod went back to his Crossword Puzzles. Good thing too! We were fast running out of interest slides. Fortunately I was able to convince Major Loomis not to show that picture of a leprechaun, that he had Ed Cogan make up. I persuaded him that it was the kind of thing that would be more appropriate for a report on a *Notre Dame* football game than a sniper war. Besides most folks thought of the *"Little Payple"* as being Southern Irish elves.

But Loomis wanted to come up with *something* new. We'd already shown the map of Northern Ireland; the picture of an armed British Soldier in front of a Belfast Pub; and a beautiful shot of the Giants' Causeway, Northern Ireland's biggest tourist attraction. Loomis had picked it up one afternoon from the British Embassy. But he didn't tell them that it was destined to be made into a transparency for an Army Intelligence Briefing. He told me that they were just so pleased that *anybody* might be interested in Northern Irish tourism, that they loaded him down with travel brochures and Airline information; pamphlets on Belfast's best hotels, and a lot of other crap that they never thought they'd be able to get rid of. We ended up tossing them into the burn bag.

## CHAPTER FIFTY

# What Happened to Your Crewcut?

A short time after that, one morning after the briefings were over, Loomis, Gilmore and I were trying to keep busy, when Sergeant Rivera at the front desk buzzed me over the intercom.

"Cap-Captain Woolsey, there's a gentleman out here in the lobby that says he's an old friend of yours. His name's LeBron, Carl LeBron. He's wondering if maybe you could meet him out here at the front desk for a few moments. What should I tell him, sir?" Rivera asked.

"Tell him that I'll be right out , Sergeant," I said. Then I turned to Major Loomis. "If it's OK with you sir, I'd like to see how the former Lieutenant of the Latin American desk, now turned civilian, is making it in the real world. Do you remember him sir? I don't recall whether he was still around when you arrived?"

"He left about a week before I got here," Loomis answered. "Sure you can go. Take him out for coffee and a Danish for *Auld Lang Syne*. I'll see ya when you're finished talking over the good old days with him. "

I grabbed my jacket from the clothes rack, and put it on while walking past the desk officers, then through the outer office where Marilyn and Sergeant Haskell sat. I finished buttoning my last button, and then opened the front door leading to the miniature lobby. I looked down at Sergeant Rivera, and then my eyes took a classic double take, as they beheld the metamorphosized form of the erstwhile First Lieutenant Carl

Lebron, who in the seven short months since his departure from ISB, had been transformed into the poster child for the hippie movement.

He was still as lean and muscular as ever, but his once neatly trimmed crew cut had sprouted into a mop of uncombed black curls that reached down to his shoulders. They were partially secured by a red sweatband around his forehead, and fastened into a ponytail by a rubber band in back. He wore wire-rimmed sunglasses, and sported a long disheveled beard that partially hid the three or four strings of beads around his neck. The tee shirt that he was wearing read *I Survived Woodstock*; and his faded blue jeans had the obligatory rips and tears that *maybe* could have been genuine if Carl had spent the last seven months living exclusively in a briar patch. His "white?" sweatsocks that had never been subjected to the wonders of bleach were partly covered by his brown sandals.

"Peace, Carl!" I blurted out, assuming that to be the customary greeting in Hippiedom.

"Peace to you too, Bob!" he responded politely.

"Let's take a walk to the coffee shop, before Colonel Black wanders by, sees what's become of his once upon a time favorite desk officer, and has a heart attack," I said. "C'mon! I'll treat you to an Imperialist doughnut and a Fascist cup of coffee."

We headed down the escalator to the practically deserted *coffeeteria* on the first floor. We met a few stares as we walked through the corridors, but most folks were already used to seeing longhaired rebels roaming the Pentagon. It was, after all, a federal building, completely open to the public—at least in *those* days anyway; and many an Admiral or General had lost a son or a daughter to the army of flower children that seemed to be everywhere. Carl might very well have been the prodigal son of Westmoreland himself paying a visit to dear old dad.

We entered the coffee shop.

"My treat!" I said. "If memory serves, you used to take your coffee black with two sugars. And you were partial to glazed sweet rolls. I guess that *now* your tastes run more to soybean cakes and herbal tea."

He tilted back his head and laughed.

"Just because I don't feel like conforming to standard dress codes anymore," he said, "doesn't mean that I've lost my craving for caffeine and junk food; or that I'm ready to join a Buddhist Monastery in Tibet, for Chrissake. I practically live on Big Macs and Kentucky Fried Chicken. I also laugh at reruns of *I Love Lucy* and Jackie Gleason. And I never miss an L.A. Dodger game if it's on TV. Don't believe all the government propaganda that we've all been hypnotized into some weird cult. By the way you can get me *two* glazed donuts with that black coffee!"

I did Carl's bidding, walked to the serve yourself food counter, picked up a tray, and loaded it with four doughnuts, two coffees, several packets of sugar, and three non dairy creamers. Then I paid the cashier and returned to our table.

"Your tee shirt says that you were at Woodstock," I said. "How was it?"

"Hot and crowded," he answered. "Most of the time I spent looking for an unoccupied toilet. During the rest I got high, got laid, and listened to the music. Meanwhile the organizers were trying too hard to cram the spirit of rebellion down everybody's throats. You know, like some hippie Storm Troopers. ' You *will* have sex! You *will* get stoned ! You *will* enjoy the rock bands blaring away over the giant loudspeakers!' After the first couple of days, I would've traded all the pleasures of the flesh for a nice hot bath."

"Now that you've gotten some of the orgy lust out of your system, what's the future look like for citizen Lebron?" I asked.

"Well, next week I begin graduate work in Latin American studies at Georgetown. I *am* a veteran, so getting a student loan was easy. Before I get down to serious work, maybe I'll call Len Roth and Gary Maggio tomorrow, and invite them over for drinks this Friday night. Feel free to come along, if you like. 7:30 P.M.—or 1930 hours, if your still thinking in military time. The address is 15 Marigold Lane, Apartment 4D, Georgetown. My telephone number's in the book in case you forget. I'll provide the drinks, but a donation by you of a bucket of extra crispy chicken wings from the *Colonel* would be greatly appreciated."

We bullshitted a bit more, took leave of each other until Friday, and I headed back to ISB. A couple of hours later Colonel Black walked into the Oral Briefers' Room. I was at my desk.

"Major Loomis tells me that Carl LeBron stopped by to see you this morning. How's he doing?" Black asked.

" He seems very *content* as a civilian, sir," I answered.

"I wonder why he didn't at least call my office to say hello?" he asked.

"I guess he figured that you and Mr. Johnson were busy preparing for your Tuesday afternoon conference with General Berelli," I said. "But I'm sure that he'll drop by as soon as he's settled into his new apartment. He's taking some courses at Georgetown, sir."

"You're probably right, Bob," Black said." I'm glad to hear that he's already made plans for a successful career. I just *know* that there are great things in store for him. He was always a first rate officer. Dependable. Loyal. A team player. You could learn a thing or two from him, Bob. Maybe do things the *Army* way a little more. Did you know that Carl had offers from the Baltimore Orioles and L.A. Rams to try out. But I suppose he's decided to make his fortune in the Corporate World. Yes indeed, with Carl's looks, intelligence, and social skills, I have no doubt that in fifteen years he'll be the President of Xerox or IBM. Don't you agree?"

I nodded yes, but thought to myself. "He'd better get a shave and a haircut before he meets with Chairman of the Board."

# CHAPTER FIFTY-ONE

# Deliverance

Carl phoned me a couple of days after his little get together. He'd just heard through the hippie grapevine that a pal of his from Woodstock had received a teaching fellowship at Princeton starting immediately. Everything in his buddy's Alexandria, Virginia apartment was on the auction block, including hundreds of books up for grabs at only a dime apiece. There were lamps , paintings, appliances, and furniture too. All you had to do was pay cash, and cart the swag away.

Carl knew that I could cram about a ton of this stuff into the trunk and back seat of my king size Bonneville, so I was the first person that he thought of. And his motives weren't entirely selfish either. *I* might be able to enhance the *Salvation Army* decor of my own place with a couple of framed posters and assorted bric-a-brac. But it was the lure of being able to plunder a good chunk of this guy's huge personal library that convinced me to go. Carl said that the card catalogue ranged from Shakespeare to Mickey Spillane. And because of my early quitting time at work, we could get the jump on all the other prospective buyers.

So we arranged to meet at a halfway point between Georgetown and the Pentagon, a mini-mall in Arlington, about fifteen minutes from the garage sale. There was a small eatery called *Nick's Diner* that would be our rendezvous.

At the Pentagon, I changed into the civilian clothes that I'd brought from home the same morning. I left the Pentagon parking lot at around

2:15, and was in front of *Nick's* by 2:30. I looked for Carl's *Carmen Ghia*, but he evidently hadn't yet arrived.

I went into the diner to wait for Carl and have a cup of coffee. The place was practically deserted except for a truck driver just finishing his hamburger with fries, and four boisterous locals, who had clearly been making good use of Nick's beer license, spending what I assumed were their unemployment insurance checks, on dozens of ice cold brews.

I sat down at a small booth, ordered a coffee from the waitress, whose nametag read Molly, and lit up a cigarette. Carl showed up five minutes later.

"Are we ready to roll?" I asked him.

"Finish your coffee first," he answered. "We have enough time. The sale of the century won't start until 3 o'clock anyway."

Then the four rednecks in the booth across from us started mouthing off.

"Hey, hippie faggot!" shouted the fat one, with the snake tattoo, wearing the dirty blue polo shirt. "You sure got some nice pony tail. Ah'm partial to long hair muhself. Y'all must be one o' them Yankee queers, come down to try an' seduce us Southern boys."

"That's a good 'un, Vern," said one of his three sycophant companions.

Carl ignored him.

"Ah'm talkin' to you, pretty boy," the flabby one continued, encouraged by the giggling approval of his toadies. "I guess yo' momma musta' took a break from smokin' dope long enough to screw some trav'lin' salesman, and have a baby girl like yo'self."

Then Carl stood up. Fatso had picked the wrong guy to mess with. The pony tailed Mr. Lebron had a second degree Black Belt in karate, and had been proficient enough in hand to hand combat at Infantry School, to be chosen as an instructor for a few months. He nonchalantly took off his sunglasses, and lay them on our table. Then he walked over to the townies.

There were four of them, squeezed into the booth—the fat, snake tattooed slob, who was the leader of the pack, and three scrawny under-lings. All of them were in their mid-thirties. Vern, the fat one, and his second in command, began standing to meet Carl's challenge. With commando quickness, Carl slammed the edge of his opened hand down across the scrawny guy's nose, dropping him back into his seat. His.2% alcohol level blood spurted all over the table and floor. Then he reached for a couple of dozen paper napkins from their heavy steel dispenser to apply to his broken nose, to stop the blood. He tilted back his head. Scrawny had been in bar fights before.

A microsecond after Carl had immobilized the first drunk, he grabbed Fatso Vern's stringy blond hair with his left hand, shoved him down in his seat, and stuck his right thumb into the rear of his jaw. From where I was sitting, he practically buried it all the way to his skull. Vern let out a high pitched scream. Then Carl released the guy's hair, and motioned him to be silent with his left index finger at his lips.

"This is your lucky day, fat boy," Carl said. "I've got to go soon, so I'm not going to kill you. But move your head an inch either way, and you'll be in a coma for six weeks. However, before my friend and I go, I'd like an apology from you—a written one. Waitress! This gentleman needs a pencil. Could I borrow yours, please?"

The stunned Molly edged cautiously towards Carl, removed the yellow #2 pencil, nestled in her bouffant hairdo, and handed it to him.

"Thank you, Miss!" he said politely, and then glaring at the defense-less redneck, "Now, you flabby son of a bitch, write down what I tell you on that menu! Start! All four of us…impotent cock suckers…apologize to…Carl…Bob…and everybody in Nick's Diner…for being such assholes…Now sign it!"

As the blubbering victim gingerly wrote down Carl's words, the rest of the now docile group, were openly indifferent to their leader's plight. Scrawny number one, with the broken nose, had improvised a cold compress for his wound, by soaking a whole bunch of paper napkins in the glass of his frosty malt liquor. Scrawny II and Scrawny III were trying to hide their embarrassment and defeat, by pretending to read the menu, and studying the ingredients of a packet of *Sweet 'n Low* respectively.

Carl finally released the trembling Vern from his death grip, and told the four whipped dogs to get out. They wasted no time wriggling out from the booth, and rushing toward the cashier's counter, where they each dropped a ten dollar bill, that more than covered their tabs. Then they scurried out the door before Nick, serving as his own cashier, could give them change. Then Nick came over to Carl, who was just about to apologize for the scuffle in the man's place of business.

But before Carl could get a word out, Nick patted him on the back. Then he said in the thickest Greek accent. "Don' 'pologize for nuthin'! For a lonk time thoss besterds been pullin' shit 'round here. Mekkin' dirty cracks to my waitresses. Insultin' customers. But I don' lak troubles. And they got lotsa frens too. Besides, callink cops iss bad for bus'-ness. Thenks to you I don' need no cops now. Thoss cripps won' be back soon. You can beeliff itt. An' my fren, nex time you come here, I gonna make you my spessiel Rack uff Lam'- Athens style—Brink you fren'! Brink anybody you lak! No charge. You remin' me Molly, OK?"

Well, we finally made it to the garage sale/auction. Carl got a great buy on a recliner, that just barely fit into my back seat. The both of us carried away a couple of boxes of books too, for less than five bucks apiece. Two of Carl's selections were Gandhi's *Policy of Nonviolence,* and *Pacifism and Politics* by James Finn.

# CHAPTER FIFTY-TWO

# Another Middle East Madman

In September 1969, US Intelligence was once again surprised by a coup in the Middle East. This time it was a young hothead from Libya. His name was Mu'umar Qaddafi, and he promised the Libyan people nationalization of everything from oil companies to pay toilets.

Of particular concern to the General Staff was the probable loss of Wheelus Air Force Base, a strategic goldmine to the American Armed Forces. We could keep our troops smack in the middle of North Africa, where we could keep close tabs on Algeria to the West, and Egypt to the East. The use of this facility had been granted us by Good King Idris, an ally who would've handed Tripoli itself over to the Western Powers if we asked him *reeaal* nice.

Qaddafi was yet one more on the growing list of unstable dictators, of the Nero variety, that were dominating Middle East Politics. A couple of months earlier, General Nimieri had seized the Sudan; Saddam Hussein and company controlled Iraq. And every two weeks a different group of revolutionaries was seizing power in Damascus. Nasser was looking more and more like the voice of reason and moderation. But our Intelligence *geniuses* were at least sure of one thing. Besides Israel, we could be absolutely certain that the *Shah of Iran* would be a staunch ally of the US for decades to come! A buffer against the Soviet Union for the next hundred years.

But in Libya it was time for the Intelligence folks at Wheelus to get out the paper shredders and dust off their passports. Because *we* were on our way out!

I had a personal reason for hating Mr. Qaddafi. Here was a guy, a year *younger* than myself, who at the tender age of twenty six, had reached the pinnacle of *his* career as a bloodthirsty tyrant. I, on the other hand , was still marking time at my go nowhere job at the Pentagon. By the time I even *started* my legal thing , *he* would already have committed hundreds of brutal murders of his countrymen, and tortured and imprisoned thousands more.

There was a minor flap over which desk was to take charge in the coup follow up. Major Cachuk, who now had seized control of the African Intelligence Desk after Pritchard's departure, insisted that Libya fell under his sphere of influence. He begrudgingly conceded Egypt to Gary Maggio at Middle East, but would not budge an inch in surrendering Libya. Colonel Black didn't want to pull rank on this dispute, but Cachuk *was* the senior officer so the Major took charge in determining what would be submitted for inclusion in the Black Book , But Gary would be responsible for any questions from the General staff on the matter

I took some interest in the radical proposals of this newest Mid East lunatic. For instance, one of these "radical"proposals was to eliminate landlords. All tenants would become windfall owners of their apartments. My own landlord at my recently rented high rise was abusing his power as Lord of the Manor. The central air conditioning was non-existent, and my car had been broken into in our "secure" parking lot twice and my stereo had been ripped off. So this "tenant takeover" sounded pretty good to me at the time. Even a madman comes up with a hell of an idea every now and then.

# CHAPTER FIFTY-THREE

# Birthday Party with Some Counter Culture

It was November 15th, 1969, my twenty-eighth birthday. Most of the guys that I graduated with from college already had careers, wives, kids, and a house with a suffocating mortgage by that time. The American dream. But I consoled myself. This would be my last birthday in uniform. In fact, in less than four months I'D be *out*. No more 4:30 A.M. alarm clock. A leisurely breakfast at 10:A.M. Not saying sir to *anybody*. *La Dolce Vita*.

Today was a special day for Washington D.C. too. A couple of hundred thousand anti-war demonstrators were invading the Capital, with their beads and flowers. The Pentagon expected a whole bunch of stragglers from the Capitol Lawn to wend their way to us before the day was out. Photographers and reporters were all over the place-you know, hoping for some kind of repeat of the Democratic National Convention last year. Their prayer was for Nixon to surround the building with a Division of armed riflemen, with orders to shoot to kill. Maybe even get a couple of good close angle shots of an innocent bystander or two being mowed down in the crossfire. But somebody with a whole lot of clout had passed the word down, that there was to be *no* confrontation. Every military man and woman was to *outChrist* Christ himself and turn the other cheek- *any* cheek if assaulted. Nixon had already taken sufficient heat from some of his nice middle class Republican supporters, who were getting sick and tired of wasting tax dollars, fighting a war that seemed endless. For Christ sake, we just put a man on the Moon! Couldn't we just exterminate ten or twenty million North Vietnamese with a little H-Bomb and get thus thing over with? *Nuke* the bastards, or bring the boys home. This war had already destroyed the 1960's. Let's start the next decade by letting whatever dictator the CIA had installed that day kick some enthusiasm into *his own* troops and have them fight their own battles.

Now I was just a Pentagon Pawn. But it was clear to me that Nixon was , in his own devious way, getting the" Peace with Honor" that he liked to talk about so much. The *Honor* part just meant that we'd get the hell out of there—but in our own sweet time. So it wouldn't look like we were being forced out. The *Peace* part just meant that the North Vietnamese would take over in a few years, and slaughter the hated opposition in the South. We Classics types called it a *Pax Romana* Burn down the temples ; massacre a few high priests; and tell the subjugated tribes that the Emperor would make everything just fine.

"Hey Sergeant!" shouted a voice behind me, as I headed for my car, at the very rear of the Pentagon's unreserved parking lot. As a mere captain I didn't merit one of those priceless bumper stickers that permitted the higher Brass to park within a quarter mile of the main entrance. So I had to *schlepp* the mini- marathon back and forth to my car each day. Only a step or two from the streets of Arlington, Virginia.

I turned around to see quartet of flower children-two boys and two girls—dressed in the uniform of the day. Torn jeans, white socks , sandals, tie dyed shirts and denim jackets. The commander of the squad wore a stovepipe hat.

"I don't do enough honest work around here to deserve to be called *Sergeant*, Citizen," I answered. "You can call me Captain, or even Bob if it makes you feel more comfortable."

The other three members of the detachment shook their signs and shouted a string of obscenities at me. The signs read *Napalm the Pentagon* , *Nixon and Charles Manson—Both Good Family Men* and *Nixon—Racism with Honor.* Outside of a lot of profanity and sign shaking they didn't look particularly threatening. But I did sneak a squint to my right and left to try and spot the Pentagon Security Police, who were probably all busy ticketing non-stickered vehicles.

"Look fellas," I said, "I've only got three months and twenty seven days of duty left at this place. One month of that I'll be on vacation in Europe. On March 12th, 1970, the moths can feast all they want on this uniform. So, you see I've really got no beef with you guys. I'm just here surviving. Out of my paycheck I take home $167.43 a week. From that I have to pay for my rent, clothes, utilities, and food. Do you believe that? The Army doesn't even pay for my *food!* To earn this glorious sum of money, I have to show up every day by 6:00A.M. Then I have to Kowtow to a lot of guys who're dumber and a lot less educated than I am. The Army's not going to give me back the two years of my life that they've taken away from me. Years when I could have been *starting* life and making a couple of bucks. And it was just through some eerie kind of Russian Roulette that I wound up here, and not in Vietnam. So if *anybody's* got a right to be pissed off at this government—it's *me!*"

"Look man," said their leader, the one with the Abe Lincoln hat, "This f—-king war has gone on too f—-king long. We're here at this f—-king building to let those f—-king war criminals inside know that we're not gonna f—-king take it any more. "Then he lit up a huge joint, big enough to accommodate a party of twelve; he took a deep drag and started to pass it around to his little troop. I hadn't smoked any pot since law school, except for that afternoon with Matt Lehrer. The piquant aroma smelled tempting.

"Hey man," I said, walking toward the community reefer, "How's about letting a fellow citizen have a puff on his birthday—a sort of peace pipe?"

He nodded to the girl that was holding the *Charles Manson* sign, and she placed the crudely formed cigarette in my hand. I put the sticky papered end to my lips and inhaled about a dozen cubic liters of smoke into my lungs. Then I forced myself not to exhale for twenty seconds or so. *Exhale!* A few moments later, after the joint had its first pass around, I took another colossal drag. I let it out in the most efficient manner as I flashed the hippies a big smile and a peace sign. Then I decided to take a pleasant stroll along the suddenly gorgeous streets of Arlington for a while. I wasn't in any condition to drive.

Whoda' thought that at that very moment across the Atlantic, in some student dormitory on the campus of Oxford, some young American Rhodes Scholar from Arkansas, who was fortunate enough not to be embroiled in the Vietnam mess, was trying his damnedest , *without any success,* to inhale a joint like the one I just did.

# CHAPTER FIFTY-FOUR

# Namesake

It was mid- morning that fall, when Len Roth asked me to stop by his desk for a few minutes. He had someone that he'd like me to meet. I took one last sip of my cold coffee, and headed for the corner of the huge desk area where Quigley and Roth held sway. Len was busy talking to another officer—a Captain wearing *my NameTag*.

"Captain Robert J. Woolsey," Len said, "meet *Captain Robert J. Woolsey!*"

"The name's Jim," said the other Captain as he offered me his hand. "Robert *James* Woolsey. Everybody's called me Jim since Grammar School. But the Birth Certificate reads *Robert James,* so that's the way the Army has me listed in its Personnel files.

"Call me Bob, I replied." John's my middle name, but it's little known fact to everybody but my mom and dad—and maybe the minister that baptized me."

We shot bull for a few minutes about Jim, who in twenty five years was to become the world's chief spy, the Supervisor of all the American *James Bonds,* the head of the CIA.

Jim, like Len had been a Rhodes Scholar, so I felt particularly stupid talking with the two of them—sort of like the solitary brown shoe between a couple of pairs of patent leathers. I don't recall where Len and Jim had met. Maybe at the annual Rhodes Scholar Picnic and Hog Calling Contest. Jim was soon to be taking his first giant step in the world of International Diplomacy. It wasn't quite yet official, but he'd been tentatively selected as a member of the American team attending the initial SALT talks. Yes sir, he was on his way up.

I never saw Jim after that brief chat, but I *was* mistaken for him twice. One month later, I called on the Pentagon Dentist, to have my last wisdom tooth pulled. I paid to have the other three yanked out. The US Army would do this one for free.

"Captain Woolsey?" the Dentist asked, knitting his brows and holding my x-rays of record to the light. "Captain Robert J. Woolsey??"

"Yes, Doctor," I said.

"We've got ourselves a mystery here," he said. "not only do you still have your lower left wisdom tooth. But you've grown back the other *three!*"

"You've probably got the charts of Captain Robert *James* Woolsey, Doc," I explained. "I'm the undistinguished Robert *John*, a humble Briefing Officer on General Mc Christian's staff. I know that the odds of having two Captains with this same unusual name stationed at the Pentagon at precisely the same time are about a trillion to one, but if you'll just check the file right next to his, I'm sure that you'll solve the *Case of the Missing Molars.*"

A harmless error. No real harm done.

But in late 1969 Colonel Black walked into the Oral Briefers' Room, accompanied by a Mr. Carruthers from the State Department. "This gentleman is here to see you, Bob. Says it's important. He's got some papers for your eyes only. Have you been moonlighting as a double agent for Henry Kissinger after office hours?" Then the Colonel left us alone.

Carruthers didn't crack a smile at the Colonel's innocent joke. This guy was all business. He formally asked my name, looked at my official DIA badge, and handed me a sealed brown package. I took a look at the thick, ominous envelope. Sure enough, it had my name and rank, a special wax seal with the emblem of the State Department, and the stamp "For Your Eyes Only". There were other threatening stamps too. "Highly Classified Data", and "State Department Use Only"! There might even have been a "Do not open till Xmas" sticker lost between all those other red warnings. I told Mr. Carruthers what probably had happened, but his orders were to deliver the envelope to me. My office number was printed clearly on the label. He was becoming more and more uncomfortable. He was doing *his* job. Why was *I* making waves?

"Please sign here Captain," he said, holding out a pen. "You can direct any questions you might have to Assistant Secretary Lindell at the State Department."

I signed. The simplest way of handling the matter was for me to follow the orders of this fellow who even Colonel Black fell over himself calling "Sir". But I didn't open the thing up. It was no doubt filled with all kinds of classified goodies that maybe Nixon, Kissinger, Melvin Laird, and a couple others of the "anointed" were privy to. Wild thoughts filled my imagination about what would happen to me if I broke the secret seal. I'd be marked as some kind of Edmund Dantes, like in the *Count of Monte Cristo.* Thrown into someplace like the Chateau d'If to keep my mouth shut. Locked up forever in some Pentagon dungeon, fifty feet below Sergeant Stempel's record room, for reading about the US position on Nuclear Disarmament.

So I brought the matter to Colonel Black's attention again. He and Mr. Johnson were used to dealing with the higher echelons. Black must've met *somebody* from the State Department, while he was trolling for chicks at one of those Embassy Parties that he was always bragging about.

But it was Mr. Johnson that came to my rescue , just like he did last Christmas with Patty De Fazio. He made a simple phone call, and twenty minutes later, a Mr. Stanton showed up. He was wearing enough security badges to carry around a Hydrogen Bomb, and he was very, very polite about the whole thing. He apologized all over the place for the confusion, as he retrieved the *unopened* package. He signed an official receipt with the State Department Seal on it, and the matter was closed. I've still got the damn thing somewhere. That is unless that guy Stanton wrote it on some kind of disintegrating paper that you see in those spy movies.

# CHAPTER FIFTY-FIVE

# War Stories

One afternoon Santini got a phone call from Tony D'Alessandro, an Infantry Lieutenant, whom Don had known ever since Officers' Training at CCNY. I met Tony briefly when he was in the First Platoon at Fort Benning.

He couldn't have been more than 5' 5" tall and he weighed about 135 lbs., but he had arms like Popeye, and could scamper up a hundred foot obstacle course rope in less than two minutes. Tony was a natural born soldier. I heard that in hand-to-hand combat back at Fort Benning that he had beat the living hell out of a fellow platoon member that outweighed him by a hundred pounds.

Anyway he came up to our apartment. He'd returned from II Corps in South Vietnam only about a week earlier and was glad to see some old faces—particularly Santini's.

Don and I had been living some pretty cloistered lives in D.C. We gathered around him as he told us what Ranger Training had been like, and how half the guys from our old Company that went through it had washed out. Some of them the fittest and most athletic in the whole outfit.

He told how the Ranger Trainees had to endure days on end of constant maneuvers, sleeping only five or ten minutes at a time, a couple of times a day. He swore that after two months of that hell, he could *actually* sleep while crawling through the thickest underbrush.

The Army made it incredibly tough; but they took precautions that nobody'd get seriously hurt. First of all, they strapped eight canteens of water to each trainee—-*two* gallons, about twenty pounds of the stuff. Add this to the other twenty pounds of equipment that had to lug around, and Tony must have been *schlepping* about a third of his own body weight. But he frankly admitted that if they'd have allowed him to carry another gallon of water he'd 've begged for it.

A lot of the guys just quit after a couple of days. No shame. No badgering. Once you gave up, it was over. Of the fellows who decided to stick it out, a lot broke down mentally. Bud Durban, who'd been in his same platoon since Benning, suddenly stopped walking one afternoon and took out some M-1 cartridges. He removed the bullets, imagined them to be Quarters, and began shoving them into a nearby tree, that he fantasized to be a Coke Machine. He began whimpering when no bottle of cold soda came out. He kept yelling "Where's my Coke? Where's my Coke?" Then Tony had to administer some amateur Psychology by telling Bud that the machine only took *dimes,* but that somebody with the right change would be around on about ten minutes. Tony radioed their exact position to the Supervising Cadre, and they picked Bud up in half that time.

But he made it through, and got to wear that little *Ranger* tag on his uniform. I sure didn't understand it. Neither did Santini.

Tony didn't talk too much about Vietnam though. He condensed a whole year of duty into about ten minutes. He led patrols on "Search and Destroy" missions in II Corps. His job was to uncover stashed materiel in surrounding villages, burn the huts of enemy sympathizers, and return to base.

One incident made it difficult for him to ever trust anybody again. He'd been in country a little more than two weeks, when he had his patrol search one of those huts that all looked alike. Some guy about eighty years old was yelling something to his interpreter. He wanted Tony to rescue his dog before he burned his house down. The pooch was sleeping under the little bench inside. Tony didn't trust the guy. He'd found rifles and munitions earmarked for the Viet Cong all over the village. But he entered the shack anyway. The old coot reminded him of his Grandfather. He decided to save the puppy. He looked around and saw the bench where the dog was allegedly snoozing. He was about to reach in and grab for it , when something didn't seem kosher. He sensed it ; he smelled it. Sure enough there was a trip wire attached to that bench. Tony ran out of the hut and ordered his Platoon Sergeant to raze it—to raze the whole stinking village. In a few seconds a flame-thrower was spewing fire all over the grass house. The booby trap inside exploded, shaking the rest of the huts.

Tony ordered that the old man be dragged out in front of him. Then he took out his 45-caliber pistol, and placed the barrel directly at the bridge of the old man's nose. He pulled the trigger once; then twice; six times. Click. Click. Tony had removed the bullets from the clip, and the firing pin was striking an empty chamber. For an instant he had thought about keeping a sixth bullet in the bottom of the clip to blow the old bastard's brains out. After five false alarm clicks, the son of a bitch would have thought that he was home free. And then Surprise, Surprise! But Tony just couldn't do it.

# CHAPTER FIFTY-SIX

# Westy in his Pajamas

One day Colonel Black asked me to deliver the Weekly Book to General Westmoreland, who was recuperating from surgery at Walter Reed Hospital. This was one of Black's weekly chores, but he'd been called away due to a death in his family. Major Kraft, who was his usual replacement, was out shooting quail or some other defenseless wildlife back home in Michigan. I was the most expendable officer he had.

Westmoreland was the highest ranking officer in the US Army. Maybe I didn't like his military strategy, or didn't appreciate the way he had handled the war under LBJ, but he did report directly to the President of the United States. The fate of over a million men was in his hands.

Sam Jefferson chauffeured me and my handcuffed suitcase to Walter Reed. I was to leave the pistol back at the office. Maybe Westmoreland was afraid of guns.

I'd always loathed hospitals, seeing nurses wheeling around doped up patients in squeaky gurneys. Looking at their frightened stares as they lay helpless, with a dozen tubes dangling out their arms and nose. Then there was that horrible antiseptic smell! And the depressing walls all painted gray and olive green.

I showed the nurse at the main desk my ID. She checked her list to confirm my appointment. Fifteen minutes later a very sharp looking

Major named Rourke, met me in the lobby, and escorted me to the General's room. I knocked at the door and he *bade me enter.*

It was a little disappointing seeing a larger than life guy, who'd had so much to do with our Nation's History over the past three or four years, sitting in front of you in a wheelchair, clothed only in a robe, pajamas, and slippers. You know something like seeing Cindy Crawford, without make-up, just after coming out of the Delivery Room.

He was reading *Time* magazine through a pair of reading glasses. One of those wheeled hospital tables was in front of him. He'd just had a gall bladder or an appendix removed , so I wasn't seeing him at his spit and polish best. In that get up, he was just some guy, with bony, vein-streaked ankles wearing bifocals. He gave me a weak smile and motioned me over.

He was very courteous, asking me the usual crap that Generals ask the troops in the movies. Like where I came from, and whether I'd considered the Army as a career. Nice guy stuff. He read the Book, just like the Secretary of the Army ordered, and he returned it to me. He thanked me and wished me luck. I said I hoped he'd have a speedy recovery. Then I marched out of the room in as military a fashion as I could.

Sam Jefferson picked me up at the Admissions Entrance, and drove me back to the Pentagon.

"Where's your hat ,Bob?" he asked. "I know that you were wearing one when you walked in the place. Maybe you oughta handcuff *that* to your head. Heh! Heh!"

This was probably more embarrassing than serious. Like being introduced to some pretty sweet thing, while your fly is open. But it meant getting my ass chewed out for pulling a real bonehead move. Major Loomis just laughed it off, He even volunteered to go out and buy me a spare. I gave him ten bucks, and he was on his way out the door, when Sergeant Rivera, at the office entrance, buzzed me over the intercom. Major Rourke was at the door. You remember, Westmoreland's Aide.

Anyway, I met him outside the door, and he tendered me the beaten up cap with the frayed gold trim.

"With the General's compliments!" he said. "Oh, by the way, he forgot to congratulate you on your splendid Czechoslovakian Briefing last year." Then he smiled, turned around, and went out into the corridor.

# An American Tragedy

The shocking news was all over television. Some Lieutenant named Calley had evidently taken some village called My Lai prisoner. Then he'd given his troops orders to massacre just about everybody in the place—women, children, and old people. I recalled how Tony D'Alessandro told us of his temptation to plug some treacherous Vietnamese Senior Citizen in the head for planting a booby trap that could've killed him. Tony had enough self discipline to hold back. Evidently this guy Calley didn't.

Major Loomis told me that he'd been in Vietnam at the time of the alleged incident He'd heard something the older officers used to call "scuttlebutt", about a whole village that had been exterminated by some trigger happy young officer. But there were always rumors about something. If you paid attention to any of them, you'd believe that we were going to drop the H- Bomb on Hanoi next week, and that Jane Fonda would be the new Secretary of State.

The General Staff talked about nothing else for the rest of the month. Although ISB was an *Intelligence* operation, and this stuff was outside our field, McChristian wanted his own personal briefing on the matter. So we gathered whatever we could from the *Operations* Branch. We got Calley's Bio from *Personnel*. We studied the background of the village. Viet Cong activity in the area. Everything that might shed some light on the tragedy.

We found out that Calley was an immature kid that barely got by Officers' Training. Then he was sent off to command fifty kids in an insane war. A few months in country and he saw an enemy behind every tree. Every hut was a potential booby trap. One morning he snapped, and his platoon snapped along with him. Estimates of the dead varied between 100-500 people. Their bodies were shoved into mass graves. Loomis' voice cracked as he told the story. The General had no questions. I turned up the lights and we left the War Room.

# CHAPTER FIFTY-EIGHT

# Europe Revisited

It was New Year's Eve 1969. My X-Rated porn supplier, Mark Clancy, along with Joe Finestra and my best friend Ed Rubin, were sitting with our dates at Geordie's, a casual East Side pub, fashionably decorated with sawdust and peanut shells all over the floor. We were all ready to welcome in the 70's, and bid a very *unfond* farewell to the decade of the 60's. Ed and I were scheduled to take advantage of *Icelandic Airline's* steerage rates, and head for Europe the following day. At midnight the eight of us clinked our glasses of Champagne; everybody hugged everybody; the horns blew; and the house stereo blared out *Auld Lang Syne*.

This vacation was going to be different than last May's disaster. No uniforms to *schlepp* around; and we had *confirmed* round trip tickets to Luxembourg and back. I also gave myself a whole week's breathing room on the return end of the trip. You know, just in case the plane crashed in the North Atlantic somewhere, and I was forced to survive in a lifeboat for a few days.

At 6:00 P. M. in New Year's Day, Ed and I were chomping at the bit to board the bargain flight. Our bags had been loaded on board, and we'd just kissed our relatives good-bye. We were ready for *Icelandic* to whisk us off to Luxembourg, after a brief stopover in Reykjavik.

But as it turned out, the tiny airline prided itself to a fault on its flawless safety record. Even the barf bags were double-checked. So the 7:00 P.M. departure would be *momentarily* delayed, the loudspeaker announced. Ed and I sat patiently in the plane until 8:30. The hospitable staff then bussed us all out to a *Howard Johnson's* near Kennedy for a late dinner; and then dumped us all back at the Airport Waiting Room, where we spent the next eight hours trying to sleep on its brittle Formica chairs. Finally at 6:00 A.M., we were ushered back aboard the aircraft. Iceland here we come.

We landed at the barren brown airstrip, at what would've been noon New York time. I hadn't felt this grungy since *Operation Overnight* back at Fort Benning. No one, except for a few disembarking Icelanders, was permitted to get their luggage from the cargo hold. I swear, I would've given twenty bucks for a pair of fresh socks. Anyway we bought the obligatory postcards of some glaciers at the little kiosk in the Reykyavik terminal, and we resumed the second leg of the flight to Luxembourg.

It was almost midnight, Western Europe Time, when we finally arrived. Twenty four hours past our scheduled departure from Kennedy. After clearing a twenty-second Customs Inspection, Ed and I rented a VW beetle. They were all out of cars with automatic transmissions, so we had to make do with a stick shift. This guaranteed that I'd do all the driving, because Ed had never even *seen* a clutch before. I tried giving him a short lesson on the deserted Luxembourgese highway into town, but that wasn't such a good idea. Ed grinded the gears a few times; we bucked and stalled, and then bucked again. I might've been a little more patient if I hadn't been awake for almost thirty-six consecutive hours. Not counting the few moments when I was able to doze off at the airport on the carborundum chairs. When I began to grit my teeth in anger, I knew that it was best to delay the driving lesson until morning.

On January 3rd we started our trip. After breakfast at the hotel, I snapped a quick photo of the Royal Palace, and then another one of the "Vous Sortie Le Grand Duchy Luxembourg" sign that concluded our fifteen minute tour of the place. We were in Belgium. From now on our itinerary wasn't really planned. A couple of days in Belgium and Holland. Maybe a week in France; a week in Italy; and then a few final days in Switzerland to visit Ed's rich kinfolk in Geneva. Then back to Luxembourg again.

For me this trip was a welcome intermission between Army life and the as yet untested civilian world of legal briefs and courtrooms. I wanted it to be special. I also wanted it to be *warmer*. January in the Benelux countries is *cold*. So we spent most of our first few days thawing out in the museums and coffee shops of Amsterdam. We also took the hush-hush tour of the City's Red Light District, but didn't "buy" anything. Mostly we just stared in amazement at the voluptuous ladies advertising their services in picture glass windows. Because we were probably the only two American tourists dumb enough to spend their vacation in the sub freezing temperature of Holland, the local pimps and hustlers followed us around offering special discount packages. *Two* for the price of one even! Time to head South.

Paris wasn't all that *far* South, unfortunately, but we couldn't travel to Italy without spending a few days there. Because we wanted to spend our extra *francs* on *haute cuisine,* we booked a room at the *Chaud Jardin*, on the left bank, a *pension* described as adequate by our *Guide to Bargains in Paris.* Our lodgings were up four flights of stairs, but we only had to make the climb once or twice a day.

Madame Passeau, our hostess, ran a very tight *pension*. The rates *were* reasonable, but everything not explicitly included in the basic *pris fixe* was extra. Breakfast rules were strictly enforced. *One* cup of coffee with milk, *two* sugars, *two* croissants, *two* pats of butter, *one* paper napkin. No charge for pepper and salt. The towels were clean, but just one per person per day was issued. I was surprised that the thrifty Madame didn't ration our squares of toilet paper, and put a limit on our flushes. Only *one* item in the place was free. The picture postcards in the lobby showing the hotel's charming dining room. But the super wide angle lens photo made the intimate six-table area look like the Banquet Hall at *Versailles*. The back of each postcard read, "The coziest *pension* in Paris", in three languages. Madame was delighted when Ed and I helped ourselves to a few, wrote a short greeting to our folks on each, stuck on a fifty *centime* stamp, and asked her to mail them to America for us.

One great thing about Paris is its compact size. You can travel from one end of the city to the other in practically no time on the *Metro,* their excellent subway. So we were able to leave our rented Volkswagen parked at curbside on front of the *Chaud Jardin* during our whole stay. And because we didn't use the car, we posed no threat to the innocent pedestrians of Paris, when we overindulged on a couple of extra glasses of Cognac while we were carousing.

We said *au revoir* to Madame Passeau after five days, and resumed our quest for some balmy weather. We stopped at the port of Nice before entering Italy. Ed wanted to make his fortune at the gaming tables. We were the only two guys in the whole place not wearing tuxedoes. But the hesitant *maitre D'* let us in after Ed explained that our formal wear was on board his Uncle Jacque's yacht, the *Bon Homme Richard* The impetuous guy had set sail without notice, late last night, for the Aegean probably, and he might not be back for a week *Je regret,* We were granted admission.

Ed and I sank into the plush purple carpet, as we walked towards the Roulette Wheel. The place was so *quiet.* I didn't hear the chinking and clanging of any slot machines, or the crashing of the coins paying off. There was some subdued shouting from the few lucky patrons at the different tables, but other than that, the place was hushed.

We went to the cashier's window. Word must've spread about the two wealthy, casually dressed Americans. But I couldn't help but notice the scowling *maitre D'*, as we walked away from the window clutching our meager hundred dollar stack of chips—all in single *one franc* pieces. I don't think that he was buying Ed's tale of old Uncle Jacque and his privately owned QE2.

In fact, about a half-hour later , after we'd blown all our chips at the Roulette Wheel, the *maitre D'* said Good-bye with a sarcastic, "I hope that the *monsieur* will come back soon. I look forward to seeing his

Uncle as well—along with Aristotle Onassis, Jackie Kennedy, and the Saudi Arabian Princes in his *entourage!*"

Next morning we were on our way to Italy. A couple of days each in Milan, Venice, Florence, and Rome. We both agreed against a visit to Naples and my cousin Aniello. The Ferraras spoke almost no English, and Ed would've felt very uncomfortable. So we'd limit ourselves to visiting *his* clan in Geneva, which had quadrilingual fluency in French, Italian, German, and English.

We'd both been pretty faithful to our budget, even considering the hundred bucks apiece that we blew at the Nice Casino. We always made it a point to get lodgings within walking distance of the University everyplace we stayed in Italy. We could pass for a couple of American exchange students, so it was a cinch to crash the school cafeteria, and get a whole meal for about a buck apiece. Mostly pasta floating in tomato sauce, but not all that bad. Besides, if you explored the thick gravy with your fork, you might even discover a meatball or two.

Florence was our shopping Mecca for gifts to bring home. Paris had its perfumes, of course, But the *real* buys were the hand crafted leather and jewelry sold on the *Ponte Vecchio*. We had our own devious purchase plan set up in advance.

We both had to buy about twenty quality items for relatives back home. Divided equally between men and women. Something small that wouldn't break in our luggage. We opted for wallets for the men, and necklaces for the women.

I went to reconnoiter a few leather goods shops. I chose a small one that was a sole proprietorship, full of fine belts, and handbags, and *wallets*. I had no doubt that this guy's great-great-great-etc. grandfather had probably sold the same quality pieces to the Medicis.

I sauntered past the small boutique, and stopped to examine the merchandise. I asked the owner in intentionally fractured Italian what the cost of *one* wallet was. He quoted me, in intentionally broken English, the sum of three thousand lire. A bargain in America, about five bucks in those days, but I had not yet begun to negotiate. We dickered price a little. I played the role of the penniless student. He made himself out to be a starving, practically bankrupt, merchant. His creditors were threatening him with prison, if he didn't pay by the end of the month. What a performance!

When I had nibbled him down a bit, I presented an offer he couldn't refuse. It was getting dark, and all the shops would soon close.

"I give you ten thousand lire for ten wallets, *signore*. Cash. No travelers Checks," I said.

"*Impossibile, signore*," he answered. "Thirty five thousand, and I *lose* money. You rich *Americano!* No take advantage!"

It was now Ed's turn to enter the bargaining process. He walked nonchalantly over to the stall at my prearranged signal.

"I'm looking for a couple of wallets, sir," he said, making no attempt to even fake a word or two in Italian.

"Look here, stranger, I'm busy talking with this gentleman," I said, interrupting Ed impolitely. "You can join the haggling, but *only* if you buy a bunch of the things , just like me. How many do you want to buy?"

"Just four or five," he answered.

The street-smart vendor had a feeling that he was being conned, but he'd already made his move.

"Signore," I continued, "You sell us both a total of twenty wallets. We pay cash. Thirty thousand lire. OK stranger? OK *signore?*"

Ed played the part of the innocent abroad perfectly. Like some backwoods clod who never wore shoes before.

"But I only need *five!*" he said.

"All right, all right *signori*," the merchant said. "Final offer. Two of you. Twenty wallets. Cash. I no wrappa. No receipta. Thirty thousand lire. Best stuff in alla Florence. Give me money now and getta hell outta here!"

We forked over the agreed amount, and grabbed the brown paper bags that the *signore* had dumped our well-earned bargains into. I thought that we did OK, for a couple of novice wheeler-dealers.

As for the *signore* leather goods dealer, he was probably also cackling to himself over the crafty deal that he'd just put over in those two *Americano* suckers.

We followed the same routine with a jewelry merchant on the opposite side of the bridge with the same result.

# CHAPTER FIFTY-NINE

# Swiss Family Rosenthal

We were off on our way over the Alps to Geneva. We were lucky. Snow hadn't fallen in quite a while and the highway was clear. No need for tire chains.

When we arrived. I put my *Bargain Lodgings in Switzerland* book away. Ed figured that there was a good chance that some of his relatives might drop up to our hotel room for a visit, so we couldn't stay in the squalor that we'd been accustomed to elsewhere during the trip.

We decided on the *Recoin Suisse,* not exactly a four star hotel, but a definite three. Bellhops, extra towels, mints on the pillows, disposable shower hats, and a view of Lake Geneva—if you stood on tiptoe.

A phone call to his cousin Bernard, and dinner for the following evening was arranged at the *Chateau Rosenthal,* the family estate. Ed was a bit apprehensive at meeting his mother's long lost kin. She hadn't laid eyes on them in over forty years. Ed's mom was as refined a lady as I ever knew, but she was very down to earth. Maybe the Swiss branch of the family were a bunch of snobs. Maybe they were stuffy. Maybe Ed would have to fake a headache, and we'd have to leave before dessert.

His anxiety was unwarranted. Bernard and his wife, Yvonne, gave Ed a big hug at the door, and made us *both* feel like prodigal sons. Before we feasted on our *"fatted calf"*, they invited us to wash up. It was the first bathroom that I'd ever been in that had a Renoir hanging opposite the commode. But I have to admit that I did feel a little uncomfortable as I conducted my business while staring at the canvas of the pretty little girl in blue and red playing the piano.

Bernard and Yvonne welcomed us into their drawing room for some aperitifs and "getting to know you" conversation. They were glad that we had no difficulties negotiating the Alps. Bernard said something about those little Volkswagens being part mountain goat, and that he liked them for their gas mileage. This sounded pretty funny to me, coming from a guy that had a Renoir hanging in his toilet. I mean, you wouldn't expect him to give a damn about gas mileage.

Then he gave us a quick tour if the place. I felt sort of like those Russian peasants back in 1917, when they burst into the Palace of Czar Nicholas, and were suddenly facing the paintings of the world's greatest masters, barely able to speak in the presence of such genius. Picassos and Degas adorned the rooms. A private art gallery. It would be hard for me to look at my mother's favorite landscape, hanging in the living room. that she picked up for fifty bucks at a garage sale,

Dinner was what I expected. Vichyssoise, squab, truffles, and *crepe suzette flambe* for dessert. I had a feeling that the fancy meal was a conscious effort to impress the pants off both of us. Maybe tomorrow's supper without us, would be something like breaded pork chops with French fries, something that Bernard and Yvonne *really* liked to sink their teeth into. And I bet they were going to have Chocolate Fudge Ripple ice cream for dessert too.

I purposely limited my alcohol consumption to a half a glass of white wine during the meal, politely refusing even an after dinner cordial. I was afraid that I'd get a little loaded, trip on the thick carpet, and break some million dollar Ming vase.

Bernard was our personal escort and tour guide for the next couple of days. His chauffeur drove us all over the place, from the Cathedral of St. Pierre to the countless parks that rimmed the city. The last day of our visit Bernard gave the chauffeur the day off and commandeered the wheel of the big Mercedes. I guess he wanted to show us that *he* could drive a car just like the rest of us. I was mischievously hoping in the egalitarian lobe of my brain that he'd get a flat tire, and would have to change it, getting his patrician hands all black and greasy mounting the spare. But we completed the tour without incident.

It was time to return to Luxembourg, and fly the friendly skies of *Icelandic Airlines*. The flight back home proceeded without a hitch. Maybe they only took those super safety precautions on planes *leaving* Kennedy Airport.

# CHAPTER SIXTY

# What? No Gold Watch?

It was the first week of March 1970. I had decided to take early leave of the Army. I discovered to my delight, that I had some unexpected vacation time left. Back in June 1968, ISB had neglected to inform Pentagon Personnel of my week furlough. So instead of leaving on March 10, 1970, I switched the departure date to March 7th.

Colonel Black and Major Loomis had already given me the obligatory line of bullshit about how great an Army career was, and how I should stay for another tour of duty. Of course they offered no guarantee of assignment. A year from now I could be serving as Intelligence Adjutant to some fruitcake like Colonel Whatsisname, back at Fort Benning. Thanks, but no thanks.

The Colonel took my tactful refusal pretty well. He even suggested that I organize a farewell celebration at some local Officers' Club to commemorate the occasion. Actually it was to be a *three* man going away party. Rod Burton, Major Carson, and I were all saying Good-bye to ISB this month.

I was still coming in every morning at six to help Major Loomis and Lieutenant Gilmore with the briefing. But since we were, frankly, overstaffed, I spent most of the time gabbing with Ed Cogan about my return to the real world, and *his* new prosperity as a visual arts entrepreneur. He'd opened a small shop in Northwest D.C. and had a young college grad manning the place during the week. Ed would take over on weekends. Right now, with the rent and the outlay of a modest salary to the college kid, he was just breaking even. But he figured that in six months he and his family could *survive* by his working full time outside ISB. He'd made enough contacts in the past year and a half to finally enjoy the fruits of capitalism. Ed had already told Colonel Black of his plans, so that he could start the search for a new graphics man.

Initially Colonel Black had given me guidelines for a modest affair at the Fort Belvoir Officers' Club. Tables for about twenty five couples; a serve yourself bar; one entree of B.F. Goodrich chicken for everybody; formal attire optional; Mr. Johnson's young nephew would spin records for background music.

But during the pre-gala week, the Colonel developed into a regular party animal, with a self-bestowed title of Toastmaster General. I had to arrange for a couple of professional bartenders to serve drinks; roast chicken wasn't fancy enough. The guests would have a choice between Prime Ribs, Baked Salmon, or Filet Mignon. I had to fire Mr. Johnson's nephew, and hire a three-piece band. Formal attire only was decreed, so I had to retrieve my dress blue uniform from storage. Naturally the pants didn't fit me any more, and I had to let them out a couple of inches.

Black also wanted floral pieces on his newly ordered dais, where I was to arrange for a small podium and a microphone, so he could award the three departees their little trophies. Instead of a "Thanks guys for a job well done", we were each to receive a little silver turtle, the symbol of the Intelligence Branch, with our names inscribed on their bellies. And to make certain that all the revelers mingled, he came up with a hokey idea that *I* was strictly to enforce.

His social brainstorm was to have each guest (men and women) wear a different nametag of one half of a famous couple, like Tarzan and Jane, or Bonnie and Clyde. The nametags would be placed in my hat for males and Lieutenant Gilmore's for females.

Party time! the guests started trickling in. Stu Rutkowski grumbled something about this being the silliest piece of bullshit since his high school prom, as he reached into my cap and picked King Arthur; his date picked Juliet. Their assignments—to search out Queen Gwynivere and Romeo!

My date for this farewell dinner was Emmy Tyler, the roommate of Don Santini's girlfriend. I thought that it would be incredibly rude to leave her alone in a roomful of strangers, while I carried out Colonel Black's socially innovative mission. So I would desert my post occasionally to make her evening tolerable, leaving Pete Gilmore in charge. Disaster. Some couples made it past Pete without the ordained nametags; some took *matching* nametags; some, thinking that this fiasco was *my* doing, refused to participate; Cleopatra didn't know if she was looking for Caesar or Mark Anthony; and one young lady had no idea who Helen of Troy's lover was, so she spent the evening looking for Hercules.

Black blew a gasket. Sure I'd seen him blow his stack when we were preparing a Black Book that might affect the lives of American forces. But to give me a formal reprimand in front of Emmy for failure to properly supervise his dumb party game? I feared that I wouldn't receive my silver turtle!

But the rest of the evening proceeded pretty much according to schedule. A couple of Vodka Martinis, and the Colonel turned into a pussycat. He even put his arm around my shoulder, and wished me all the best in my new life. Tomorrow, when he became pissed off at me again, I would be officially gone from ISB, and he'd have to vent his hangover on somebody else. I looked over at his stunning date, probably a stewardess on a short layover at National Airport. I *knew* that she wasn't the type to take any of his crap, after doing him sexual favors in bed.

Emmy and I were seated at the dais, with Colonel Black and Stewardess Black; Major and Mrs. Carson; and Rod Burton and his girlfriend. At about 10:30 P.M., Black staggered to the podium, and turned on the microphone to address the crowd. He went on to congratulate Rod , Major Carson and me. Then he congratulated the chef, and the band, and the bartenders. Even the busboys. Then he raised his cocktail glass and gave a toast to "three of the most outstanding officers he'd ever had the privilege to command." We applauded ourselves. The whole place stood up to clink their glasses together. The four Bloody Marys that I'd drunk were making me blush. I accepted my little turtle, which would be given a place of honor at the bottom of my trunk along with my Erect Penis Soldier of the Year Award, that I received from Barney Watson at Fort Benning.

"Captain Woolsey," the Colonel announced at the end of the presentation, "feel free to visit ISB whenever you get the chance. You're always welcome. Of course, tomorrow, when your security clearance has been revoked, we'll have to talk out in the corridor. Heh, heh. But as far as I'm concerned, nothing has changed. Don't you agree, Bob?"

I smiled back at him and said, "You betcha, *Rog, baby,* nothing has changed at all!"

# CHAPTER SIXTY-ONE

# Fade to Black

About 1:00 A.M. I took Emmy back home. To put it more precisely, she drove *me* home, and I phoned her a cab. As with Colonel Black, my libations had produced a "Thank You" jag. I thanked Emmy for being so nice and understanding. Then I thanked my apartment doorman for opening the taxicab door. I even gave him a buck. Boy was I drunk! Then I took the elevator back to my studio, that I'd been renting since I moved out of the two bedroom with Santini, so I could be closer to work. I peeled off that scratchy blue uniform that I vowed never to wear again. Then I went to sleep.

Next day was March 7, 1970. I woke up at 7:00 A.M. Then I went back to sleep, waking up at 7: 30. I tried forcing myself back to sleep, but my body's supply of melatonin was tapped out. So I went to the kitchen to prepare a big heavy breakfast of French toast, sausage, coffee, and orange juice—several glasses of orange juice.

I got dressed and went downstairs to the little deli. I bought a copy of the *Washington Post*. I glanced at the headlines, before turning to the basketball scores. There was an extraordinary item on page one. This afternoon the East Coast would experience a Total *Solar Eclipse*. The first one in about sixty years, and the only one for another hundred. A nice way to celebrate my new freedom. I packed a lunch of two roast beef sandwiches, a bag of potato chips, and a thermos of coffee. I put it in a shopping bag together with a copy of *Portnoy's Complaint*, that Carl

Lebron had given me before leaving ISB, but which I hadn't yet started. Then I headed for Rock Creek Park in D.C. to view the event.

But before going to Rock Creek, I had to make the trip to the Pentagon to park in the Visitors' Lot just once. I pulled into a spot close to the South Entrance, and walked inside. I'd given up all my security badges the afternoon before, so I was just another common citizen roaming the halls. But I didn't stay too long. I was afraid that I might see somebody I knew, and I'd be forced into an embarrassing conversation about my plans for the future and stuff like that. I left. Maybe I was afraid because I *had* no plans for the future. The Army wouldn't be there any more to tell me what to do.

So I returned to my car and drove to Rock Creek Park. I parked and wandered towards one of the deserted picnic tables. Aside from a couple of folks walking their dogs, and a few unemployed teenagers playing touch football, I had the place to myself.

I'd put together a cardboard contraption that allowed you to witness the eclipse without going blind. You just punctured a piece of cardboard and viewed the spectacle backwards. It sounds a little confusing, but I'll have plenty of time to get it down pat the next time, in the year 2076.

The time was precisely 1:17 P.M. The sky was becoming black—not dim, like when there's heavy cloud cover, but almost pitch black. The universe was even fooling the birds in the park into believing that the Sun had set. They stopped chirping and returned to their nests. It was an eerie feeling. For about three minutes the Cosmos was putting on its classiest show. No encore for about a hundred years.

Then, on cue, the Sun began to creep out from behind the Moon, and resume its rightful place at center stage. God said "Let there be light" again, and sure enough there was light. And it was good. I ate my remaining sandwich and emptied the half-full thermos of coffee on the grass. Tomorrow I began my life.